$24.99

Outdoor Cooking

by
THE EDITORS OF TIME-LIFE BOOKS

TIME-LIFE BOOKS·AMSTERDAM

$24.99

TIME-LIFE BOOKS
EUROPEAN EDITOR: Kit van Tulleken; *Design Director:* Ed Skyner; *Photography Director:* Pamela Marke; *Chief of Research:* Vanessa Kramer; *Chief Sub-Editor:* Ilse Gray

THE GOOD COOK
The original version of this book was created in Alexandria, Virginia for Time-Life Books Inc.

U.S. Editorial Staff for *Outdoor Cooking: Editor:* Gerry Schremp; *Designer:* Ellen Robling; *Chief Researcher:* Barbara Levitt; *Associate Editors:* Adrian Allen (pictures), Anne Horan (text); *Text Editor:* Sarah Brash; *Researchers:* Robert Carmack (techniques), Patricia McKinney (anthology), Denise Li, Ann Ready; *Assistant Designer:* Peg Schreiber; *Copy Co-ordinators:* Tonna Gibert, Nancy Lendved; *Art Assistant:* Mary L. Orr; *Picture Co-ordinator:* Alvin Ferrell; *Editorial Assistants:* Andrea Reynolds, Patricia Whiteford; *Special Contributor:* Leslie Marshall

European Editorial Staff for *Outdoor Cooking: Editor:* Ellen Galford; *Series Co-ordinator:* Debbie Litton; *Text Editor:* Nicoletta Flessati; *Anthology Editor:* Anne Jackson; *Staff Writers:* Alexandra Carlier, Sally Crawford; *Researchers:* Joy Davies (principal), Susie Dawson; *Designer:* Cherry Doyle; *Sub-Editors:* Charles Boyle, Kate Cann, Frances Dixon, Sally Rowland; *Anthology Researcher:* Debra Raad; *Anthology Assistant:* Lesley Kinahan; *Proofreader:* Judith Heaton; *Editorial Assistant:* Molly Sutherland

EDITORIAL PRODUCTION FOR THE SERIES
Chief: Ellen Brush; *Traffic Co-ordinators:* Stephanie Lee, Jane Lillicrap; *Picture Co-ordinator:* Ros Smith; *Art Department:* Janet Matthew; *Editorial Department:* Theresa John, Debra Lelliott, Sylvia Osborne

ISBN 7054 0616 4

TIME-LIFE is a trademark of Time Incorporated U.S.A.

LIBRARY OF NATIONS
CLASSICS OF EXPLORATION
PLANET EARTH
PEOPLES OF THE WILD
THE EPIC OF FLIGHT
THE SEAFARERS
WORLD WAR II
THE GOOD COOK
THE TIME-LIFE ENCYCLOPAEDIA OF GARDENING
THE GREAT CITIES
THE OLD WEST
THE WORLD'S WILD PLACES
THE EMERGENCE OF MAN
LIFE LIBRARY OF PHOTOGRAPHY
TIME-LIFE LIBRARY OF ART
GREAT AGES OF MAN
LIFE SCIENCE LIBRARY
LIFE NATURE LIBRARY
THE TIME-LIFE BOOK OF BOATING
TECHNIQUES OF PHOTOGRAPHY
LIFE AT WAR
LIFE GOES TO THE MOVIES
BEST OF LIFE
LIFE IN SPACE

Cover: Sizzling on an outdoor grill, kebabs of scallops and cucumber are basted with the marinade in which they were steeped (*page 72*). The oil in the marinade protects the delicate flesh and flame-coloured coral from drying; the dill complements the subtle flavour of the seafood.

THE CHIEF CONSULTANT:
Richard Olney, an American, has lived and worked since 1951 in France, where he is a highly regarded authority on food and wine. He is the author of *The French Menu Cookbook* and the award-winning *Simple French Food,* and has contributed to numerous gastronomic magazines and journals. He has directed cooking courses in France and the United States and is a member of several distinguished gastronomic and oenological societies, including *L'Académie Internationale du Vin, La Confrérie des Chevaliers du Tastevin* and *La Commanderie du Bontemps de Médoc et des Graves.* Although he is chief consultant for the series, this volume was prepared under the guidance of other consultants.

SPECIAL CONSULTANTS:
Carol Cutler lives in Washington D.C. and is the author of a number of cookery books, including *The Six-Minute Soufflé and Other Culinary Delights.* During the 12 years she lived in France, she studied at the Cordon Bleu and the École des Trois Gourmandes, and with private chefs. She is a member of the *Cercle des Gourmettes* and is also a charter member of *Les Dames d'Escoffier.*
Jeremiah Tower is an eminent American restaurateur who lived in Europe for many years. He is a member of *La Commanderie du Bontemps de Médoc et des Graves* and of *La Jurade de Saint-Émilion.* He was responsible for the majority of the step-by-step sequences in this volume.
Pat Alburey is a member of the Institute of Home Economics of Great Britain. Her wide experience includes preparing foods for photography, teaching cookery and creating recipes. She was responsible for many of the demonstrations in this volume.

THE PHOTOGRAPHERS:
Aldo Tutino has worked in Milan, New York City and Washington D.C. He has received a number of awards for his photographs from the New York Advertising Club.
Bob Komar is a Londoner who trained at both Hornsey and Manchester Schools of Art. He specializes in food photography and in portraiture.

THE INTERNATIONAL CONSULTANTS:
Great Britain: *Jane Grigson* was born in Gloucester and brought up in the north of England. She is a graduate of Cambridge University. Her first book on food, *Charcuterie and French Pork Cookery,* was published in 1967; since then, she has published a number of cookery books, including *Good Things, English Food* and *Jane Grigson's Fruit Book.* She became cookery correspondent for the colour magazine of the London *Observer* in 1968. *Alan Davidson* is the author of *Fish and Fish Dishes of Laos, Mediterranean Seafood* and *North Atlantic Seafood.* He is the founder of Prospect Books, which specializes in scholarly publications on food and cookery, and of the Oxford Symposia on food history. **France:** *Michel Lemonnier* was born in Normandy. He began contributing to the magazine *Cuisine et Vins de France* in 1960, and also writes for several other important French food and wine periodicals. The co-founder and vice-president of the society *Les Amitiés Gastronomiques Internationales,* he is a frequent lecturer on wine and a member of most of the vinicultural confraternities and academies in France. **Germany:** *Jochen Kuchenbecker* trained as a chef, but worked for 10 years as a food photographer in many European countries before opening his own restaurant in Hamburg. *Anne Brakemeier,* who also lives in Hamburg, has published articles on food and cooking in many German periodicals. She is the co-author of three cookery books. **Italy:** *Massimo Alberini* divides his time between Milan and Venice. He is a well-known food writer and journalist, with a particular interest in culinary history. Among his 18 books are *Storia del Pranzo all'Italiana, 4000 Anni a Tavola* and *La Tavola all' Italiana.* **The Netherlands:** *Hugh Jans,* a resident of Amsterdam, has been translating cookery books and articles for more than 25 years. His own books include *Bistro Koken, Koken in een Kasserol* and *Vrij Nederlands Kookboek,* and his recipes are published in many Dutch magazines.

Valuable help was given by the following members of Time-Life Books: *Maria Vincenza Aloisi, Joséphine du Brusle* (Paris); *Berta Julia* (Barcelona); *Janny Hovinga* (Amsterdam); *Elisabeth Kraemer* (Bonn); *Ann Natanson, Mimi Murphy* (Rome); *Bona Schmid* (Milan); *Enid Farmer* (Boston); *Susan Jonas* (New York).

CONTENTS

The Renaissance of an Ancient Art

Revered as a gift from the gods in aeons past, fire has magical powers. After its leaping flames die down, its embers form an incandescent bed above which foods of almost every description can be grilled or roasted—and in the process become permeated by the delicate but distinctive fragrance of smoke. Depending on the weather, the fire can burn outdoors or in a fireplace; depending on taste, the fare can be as plain as hamburgers or as elaborate as a whole, stuffed, spit-roasted rabbit.

Achieving predictably delicious results when cooking any food over glowing embers is the subject of this book. The following pages address the basics: the equipment and how it works, the fire and how to build it, the marinades that aid in the preparation of foods, and the sauces and relishes that enhance their presentation. Four chapters then deal with the techniques for handling the primary ingredients: vegetables and fruits, meats, poultry and game, fish and shellfish. A final chapter describes ways to manage such diverse techniques as smoking meats and grilling cheese, and how to succeed in such ambitious undertakings as spit-roasting a whole pig or staging a clambake. The second half of the volume consists of an anthology of over 220 of the best published recipes for outdoor cooking.

International in scope, the recipes reflect the universality of the art. In every part of the world, the outdoors was the first kitchen and an open fire the first stove; the first cooking method was to lay the food in the smouldering embers or impale it on sticks held over them. An early description of outdoor cooking appears in the *Iliad* of the Greek poet Homer, who recounts that Trojan warriors slew "a sheep of silvery whiteness" and "cut the meat carefully up into smaller pieces, spitted them, and drew them off again when they were well roasted".

For soldiers and civilians alike, such feasts became rarer as cities grew and cooks took their fires indoors to clay ovens, fireplaces and—eventually—metal stoves. Outdoor cooking was left to hunters and fishermen, shepherds and adventurers.

In the New World, early explorers and settlers rediscovered the rewards of cooking over coals. The Spaniards found the Caribbean Indians cooking their game and fish on green-wood grills called *barbacoas*, which were suspended above pits heated with wood fires. The colonists of Virginia learned from the Indians to barbecue pigs in a similar manner, and farther north the settlers adopted the New England Indians' technique of baking clams and fish in pits lined with seaweed-covered stones.

In the Old World as well as the New, public celebrations and ceremonies were the occasion for outdoor feasting on a grand scale. Among the most bizarre of these events was the great Frost Fair on the River Thames in the arctic winter of 1683-84, when whole oxen were roasted over fires set on the ice. And even today, the people of Munich commemorate a royal wedding of 1810 with their annual Oktoberfest, when fish, chicken, pigs and oxen are spit-roasted outdoors in a suburb of the city.

Until the middle of the present century, however, only campers and picnickers regularly paid much attention to outdoor cooking. Then, exuberantly changing their lifestyle, city-dwellers traded their flats for suburban houses and turned their new back gardens into outdoor living rooms—or, with increasing affluence, acquired weekend retreats in the country. Cooking and eating alfresco became the vogue. No longer an occasional summer treat, cooking over coals developed into an everyday affair whose popularity has grown in recent years, first in the United States and more recently in Europe.

Basically, modern techniques of outdoor cooking mirror ancient practices. Food is still grilled, but on a metal rack instead of a *barbacoa*, and the fire is contained in a metal bowl or box instead of a pit. Spitting is now done with a metal rod rather than a stick; an electric or battery-powered motor keeps the rod turning smoothly. Even the smoking of food, which once required building a shed, is accomplished today in a portable cooker.

Such refinements in equipment tame the fire, so the cook can concentrate attention on the preparation, embellishment and presentation of the food itself. The result, as the demonstrations in this book show, can be spectacular finished dishes with an elegant appearance and matchless flavour.

Because any food cooked over coals takes on an assertive flavour, experience has proved that the most appropriate beverages to accompany it are light and simple ones. Among wines, a practical choice may well be a rosé, which complements virtually everything from beef to pork, from poultry to seafood. Tavel from Provence is a good choice; so are California rosés made from Cabernet, Pinot Noir or Zinfandel grapes. Among white wines, Muscadet from the Loire valley marries well with fish or shellfish, as do clear-tasting, refreshing dry wines from Germany's Palatinate region, the Chardonnays and Chablis from France and Soaves from Italy. Among red wines, young Beaujolais has a strong, fresh bouquet that will harmonize with beef and poultry; the wines of the Côtes du Rhône are equally suitable.

But beverages for outdoor meals need not be restricted to wine. Cold lager, with its mildly bitter taste, is always welcome. And for those who prefer non-alcoholic beverages, iced tea is refreshing and flavourful, particularly if it is laced with slices of lemon or lime and sprigs of fresh mint.

A Guide to Outdoor Cooking Equipment

The battery of basic equipment used for cooking outdoors ranges from tiny collapsible boxes to huge masonry structures. Many are designed for grilling only, although some can incorporate rotisseries for spit-roasting and others are intended mainly for smoking food. Some employ gas or electricity instead of—or in addition to—wood or charcoal.

Despite obvious differences in size, shape and design, all outdoor cooking equipment is based on two components: a firebox that holds the fuel and a rack or spit that holds the food. As the five types of portable charcoal cookers below demonstrate, these elements can be put together and refined in various ways.

The brazier, for example, is no more than a firebox and rack, and the fire is laid directly on the bottom of the firebox. In the model shown, the rack is supported on a central post that can be raised or lowered with a crank to adjust the temperature at which foods cook; in other models,

the rack rests on notched brackets attached to the rim of the firebox and the rack is adjusted by moving it from one set of notches to another. Long legs with wheels elevate the cooker to a convenient height. Some braziers also have a windscreen, or hood, that can be attached to the firebox rim. Shaped like a half cylinder, the hood can be fitted with an electric or battery-powered rotisserie.

In a hibachi, by contrast, the fire is laid on a grate rather than on the bottom of the firebox. (The model that is shown here has a double grate.) The presence of a grate permits air-flow underneath the coals, which consequently burn hotter and more evenly. Vents near the bottom of the firebox can be opened or closed to regulate the air supply and thus the rate of burning. Hibachis—which are available in many sizes—usually have brackets for adjusting the height of the racks.

The principal feature of a kettle grill is its vented cover. Grilling food under a

cover shortens its cooking time by as much as 25 per cent and intensifies its smoky flavour. A kettle grill also contains a grate for the fire and has firebox vents to regulate the heat. The rack of a kettle grill, however, is not adjustable. In the model shown, the vent closure beneath the grate can be used to clear ashes from the firebox into a tray below.

A rotisserie grill is designed to spit-roast food as well as grill it. The rack height can be adjusted by means of levers at the front of the grill. The rotisserie is supported by brackets that permit raising and lowering of the spit rod. The model shown has a grate, vents in the firebox, a vented cover and a chopping board that can be fixed to the edge of the firebox at either side. In some rotisserie grills, the coals can be placed behind a vertical grate at the back of the cooker to provide a wall of heat for spit-roasting.

A charcoal-water smoker cooks food, but is not designed for preserving it. The

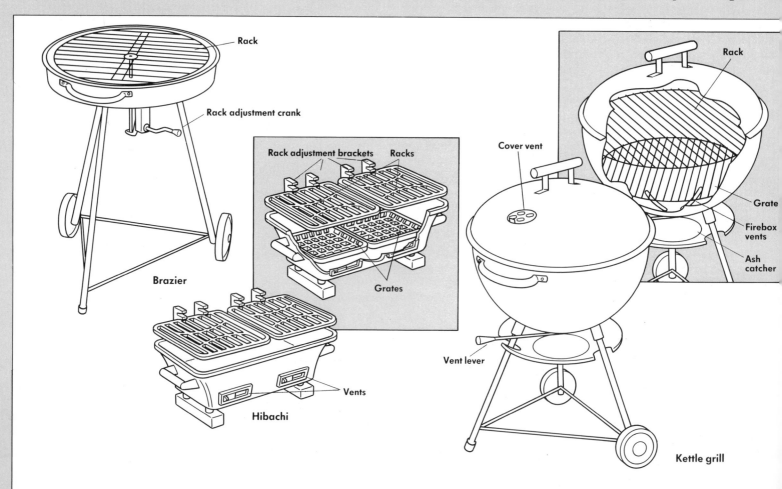

Rack

Rack adjustment crank

Brazier

Rack adjustment brackets   **Racks**

Grates

Hibachi

Vents

Cover vent

Vent lever

Kettle grill

Rack

Grate

Firebox vents

Ash catcher

smoker holds a pan for fuel and—above it—another pan for water, and one or two racks for food. Its tight-fitting cover traps smoke released by the damp wood that is used to augment the charcoal fire; meanwhile the water pan provides steam to keep the food on the racks above it moist (*pages 86-88*). The model shown has a gauge to help monitor the heat inside, and doors through which the charcoal and water supplies can be replenished. In addition to serving as a smoker, the device may be used as a grill if the cover and water pan are removed and the charcoal pan placed directly under a rack. If a smoker is not available, it is possible to smoke food in an ordinary grill that can be completely covered, either with its own lid or with an improvised cover of heavy-duty foil and wire.

The cookers shown on these pages are all portable models, but you may decide to build a more permanent brick structure. The one used in many of the demonstra-

tions in this book has brick walls on three sides and includes brick supports for a rack at different levels above the coals (*page 8*). For a well-ventilated firebox, set the grate that holds the coals above a metal tray to catch the ash.

Choosing an outdoor cooker requires careful shopping. Except for the hibachi, which is often made of cast-iron, the fireboxes and covers of outdoor grills and smokers are usually formed out of sheet steel. For durability and good heat retention, the sheet steel should be 20-gauge or heavier; hot coals may burn a hole in light-gauge steel. The finish may be either porcelain enamel or heat-resistant paint. Of the two, porcelain enamel will stand up better to rust and heat.

All wire racks should be coated with nickel chrome, which resists flaking or pitting and thus keeps the wires easy to clean. Be sure that the rack is sturdy enough not to bend under the weight of food. Legs should be widely based for sta-

bility and firmly fastened to the firebox. Wooden handles will absorb less heat than metal ones.

Regular maintenance will extend the life of any cooker. To preserve the finish, you can line the firebox with heavy-duty aluminium foil before building a fire, remembering to cut holes in the foil for the vents. After use, the cooker is left to cool; then the rack or rotisserie and grate can be removed and the ashes wrapped up in the foil and discarded. If, however, the firebox is not lined with foil, the cold ashes can be shovelled out or the grill inverted to dump them. To clean the rack, use a stiff wire brush to remove grease and food. Wash the spit rod and holding forks of a rotisserie with hot soapy water and dry them well.

Before storing a grill or smoker for the winter, wash and dry each part. Then place it indoors in a dry place; if it must be stored outdoors, use a tarpaulin or plastic cover to ward off rust.

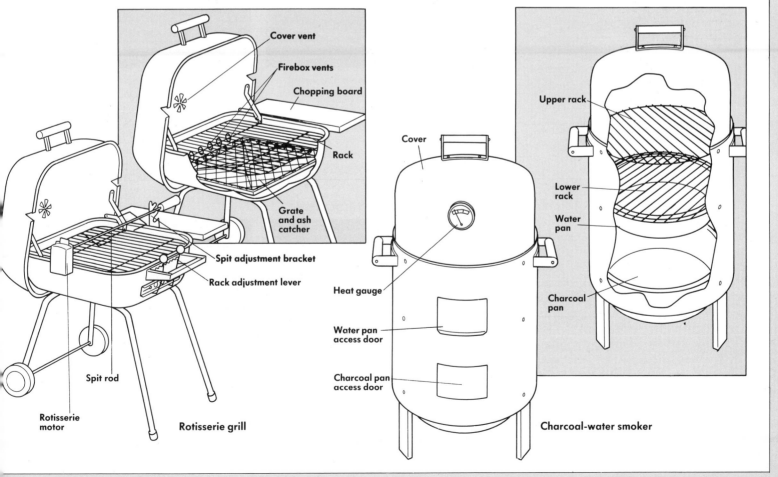

Rotisserie grill

Charcoal-water smoker

Handling Fuel and Fire

Successful cooking out of doors depends on a good fire—a bed of glowing coals that produces constant heat without flames to burn the food. The most widely used fuel for an outdoor fire is charcoal, which burns slowly and evenly and is also convenient to store and handle. You can also make the fire with logs or aromatic fruit woods (*opposite page*); in either case, tossing branches of rosemary, thyme or bay on to the fire towards the end of cooking will give a delicious flavour to the food.

Charcoal is generally available in two forms—briquets or lumps. In briquets the charcoal has been pulverized, bound with starch and compressed into nuggets of uniform size that burn for a long time and produce even heat. Lump charcoal contains no additives and is easy to light but, being less dense than briquets, it will not burn as long. For most grilling, you will require a bed about 5 cm (2 inches) deep and 2.5 to 5 cm (1 to 2 inches) larger all round than the area the food covers. For spit-roasting, you will need enough coals to form rows about 10 cm (4 inches) deep on either side of the drip pan.

An efficient device for igniting charcoal is a gas lighter (*Step 2, right*)—a replaceable cylinder of butane gas attached to a long metal nozzle. Electric starters are also available. Petroleum-based jellies and liquids or firelighters in the form of blocks or granules can be spread among the coals to facilitate lighting. Such products are convenient but, unless an odourless type is used, they may impart an undesirable taste to the food. Never use petrol or paraffin to start a fire; both are dangerously explosive.

Once they have burnt long enough to acquire a coat of ash, the coals should be rearranged to spread the heat effectively for grilling (*right, above*) or spit-roasting (*right*). To judge the temperature of the coals, hold your hand 10 to 15 cm (4 to 6 inches) from the fire and count the seconds. If you must withdraw your hand after 2 seconds, the fire is hot enough to sear foods. If you can tolerate the heat for 4 seconds, the fire is medium-hot.

Opening all the vents of a grill will increase the temperature of the fire; closing them partially will reduce it. Pushing the coals together will increase the heat; spreading coals apart will cool the fire.

A Bed of Coals for Grilling

1 Arranging the charcoal. On the grate at the bottom of the grill, place sufficient charcoal to cover an area slightly larger than the food to be cooked. Pile the charcoal into a mound to start the fire.

2 Using a gas lighter. Carefully following the manufacturer's instructions, ignite the gas lighter. Hold the lighter with the end of the nozzle under the grate beneath the mound of charcoal; keep it in position until the coals start to glow.

3 Letting the fire burn down. Leave the charcoal to burn undisturbed until—after 30 to 45 minutes—the flames have died and a film of fine white ash covers the surface of the coals.

4 Spreading the coals. Use a small metal rake to spread the coals in a single layer; the closer the coals, the more intense the heat. To replenish the fire if necessary, add fresh charcoal round the edges. Position the rack over the coals.

Rows of Coals for Spit-Roasting

1 Rearranging the coals. Start the fire (*Steps 1 to 2, above*). When the coals are ash-covered, rake them into two parallel rows with a space in between for the drip pan. To improve the air-flow, bank the rear row slightly higher.

2 Positioning the drip pan. Place a foil drip pan—longer and wider than the food to be spitted—between the two rows of coals. Check that the drip pan is directly under the spit (*above*).

A Log Fire for Indoor Cooking

For grilling or roasting at a fireplace indoors, wood logs make the best fuel. Neither charcoal briquets nor lumps are safe to use in a confined space since they release carbon monoxide.

Hard woods such as oak, beech or ash burn well without spitting. Fruit woods such as apple, cherry or vine prunings lend food flavour. Avoid soft woods—conifers, for example—since they burn rapidly and give off resinous smoke which impairs the taste of food. The wood you use should have dried out for at least six months; freshly cut green wood is too moist to burn well—use it only for smoking food (*pages 86-88*).

To cook at an indoor fire, you will need to build a support for the rack or spit. On the hearth in front of the fire, set bricks in two parallel stacks about 30 cm (12 inches) high. Some spits are supplied with metal clamps that fit over the top of bricks; otherwise, split a cored brick in two and rest the ends of the spit in the hollows. For cooking, rake out hot embers between the bricks.

1 Laying a fire. Check that the damper—the metal plate in the chimney flue—is open. Put crumpled newspapers under the grate. Arrange three criss-crossed layers of kindling in the grate. Place a split log on the kindling at the back of the grate (*above*) and another at the front.

2 Adding more kindling. Place several pieces of kindling on top of the two logs to allow room for air to circulate between the layers of wood (*above*). Set another split log on top.

3 Lighting the fire. Twist a newspaper into a fairly tight roll. Light it, and hold it up the chimney for a few seconds to start an updraft. Use the newspaper to ignite the crumpled papers (*above*), then push the lighted roll of paper under the grate.

4 Letting the fire burn down. The kindling will blaze for about 10 minutes, igniting the surfaces of the logs. Allow the fire to burn undisturbed, but not unattended; it may take an hour or longer to burn down to usable coals.

5 Checking the coals. When the glowing embers that fall from the logs form a thick layer under the grate (*above*), the fire is ready. To support a rack or spit, set two stacks of bricks on the hearth. Rake hot embers between the bricks.

Marinades: Preliminary Enhancements

Almost everything that you cook over coals will benefit from being marinated beforehand. The marinade may be mild or spicy, and based on one or two flavourings, or on several. It may be a dry blend designed chiefly to flavour food, a paste or aromatic oil to moisten the food's surfaces, or an acid-based mixture that will act as a tenderizer.

A dry marinade may be as simple as a blend of crushed dried herbs and spices, usually—but not necessarily—combined with salt (*right; recipe, page 161*). If salt is included, it forms a brine with the juices of meat or fish and permeates the flesh, carrying the flavour of the herbs and spices with it. Such a marinade is particularly useful for pork, because the salt attenuates its sweetness.

In a paste marinade, fresh or dried spices, herbs and aromatic elements such as garlic or grated citrus peel are crushed or chopped, and then combined with just enough oil to bind everything together (*opposite page, above; recipe, page 161*). In Oriental cookery, paste marinades are often bound with soy sauce rather than oil. Paste marinades not only flavour meat or fish in advance, but adhere to the food as it cooks, keeping it moist.

An oil-based marinade—much wetter than a paste—is ideal for protecting and nourishing vegetables and lean meat or fish. For this type of marinade, a generous quantity of oil is combined with just enough aromatic ingredients to flavour it (*opposite page, below; recipe, page 161*).

An acidic marinade may be based on wine (*right, below; recipe, page 162*), lemon, orange or lime juice, wine vinegar or yogurt. Aromatics add zest to the mixture, and the addition of oil ensures that the food does not dry out.

Marinating time will vary according to the type of food and the intensity of flavour you desire. You can marinate meat, poultry and vegetables for about 2 hours at room temperature—which promotes a rapid exchange of flavours—or for up to 24 hours in a refrigerator. If you are tenderizing meat in an acid-based marinade, it can be kept in a refrigerator for up to 48 hours. For fish and shellfish, which deteriorate more quickly than meat, allow only about an hour at room temperature or about 2 hours in the refrigerator.

A Dry Marinade of Spices and Salt

1 **Crushing flavourings.** With a mortar and pestle, crush dried spices and herbs—in this case, juniper berries, whole allspice, black peppercorns and thyme leaves— to make a coarse powder. Crumble bay leaves into tiny bits with your fingers; add them to the mixture.

2 **Adding salt.** Pour coarse salt into the mortar and stir it together with the herbs and spices. Use the pestle to grind the ingredients until they are evenly blended; the marinade is now ready for use.

Acidic Liquid to Tenderize

1 **Preparing vegetables.** Cut an onion into thin slices and place them in a shallow dish large enough to hold the food to be marinated. Cut peeled carrots into thin rounds and place them in the dish. Add chives and sprigs of fresh parsley and dill. Grind in pepper.

2 **Adding liquids.** Moisten the ingredients with enough olive oil to coat the bottom of the dish. Pour in wine—in this case, white wine is used. Use your hand to mix the ingredients together; the marinade is now ready for use.

Herbs and Spices in a Mixture that Clings

1 **Preparing the dry ingredients.** With a mortar and pestle, pulverize dried spices and herbs—here, whole allspice and blades of mace. Use your fingers to open cardamom pods (*above*); spill the seeds into the mortar and discard the pods.

2 **Grinding.** Crumble bay leaves and dried chili peppers (*above*) with your fingers; add them to the mortar. Grind the mixture with the pestle until it forms a fine powder.

3 **Adding oil.** Dribble olive oil into the mortar and stir it gradually into the dry ingredients. Incorporate just enough oil to moisten the mixture evenly and make it sticky enough to adhere to food.

Aromatic Oil for Moistening

1 **Chopping herbs.** Peel shallots and garlic cloves and set them aside. Remove the leaves from sprigs of fresh thyme and discard the stems. With a sharp, heavy knife, chop the leaves, using a rocking motion while steadying the back of the knife blade near its tip with one hand.

2 **Combining ingredients.** Finely chop the shallots and garlic and mix them with the thyme in a shallow dish large enough to hold the food to be marinated. Grate the rind of an orange, being careful not to include any of the bitter white pith. Add the grated rind to the dish.

3 **Incorporating oil.** Pour enough olive oil into the dish to saturate the aromatics. Add a pinch of coarse salt and grind in pepper to taste. Stir to mix the ingredients well before using the marinade.

A Gallery of Accompaniments

The smoky taste of foods cooked over coals is best accented and complemented by sauces, relishes and garnishes that have an assertiveness of their own. Herbs, spices and aromatic vegetables will supply the essential zest to accompaniments that range from tangy barbecue sauces and relishes to more subtly flavoured mayonnaises and butters.

Barbecue sauces are used to marinate meat or poultry and to baste the food as it cooks, forming an attractive glaze. Such sauces may be hot and spicy, or sweet and sour; the mixture shown on the right combines honey, soy sauce, orange juice, tomatoes and vinegar (*recipe, page 164*).

Relishes consist mainly of chopped raw vegetables bound with oil and citrus juice or vinegar. The chili relish shown here (*right, below; recipe, page 162*) is a colourful amalgam of onions, garlic, tomatoes and coriander, with chili peppers to give it bite, making a piquant garnish for hamburgers or steak. For a pungent accompaniment to meat—lamb in particular—you can pound spices and aromatic ingredients such as garlic and parsley in a mortar, then add generous amounts of lemon juice, oil, diced lemon and olives (*opposite page, below; recipe, page 113*).

Another spicy sauce is based on ground peanuts cooked with Oriental seasonings and aromatics (*page 15; recipe, page 111*). This crunchy sauce is traditionally served with satay, the marinated grilled kebabs of South-East Asia.

Mayonnaise, an emulsion of egg yolk and oil, makes a perfect complement to the delicate flavour of grilled fish. By adding other ingredients you can create a spectrum of effects from the aromatic sweetness of a basil mayonnaise (*page 14, above; recipe, page 163*) to the pungency of a garlic-laden aïoli (*recipe, page 163*).

Flavoured butters provide some of the simplest garnishes for meats, fish and vegetables. Made by beating softened butter with a flavouring, the mixture will mingle with the juices of hot food. You can season the butter with mustard, chopped herbs or crushed garlic; or make an unusual complement for grilled seafood by incorporating fish roe—here, scallop corals (*page 14, below; recipe, page 156*).

A Classic Barbecue Sauce

1 **Softening the tomatoes.** Finely chop onions and sauté them in a little oil until they are soft. Cut tomatoes into wedges about 5 mm (¼ inch) thick and add them to the onions with a sprig of thyme, a bay leaf and salt and pepper. Over a gentle heat, cook the tomatoes, stirring them occasionally, until they are reduced to a thick pulp—about 30 minutes.

2 **Sieving.** Transfer the tomato mixture to a nylon sieve set over a bowl. Using a broad wooden pestle, press the mixture through the sieve (*above*). Discard the tomato skins and seeds and the herbs that remain in the sieve.

A Piquant Relish with Hot Chili Peppers

1 **Seeding chili peppers.** Chop onions and garlic cloves and place them in a bowl. Nick the skins of tomatoes, plunge them into boiling water, then remove the skins and seeds. Stem fresh chili peppers—in this case, *jalapenos*—quarter them lengthwise, then cut out the seedy cores. Finely chop the peppers and add them to the bowl. Stem fresh coriander leaves.

2 **Blending the relish.** Chop the coriander leaves and tomatoes coarsely and add them to the bowl. Add a large pinch of coarse salt, then pour in vinegar or fresh lime juice and mix well. Stir in olive oil. Cover and set the mixture aside for 30 minutes to allow the flavours to blend.

3 **Crushing garlic.** Peel garlic cloves. Put the peeled cloves and coarse salt in a large mortar; use a pestle to crush them to a smooth paste (*above*). Add paprika to the mortar and stir it in. Spoon in honey and pound to mix the ingredients.

4 **Blending.** One by one, add the other ingredients to the mortar—the tomato purée, orange juice, wine vinegar and soy sauce—and stir with the pestle after each addition. Stir the mixture until it is perfectly blended (*above*). The sauce is now ready for use as a marinade.

5 **Reducing the sauce.** To use the sauce as a basting liquid, transfer the mixture to a small pan. Bring the mixture to the boil; lower the heat and simmer until the sauce has reduced to a coating consistency. Stir frequently to prevent the sauce from sticking to the pan.

A Heady Combination of Garlic and Spices

1 **Pounding the dry ingredients.** Peel garlic cloves; finely chop parsley. Remove the seeds from dried chili peppers (*Step 1, opposite page*); discard the seeds. In a mortar, pound the chili peppers, cumin, paprika and coarse salt to a powder (*above*). Add the garlic and parsley, and pound the ingredients to a paste.

2 **Adding oil.** Cut the flesh and rind of a lemon into fine dice. Squeeze the juice from another half lemon. Halve and stone black olives. Dribble olive oil into the mixture in the mortar (*above*) and stir it in with a spoon.

3 **Stirring the sauce.** Add the lemon juice and cold water to dilute the mixture. Finally, add the diced lemon and the halved olives. Using a wooden spoon, stir the sauce to combine the ingredients.

A Colourful Basil Mayonnaise

1 **Whisking egg yolks.** Blanch fresh basil leaves in boiling water for 3 seconds. Drop them into cold water, dry the leaves and chop them finely. Separate eggs that are at room temperature, dropping the yolks into a bowl; reserve the whites for another use. Add the basil to the yolks and whisk vigorously for a minute.

2 **Adding olive oil.** Stir in lemon juice until the mixture is smooth. Then, whisking constantly, add olive oil a drop at a time. When the mixture begins to thicken—indicating that the emulsion has begun to form—increase the flow of oil to a thin, steady stream (*above*).

3 **Seasoning.** Continue to whisk and add oil until the mayonnaise is thick enough to form soft peaks. Stir in salt and freshly ground pepper, and add a little more lemon juice if desired. Tightly covered, the mayonnaise can be kept for several days in the refrigerator.

A Subtle Seafood Butter

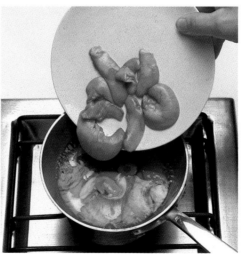

1 **Preparing coral.** Holding a scallop shell flat side up, insert a short knife and run the blade across the roof to sever the muscle. Part the shells and slide the knife beneath the scallop to free it from the lower shell. Discard all but the white muscle and orange coral. With your fingers, divide the coral from the muscle (*above*).

2 **Poaching the corals.** Prepare a court-bouillon: pour equal quantities of wine and water into a pan and add a finely sliced carrot and onion, and sprigs of fresh parsley and dill. Bring the court-bouillon to a simmer and add the corals.

3 **Reducing the court-bouillon.** Poach the corals for about 3 minutes, then use a slotted spoon to transfer them to a sieve. Let them drain. Strain the court-bouillon into another pan. Discard the aromatics. Bring the court-bouillon to the boil, then boil over a medium heat (*above*) until the liquid has reduced to a spoonful.

An Exotic Blend of Nuts and Spices

1 **Starting the sauce.** Finely chop onions and garlic. In a heavy pan, fry the onions and garlic in oil until they are slightly softened. Finely chop lemon grass—here, dried lemon grass is used—and add it to the mixture in the pan (*above*). Cook for about 5 minutes.

2 **Adding ground peanuts.** Squeeze lime juice. Prepare coconut milk (*recipe, page 167*). Add a stick of cinnamon, a pinch of sugar, salt and chili powder to the mixture in the pan. Finely grind peanuts and add them to the pan (*above*).

3 **Finishing the sauce.** Add water, peanut oil, the prepared coconut milk and lime juice to the mixture in the pan. Bring the mixture to the boil, stirring. Turn down the heat and simmer, stirring, for 15 to 20 minutes, until the sauce is fairly thick.

4 **Sieving the corals.** Set a nylon sieve over a bowl—a metal one would impart a metallic taste. Using a wooden spoon or a pestle, push the corals through the sieve. Scrape the base of the sieve and add the sieved coral to the bowl.

5 **Adding the court-bouillon.** Whisk butter until light and fluffy. Add the sieved corals to the butter and pour in the reduced court-bouillon (*above*). Whisk all the ingredients until they are well blended. Whip cream until it forms soft peaks.

6 **Finishing the butter.** Add the whipped cream to the bowl and whisk the mixture gently until the cream is well combined and the butter is smooth. Season to taste with salt and freshly ground pepper.

1
Vegetables and Fruits
Imaginative Treatments for Garden Produce

What better way to accompany or round off an outdoor meal than with vegetables piping hot from the coals, or fruits transformed into a range of delicious desserts? Many vegetables and fruits—large or small, tender or firm—are potential candidates for grilling on a rack, baking in hot ashes, or steaming in their skins or in a wrapper of foil.

Whole vegetables with sturdy skins—courgettes and aubergines among them—soften and acquire a subtle smoky taste when grilled on a rack. To keep their skins moist, oil them liberally, and pierce or score them to prevent the skins from bursting when their juices expand as steam (*page 19*). The vegetables should be cooked 10 to 15 cm (4 to 6 inches) above the coals, where the temperature is hot but not scorching, and turned periodically to ensure even cooking.

Potatoes, too, can be oiled, pierced and grilled on a rack; parboiling them first speeds the process. Slicing the vegetables will shorten the time required to cook them. Other firm vegetables such as onions, or juicier specimens such as tomatoes or sweet peppers, respond equally well to this treatment. The oil that protects the slices will contribute additional flavour if blended with spices or herbs. To make turning easy, the slices can be assembled in a hinged basket or threaded on to skewers (*pages 20-21*).

The grill also provides an unusual method for steaming vegetables. Ears of sweetcorn, protected by their own husks, can be moistened with water to create steam, and set directly on the oiled rack (*page 22*). Other vegetables, either whole or cut up, need only be wrapped in foil with a little water, wine or butter. Another simple way to cook vegetables is to bake them in hot ashes (*page 19*); this is particularly suitable for vegetables protected by firm or fibrous skins such as potatoes or onions.

Fruits can be treated by the same methods used for vegetables. Whole bananas can be grilled in their skins, as can other firm-skinned fruits such as mangoes and papayas. Fruit can also be cut into pieces and skewered; the pieces stay juicy if basted with alcohol or melted butter and spices, and can be sprinkled with sugar for a caramelized surface (*page 24*). For baking in ashes, fruits such as apples, pears or peaches can be flavoured with sugar and spices before they are wrapped in foil. A packet containing a peeled, segmented orange, sprinkled with brown sugar, rum and cinnamon, makes a perfect finale for a meal cooked over coals (*page 22*).

To flavour and coat them with a protective film of oil, a selection of vegetables are tossed in a herb-scented marinade. The vegetables—aubergines, courgettes, mushrooms, shallots and sweet peppers—were first cut into equal-sized pieces so that they could be threaded on to skewers to make vegetable kebabs (*page 21*).

17

Tactics for Whole Vegetables

Whole vegetables retain their natural moisture and flavours when grilled over coals or baked in the hot ashes of an open fire. Almost all vegetables can be grilled; those with thick protective skins also lend themselves to baking.

New and old potatoes, sweet potatoes and yams are examples of vegetables that can be grilled or roasted. Here, new potatoes are boiled until almost tender, brushed with oil and seasoned, and then grilled over coals to finish cooking and to develop crisp skins (*right*). The boiling is optional, but it shortens the grilling time and also ensures that the potatoes cook evenly. To facilitate turning, the potatoes are impaled on skewers; if they are not skewered, pierce them instead, to keep them from bursting when their moisture turns to steam and expands.

Potatoes for baking in ashes (*opposite page, above*) should be scrubbed and then pricked. Sweet potatoes and yams do not require piercing since their porous skins allow steam to escape. Onions and heads of garlic can be baked in their skins like potatoes. Beetroots need a wrapping of foil to keep them from losing their juices.

Well-coated with oil, large mushroom caps can be grilled flat on the rack, and they form natural containers for a stuffing (*right; recipe, page 165*). Choose a filling that needs little cooking because, once they are stuffed, the caps cannot be turned on the rack. Here, the stuffing contains chopped sautéed shallots, garlic and sweet red peppers, mixed with breadcrumbs, parsley and lemon juice.

Other whole vegetables that can be simply set on the rack for grilling include courgettes and aubergines, spring onions and sweet peppers (*opposite page, below*). Make long incisions in courgettes and aubergines to prevent them from bursting and to allow the piquant aroma of the coals to penetrate their flesh. Otherwise, the vegetables merely need to be well oiled. Bear in mind that when different vegetables are grilled together the timing must be orchestrated. Slow-cooking varieties should be started first and fast-cooking ones added last so that all of them will be done at the same time.

Potatoes Impaled on Skewers

1 **Skewering.** Boil unpeeled new potatoes until barely tender—12 to 15 minutes. Drain them and toss them in oil seasoned with salt and, if you like, crushed dried chili peppers. Thread five or six potatoes on to each skewer. Pour the remaining seasoned oil over the potatoes and lay the skewers on an oiled rack 10 to 15 cm (4 to 6 inches) above medium-hot coals.

2 **Grilling.** Turn the skewers frequently, using long-handled tongs or a cloth to protect your hand. Grill the potatoes for 3 to 4 minutes in all, until the skins are crisped evenly. To serve the potatoes, use a fork to push them off the skewers and on to plates. □

Mushroom Caps with a Stuffing

1 **Stuffing mushrooms.** Remove the stems from large mushrooms; wipe the caps. Marinate them for up to 2 hours in olive oil and lemon juice. Remove them from the marinade. For the stuffing, combine sautéed chopped sweet red peppers, shallots and garlic with parsley, a little marinade and fresh breadcrumbs; add seasoning. Spoon into the mushrooms.

2 **Grilling the mushrooms.** With a long-handled spatula or tongs, place the stuffed mushroom caps on an oiled rack 10 to 15 cm (4 to 6 inches) above medium-hot coals. Grill them for 8 to 10 minutes. The mushrooms are done when the caps feel slightly soft to the touch and the stuffing is cooked through. □

Potatoes Roasted in Ashes

1 **Burying potatoes in ashes.** Thoroughly scrub potatoes—in this case, a mixture of red-skinned potatoes and sweet potatoes. Pierce the red-skinned potatoes in several places with a fork or skewer. Using long-handled tongs, lay the potatoes in hot ashes—at the side of a fireplace, as here, or in the embers of an outdoor grill. Using a small shovel, scoop hot ashes over the potatoes to bury them completely (*above*).

2 **Serving.** Bake the potatoes until they feel soft when pierced with a long-handled fork—about 45 minutes. Remove the cooked potatoes from the ashes with tongs. Protecting your hand with a cloth or oven glove, brush ash from the potatoes. Cut a cross in one side of each potato and squeeze the potato at both ends to widen the opening and reveal the potato's flesh. Serve the potatoes at once with butter or soured cream.□

A Mélange of Aubergines, Peppers and Spring Onions

1 **Scoring vegetables.** Pour olive oil into a dish; turn sweet red peppers in the oil to coat them. Cut four lengthwise grooves 5 mm (¼ inch) deep in an aubergine; rub olive oil into the grooves and over the surface. Trim roots and damaged leaves from spring onions; brush the onions with olive oil and season them.

2 **Grilling.** Place the sweet peppers and aubergine on an oiled rack 10 to 15 cm (4 to 6 inches) above medium-hot coals. Turning them often, grill until their skins are blistered all over and their flesh is tender—20 to 30 minutes. During the last 5 minutes, add the spring onions and grill them until the green tops wilt.

3 **Serving.** Transfer the spring onions to a platter. Quarter the aubergine by cutting through the grooves; divide the quarters in half crosswise, then arrange them on the platter. Halve the peppers, scoop out and discard the cores and seeds, peel off the skin and add the peppers to the platter. Serve at once.□

Slices for Speedy Grilling

Vegetables that have been cut into slices, chunks or segments cook fast over coals and acquire an appetizing brown finish. Because they are exposed to direct heat, the pieces must be well coated with oil to remain moist. However, necessity can be turned to advantage by adding seasonings and herbs to the oil to endow the vegetables with extra flavour.

The best candidates for such treatment are vegetables with firm, moist flesh—among them, aubergines, sweet peppers, onions and green or underripe tomatoes. Root vegetables such as potatoes and turnips, and bulb fennel or celery sticks are also suitable, but they must first be parboiled until about half-cooked, lest they char on the outside before they become tender inside.

If, like the potatoes on the right, the pieces are large enough for easy turning with tongs or a spatula, they can go individually on to the grill rack. If the pieces are small or fragile—or if there are so many that turning them one by one would be tedious—you can protect their structure and lighten your task in two ways. You can either impale the pieces on a skewer to form kebabs (*opposite page, above*), or you can assemble them in a hinged grill basket, as demonstrated with the tomato and onion slices on the right.

For grilling on a rack or in a basket, vegetables should be cut into slices that are thick enough to hold together yet thin enough to cook through evenly in the time they take to brown. As a rule, a thickness of about 8 mm ($\frac{1}{3}$ inch) is appropriate, although especially juicy specimens might be cut 1 cm ($\frac{1}{2}$ inch) thick. Make sure that all the pieces are the same thickness so that they will be done simultaneously.

For skewering, the pieces should all be approximately the same size—about 2.5 to 4 cm (1 to 1½ inches) square, although the thickness will vary according to the vegetable. In the kebabs, or brochettes, shown here, mushrooms, courgettes, aubergines, sweet red and green peppers and onions are marinated in an oil marinade (*page 11, below*), then arranged in a sequence of alternating colours. You can, of course, vary the selection and arrangement to make whatever design of colours and textures you like.

Potatoes with a Lattice Design

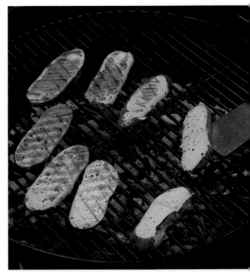

1 **Cutting slices.** Pour olive oil into a dish; add salt and pepper. Scrub potatoes but do not peel them. Parboil them for 7 minutes, or until a fork can penetrate the flesh but meets firm resistance towards the centre. Drain, then cut the potatoes lengthwise into 8 mm ($\frac{1}{3}$ inch) thick slices (*above*). Place the slices in the oil and turn them to coat both sides.

2 **Grilling.** Arrange the slices diagonally on an oiled rack 10 to 15 cm (4 to 6 inches) above medium-hot coals. After about 3 minutes, rotate the slices through 90 degrees so that the grill bars sear a crisscross pattern on to them. Cook for a further 2 minutes. Turn the slices and grill them, rotating them as before, until they are tender when pierced with a fork.□

Tomatoes and Onions in a Hinged Basket

1 **Preparing slices.** Pour olive oil into a shallow dish and toss fresh rosemary sprigs in the oil. Slice onions—here, red onions—8 mm ($\frac{1}{3}$ inch) thick and lay them in the dish. Turn them to coat both sides. Core large, firm tomatoes and slice them 8 mm thick (*above*). Place the tomatoes in the dish and turn them in the oil.

2 **Filling the basket.** Place a few sprigs of rosemary in the base of a hinged wire basket. Lay the onion and tomato slices in the basket and place the remaining rosemary on top. Season to taste. Lower the lid of the hinged basket over the vegetables (*above*) and fasten the two handles with the sliding clasp.

Composing Kebabs

1 **Preparing vegetables.** Cut aubergines into 2.5 cm (1 inch) cubes, salt them and leave for 30 minutes to draw out excess moisture; dry them. Cut courgettes into 2.5 cm pieces. Peel shallots; halve them lengthwise. Wipe mushrooms. Remove the seeds and ribs from sweet peppers; cut the flesh into 2.5 cm squares (*above*).

2 **Marinating.** Sprinkle all the vegetables with salt, chopped garlic, finely chopped parsley and mixed dried herbs. Pour on olive oil and mix the vegetables with your hands to coat them. Thread the pieces on to skewers (*above*), making sure that each skewer holds a selection of all the vegetables. Reserve the marinade.

3 **Grilling.** Place the skewers on an oiled rack set 10 cm (4 inches) above medium-hot coals; baste the vegetable pieces frequently with the reserved marinade. Turn the skewers after about 10 minutes (*above*). Grill them for a further 5 to 10 minutes, basting frequently, until they are lightly browned.□

3 **Grilling and serving.** Place the basket on a rack 10 to 15 cm (4 to 6 inches) above medium-hot coals. Grill the slices for about 3 minutes, then turn the basket over and grill the other side of the slices for a further 3 minutes, or until they are lightly browned (*above*). The onions will still be slightly crisp but the tomatoes will be soft. Remove the basket from the rack and open it. Slide the slices on to a warmed serving dish (*right*). Serve at once.□

Wrapping to Seal in Juices

When moistened vegetables and fruits are enclosed in wrappers before being grilled or baked, steam is created inside the wrapper, yielding remarkably succulent results. Furthermore, wrappers keep their contents piping hot for 10 minutes or longer, thus simplifying the timing of an outdoor meal.

Among vegetables, sweetcorn (*right*) comes with its own wrapping material—its fibrous husk. Once the silky fibres beneath the husk are removed, the ears are soaked in water to ensure they are moist enough for steaming. For other vegetables, and also fruit, heavy-duty aluminium foil can be shaped into sturdy packets (*right, below*). Wrapped in this manner, any vegetable can be safely steamed; so, too, can firmer fruits that will soften but will hold their shape for serving.

Prior to being wrapped, vegetables and fruits should be peeled, cored, shelled or stemmed as necessary. Vegetables may then be left whole or cut up. If a single kind of vegetable is packeted on its own, all the pieces must be of similar size so that they steam at the same rate. When cooked in combination, firmer-textured varieties should be cut into smaller pieces than softer types, and placed at the bottom of the packet where the temperature will be highest.

Juicy vegetables such as tomatoes or courgettes supply all the moisture required for steaming; drier kinds should be dipped in water before being wrapped. A chunk of butter will contribute enrichment, or you can add other liquids and flavourings. Lemon juice, stock or wine might replace water when steaming carrots, cabbage or broccoli, for example.

Liquids added to parcels of fruit create a flavourful sauce within the wrapper. The oranges on the right are packaged with rum, brown sugar and cinnamon, then baked in hot ashes. Whole peaches could be moistened with brandy and flavoured with macaroons; pears would go well with Sauternes and almonds.

Although the sizes of the packets can be adjusted to yield an individual serving or a platterful, they must always be kept small and light enough to be handled without risk of splitting. Two layers of foil make the packets strong, and double folds or twisted tops seal them tightly.

Sweetcorn Protected by Its Own Husks

1 Preparing sweetcorn. One strip at a time, carefully peel back—but do not remove—the fibrous husk of each ear of sweetcorn. Pull off the thread-like silk inside and discard it.

2 Tying the ears. Fold the husk back to its original position, and secure it by tying a piece of string round the tip of the ear. Soak the ears in cold water for about 10 minutes, then drain but do not dry them.

Rum-Soaked Oranges Baked in Foil

1 Removing peel and pith. Using a small, sharp knife, cut off the top and bottom of an orange to give level surfaces; stand the orange upright. Slice down the sides of the orange to cut away the peel together with the thick white pith (*above*). Peel the rest of the oranges in the same manner and discard the peels.

2 Making foil parcels. For each orange, cut two 30 cm (12 inch) squares of foil; arrange the squares, shiny side down, in a stack. Slice an orange crosswise into 8 mm ($\frac{1}{3}$ inch) rounds; pick out any pips. Reassemble the orange in the middle of the top square of foil, spooning brown sugar and a little cinnamon on to each slice before adding the next (*above*).

3 **Grilling the sweetcorn.** Lay the ears on an oiled rack 10 to 15 cm (4 to 6 inches) above medium-hot coals (*left*). Turning the ears often, grill them until the husks are dark brown on all sides—about 15 minutes. Use tongs to remove the corn from the rack; discard the string, open the husks and butter the kernels (*above*) before serving the corn.□

3 **Adding rum.** Bunch the top two squares of foil round the orange. Steadying the foil and orange with one hand, pour a generous splash of rum into the packet (*above*). Gather up the foil to enclose the orange completely and twist the top of the foil into a tuft. Make similar parcels of all the oranges.

4 **Burying the parcels.** With a small shovel, dig holes about 10 cm (4 inches) deep in a bed of hot ashes. Put the parcels, with their tufts of foil upright, into the hollows. Shovel ash round each parcel (*above*), ensuring that it is completely buried; leave the tuft exposed. After 15 minutes, use the tufts of foil to lift out the parcels.

5 **Serving the oranges.** When you are ready to serve the oranges, undo the parcels and remove and discard the outer layer of foil. Serve the oranges straight from the inner foil, sliding each orange on to an individual plate and pouring the hot rum and juices over the slices (*above*). Serve the oranges just as they are or with cream.□

Special Effects for Outdoor Desserts

The fresh flavours and firm textures of many fruits make them a perfect conclusion to an outdoor meal. Morsels of mixed fruit cooked on skewers form an unusual hot fruit salad, while whole fruit, protected by its own skin or wrapped in foil, is just as quick and easy to grill. In the demonstrations here, segments of orange, lemon, pineapple and banana on skewers are sprinkled with sugar to give them a caramelized finish (*recipe, page 97*), and bananas are grilled in their skins and flambéed with kirsch (*recipe, page 96*).

For kebabs, select fruits that will hold together when subjected to the direct heat of the grill. Instead of those shown here, you could substitute chunks of apple, pear, peach or apricot. Include no more than three or four varieties so that the individual flavours can be distinguished. Interspersing the fruit with bread pieces that have been coated with butter and tossed in sugar adds a crisp contrast in texture to the juicy fruit.

Once the fruits have been cut into bite-sized pieces, you may like to macerate them before grilling to enhance their flavour. Here, a mixture of rum and sugar was used but you could substitute vermouth or a medium-sweet white wine for the rum, and add ginger, cinnamon, honey or lemon juice. The marinade can be used to baste the fruit as it grills; alternatively, baste with melted butter mixed with cinnamon, nutmeg or cloves.

Even less preparation is required for grilled whole fruits. Bananas, which have thick, protective skins, can be laid on the rack just as they are or, if you intend to flambé them, their skins can be partially removed. Other fruits, such as halved papayas or mangoes, can be grilled skin side down in the same way. Whole apples, pears or peaches will need a wrapping of foil to protect them and conserve their juices. The core or stone should be removed and the cavities filled with raisins or cinnamon mixed with sugar, and a knob of butter.

After grilling, you can sprinkle a liqueur over the fruit and set light to the alcohol. Flambéing leaves a flavourful residue on the fruit. Rum or cherry-based kirsch will enhance just about every fruit; orange-flavoured liqueurs have obvious affinities with citrus fruits.

1 Preparing fruits. Cut unpeeled oranges and lemons crosswise into slices 1 to 2 cm ($\frac{1}{2}$ to $\frac{3}{4}$ inch) thick, then quarter each slice; the peel will help keep the fruit together during cooking. Peel a pineapple and quarter it. Cut the core from each quarter (*above*). Slice the flesh into 4 cm ($1\frac{1}{2}$ inch) cubes. Peel bananas and cut them into 4 cm slices. Discard all the peelings.

2 Macerating the fruits. Place the cut fruits in a large bowl and sprinkle them liberally with castor sugar. Add rum (*above*). Mix gently with your hands or with a wooden spoon to make sure each piece of fruit is thoroughly coated. Allow the fruits to stand in a cool place for about 30 minutes to absorb the marinade.

3 Preparing bread batons. Cut the crusts from a white loaf, then slice the bread 2 cm ($\frac{3}{4}$ inch) thick. Cut the slices into 2 by 4 cm ($\frac{3}{4}$ by $1\frac{1}{2}$ inch) pieces. Melt butter in a small pan over low heat. Brush all sides of each baton of bread with melted butter. Toss the bread pieces in a dish of castor sugar, until all the surfaces of the bread are encrusted with sugar.

4 Assembling the fruit kebabs. Thread the pieces of macerated fruit and bread batons on to skewers. Include a selection of all the fruits and one or two pieces of bread on each skewer.

Bananas Flamed in Their Skins

1 **Preparing the fruit.** Choose medium ripe bananas. Starting at the tip of each banana, nick the skin lightly and run the point of a sharp knife along each side to the other end, taking care not to cut into the flesh. Peel off the top half of the skin, leaving the bottom half intact.

2 **Grilling the fruit.** Place the bananas, skin side down, on the grill about 10 to 15 cm (4 to 6 inches) above medium-hot coals. When the skins have blackened—after about 5 minutes—carefully sprinkle each fruit with castor sugar (*above*).

3 **Serving the bananas.** When the sugar has melted, use tongs to transfer the bananas to heated serving plates. Warm liqueur—here, kirsch—in a small pan and pour it over each serving. Ignite the liqueur with a match. When the flames have died, serve the hot bananas with whipped cream (above).

5 **Grilling the kebabs.** Place the kebabs on the rack about 10 cm (4 inches) above medium-hot coals. Sprinkle the fruit with castor sugar, holding the spoon near to the fruit so that only a minimum of sugar falls on the coals. When the sugar starts to turn brown and caramelize—after about 7 minutes—turn the kebabs, using a metal spatula to steady each skewer.

6 **Serving the kebabs.** When the fruit and bread surfaces have caramelized—after another 5 minutes—remove the kebabs from the grill. For serving, push the fruit and bread gently off the skewers with the aid of a fork. Accompany, if you like, with fresh cream.□

2
Meats
Matching the Cut to the Method

Searing over hot coals
Making the most of natural fat
Mincing meat at home
The basics of spit-roasting

Long-handled tongs are used to turn thick loin of lamb chops—each with its apron wrapped round a halved kidney—that are grilling over hot coals (*page 30*). After being seared quickly on all sides, the chops will be moved to the side of the rack to cook through more slowly.

Nothing so epitomizes the pleasures of cooking outdoors as the preparation of meats, their juices sizzling and their aromas blending with the scent of smoke. Getting good results outdoors starts with choosing a prime, lean cut that will withstand direct, dry heat without becoming tough. The next step involves matching the shape of the cut and the characteristics of the meat—whether beef, veal, pork or lamb—to the appropriate cooking method: grilling or spit-roasting.

In grilling, the meat is exposed one surface at a time to the heat. Thus, in order to brown evenly, the meat should be reasonably flat—a qualification that makes all manner of prime beef steaks (*page 28*) and chops of pork and lamb (*opposite*) unmistakable candidates for grilling. Less obvious choices, but as suitable, are shoulder and short saddle of lamb and, also, boned loin of pork (*page 32*). And a vast range of cuts become appropriate for grilling when reduced to small pieces for skewering (*page 38*), or when minced for hamburgers (*page 34*) or sausages (*page 36*).

A bulky, irregularly shaped cut—a leg of pork or lamb (*page 42*), for instance—which would cook unevenly on the rack, is ideally suited to spit-roasting. As the spit rod turns with the cut of meat impaled, all the meat's surfaces are exposed to the heat, which penetrates slowly and evenly through thick flesh without overcooking the outside. A rack of pork spareribs is another awkwardly shaped cut that the spit handles magnificently: the rod can be threaded through the whole rack so that the ribs stay attached to each other—and remain juicy (*page 44*).

Some cuts—spareribs are an example—possess an interlarding of fat that helps to keep them moist and succulent as they cook. Leaner cuts, such as steaks or chops, require additional basting with oil or melted butter. But a large cut of very lean meat, such as a boned loin of veal, needs to be wrapped in a layer of extra fat to prevent it from drying out during its lengthy exposure to the heat (*page 46*). Caul—a lacy membrane of pork fat obtainable from butchers—is an excellent covering that adheres of its own accord. It can be used to protect delicate offal meats. Enrobed in caul, skewered morsels of sweetbreads, heart, liver and kidneys can be placed safely on a hot rack without risk to their fragile texture (*page 40*).

A Two-Stage Strategy for Steak

The paradigm of grilled meats is a beef steak, crisp and mahogany-coloured outside but juicy and pink within. Achieving this effect takes practice, but the process itself is simple: first the steak is seared over intense heat to firm its surfaces, then it is cooked through over reduced heat.

The tenderest steaks come from prime cuts—rib, fillet, rump, T-bone, entrecote, porterhouse and sirloin steaks. However, tougher cuts, such as skirt, are also suitable candidates for the grill, providing that they have first been tenderized in a marinade (*pages 10-11*).

Whatever the cut, the best beef is fine-textured and streaked with internal fat, or marbling, that melts during grilling to keep the meat moist. To cook through without drying and toughening or becoming charred, the beef steak must be at least 2.5 cm (1 inch)—but no more than 7.5 cm (3 inches)—thick.

The border of fat on most steaks protects the edges, but may drip into the fire and cause flare-ups unless trimmed to 5 to 10 mm (¼ to ½ inch). Even then the fat will cook faster than the meat and shrink in the process, thus making steaks buckle if they are less than 5 cm (2 inches) thick. To prevent this, cut through the border of fat at 3 cm (1¼ inch) intervals.

A porterhouse such as the one shown here contains sections of fillet and loin at either side of the bone. To keep the meat juicy, ask the butcher to leave on the long tail, or strip of meat, at the narrow end of the steak. Before grilling, wrap the tail round the loin and attach it with toothpicks. To prevent sticking, grease the rack with scraps of steak fat or a piece of fat bacon and—unless the meat has been marinated—oil the steak itself.

Grilling time depends on the thickness of the steak and the degree of doneness you require. Including the searing, which should take no more than 5 to 6 minutes in all, allow 8 to 10 minutes for each 2.5 cm (1 inch) of thickness to produce rare steak, about 12 minutes for medium steak and 15 to 20 minutes for well done. Before removing the steak from the grill, press the meat with the back of a fork, or with your fingers, to test its resilience (*Step 6*), or make a cut near the bone to check the colour of the juice: red for rare meat, pink for medium, clear for well done.

1 **Trimming the steak.** Place the steak—a porterhouse steak 6 cm (2½ inches) thick is used here—on a chopping board. With a sharp knife, slice off the excess fat from the edges, leaving a border 5 to 10 mm (¼ to ½ inch) wide. If there is a large deposit of solid fat between the fillet and the tail, cut it out. Reserve the pieces of fat.

2 **Seasoning the steak.** Pour a few drops of oil on both sides of the steak, then sprinkle it with salt and freshly ground pepper, and rub the seasonings into the flesh with your hand (*above*). Wrap the tail of the steak round the fillet and secure it with two or three toothpicks that have been soaked in water for about 10 minutes to prevent them from burning.

6 **Cooking.** Move the steak to one side of the rack where the heat will be less intense, or reduce the heat by raking out the coals or by raising the rack 2.5 to 5 cm (1 to 2 inches). Grill the steak, turning it once, until done to your taste. Press the back of a fork against the meat. If it is soft, the meat is rare; if springy, it is medium; if stiff, it is well done.

7 **Removing the bone.** Transfer the steak to a carving board and let it rest for 10 minutes. Pull out the toothpicks, then cut off the tail. Holding the steak steady with the back of a fork, cut round one side of the T-shaped bone to free the fillet and round the other side of the bone to free the sirloin section.

3 **Greasing the rack.** About 5 minutes before you plan to grill the steak, set the rack 10 to 15 cm (4 to 6 inches) above the hot coals to preheat it. Grip a piece of reserved fat in long-handled tongs and push the fat along the wires of the hot rack to grease it.

4 **Searing the steak.** Place the steak in the centre of the rack where the fire is hottest, and sear the steak for a minute or two. When small red beads of juice appear on the top surface, turn the steak over and sear the second side for about a minute, until juices rise to the top again.

5 **Searing the fat.** Using the long-handled tongs to hold the steak upright, sear the fat along one edge for a minute to brown it. Then turn the steak and sear the fat bordering the opposite edge.

8 **Slicing the steak.** Cut across the grain to carve the sirloin, the tail and the fillet, section by section, into slices 5 mm ($\frac{1}{4}$ inch) thick (*above*). Overlapping them slightly, arrange the slices in separate rows so that every diner can take some of each kind of meat. Garnish the steak with sprigs of fresh watercress and serve immediately (*right*).□

Wrapping a Lamb Chop in Its Apron

Like beef steaks, lamb and pork chops reach perfect succulence if grilled in two stages—fast searing and slow cooking. To ensure that the chops stay juicy inside, they should be between 2.5 cm (1 inch) and 7.5 cm (3 inches) thick.

With both lamb and pork, the best candidates for grilling are tender rib and loin chops. Steeping the chops in a marinade (*pages 10-11*) will enrich their flavour and moisten their surfaces. Chops that are not marinated should be rubbed with oil to prevent them drying out on the grill.

Lamb loin chops, such as those used in this demonstration, can be further protected and flavoured if the butcher leaves the long tails—or aprons—of the chops untrimmed. Each apron can be wrapped round the loin to shield the tender meat; for additional flavour, mushroom caps, blanched pieces of bacon or salt pork, or the lamb kidneys shown here can be tucked into the apron before it is rolled round the loin.

To prevent too much fat dripping on to the fire and flaring up, the borders of fat round the chops should be cut back to about 5 mm ($\frac{1}{4}$ inch). On lamb loin chops, the aprons also need trimming.

For lamb chops, allow 8 to 10 minutes of total searing and cooking time for each 2.5 cm (1 inch) of thickness. Unlike lamb, pork chops must always be cooked until well done. Including searing time, grill them for at least 15 minutes per 2.5 cm.

As with beef, you can test lamb for doneness by pressing it with the back of a fork or with your fingers. The meat will feel slightly soft at the rare state, slightly firm at medium and very firm at well done. Pork chops should be tested by inserting a skewer into the flesh near the bone: the juices should run clear, with no trace of pink, when the pork is done.

Grilled vegetables make perfect accompaniments for chops. In this demonstration, cherry tomatoes and mushroom caps, well oiled to keep them from drying out, share space on the rack with the chops during the last minutes of grilling.

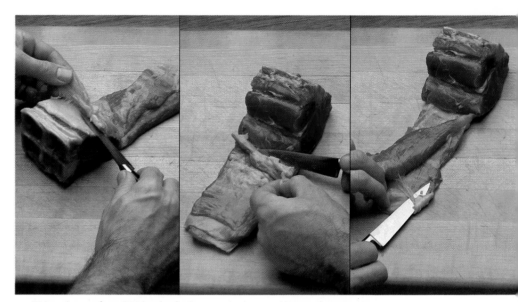

1 Trimming a chop. With a knife, loosen the layer of fat surrounding the chop—here, a lamb loin chop 6 cm (2½ inches) thick—and use your fingers to pull the fat away, leaving a border only 3 to 5 mm ($\frac{1}{8}$ to $\frac{1}{4}$ inch) thick (*above, left*). Turn the chop over and cut out the wedge of fat lodged between the loin and the apron (*above, centre*). Cut into the apron and separate the layers of lean from fat; remove the fat (*above, right*) and reserve it.

5 Marinating the chops. Place the chops in the dish with the marinade and rub their surfaces with the mixture. Cover the dish and set the chops aside for up to 2 hours, periodically turning them and brushing them with the marinade (*above*). At the last minute, rub salt and pepper into both sides of each chop.

6 Searing the chops. Set the rack 10 to 15 cm (4 to 6 inches) above hot coals and grease it with pieces of the reserved fat (*Step 3, page 29*). Place the chops in the centre of the rack and sear them for 1 to 2 minutes on each side. Stand each chop on end and sear the apron surfaces, rolling the chop to crisp it all round.

2 **Preparing a lamb's kidney.** Make a slit about 3 mm ($\frac{1}{8}$ inch) deep along the rounded side of a kidney to split the membrane. Pull the membrane away, then cut through the rounded side to open the kidney out into a butterfly shape. With the tip of the knife, remove the fatty core of the kidney.

3 **Stuffing a loin chop.** In a shallow dish, prepare a marinade for the chops—here, finely chopped rosemary, parsley and spearmint leaves combined with a little olive oil. Rub the marinade over all the surfaces of each chop. Place an opened kidney, cut side down, at the juncture of the loin and apron.

4 **Skewering the loin chop.** Pull the apron tightly round the kidney and the loin, and fasten it with a skewer—in this case, a bamboo skewer that has been soaked in water for 10 minutes to prevent it from burning on the grill. Push the skewer into the end of the apron, through the loin and kidney, and out the other side.

7 **Serving.** Move the chops to the side of the rack, or reduce the heat by raking out and separating the coals, or by raising the rack 2.5 to 5 cm (1 to 2 inches). Grill the chops until done to your taste, turning them once. Meanwhile, skewer oiled cherry tomatoes and mushroom caps (*above*) and grill them for 5 minutes, or until delicately browned. Arrange the chops and vegetables on a platter, and garnish with watercress (*right*). □

Ensuring Juiciness in a Boned Loin

Loin of pork or lamb and beef fillet yield boneless roasts that are small enough in diameter—usually 5 to 7.5 cm (2 to 3 inches)—to be grilled flat on a rack like steaks or chops. The pork roast shown here consists of a whole middle loin plus a section of the chump end. A whole beef fillet can range from 25 to 35 cm (10 to 14 inches) in length; a similarly long lamb roast can be made by leaving part of the rib section attached to the loin.

Butchers can supply the roasts already trimmed for grilling, but preparing them yourself is a simple process. The beef only needs to be freed of its fatty covering and the membrane or connective tissue that runs the length of the fillet. A pork or lamb roast is boned by cutting down the inside edge of the ribs along the length of the loin, then across the chine bone to free the meat. After that, the fat is trimmed.

To enhance flavour, the roasts should be marinated in an oil-based blend of seasonings such as the orange rind, ginger, garlic and sage used here. The oil in the marinade will also keep the meat moist and prevent it from sticking to the grill.

As with steaks, boneless roasts are first seared, then cooked. The fat bordering loins will baste the meat during grilling; fillets should be basted regularly with oil or reserved marinade. Allow a total grilling time of 8 to 10 minutes per 2.5 cm (1 inch) of thickness if you like beef or lamb rare, 12 minutes if you prefer it medium and about 15 minutes for well-done meat. Pork requires 15 minutes per 2.5 cm to reach a safe internal temperature of 75°C (170°F). After grilling, the roast should be left to rest for 10 minutes—a process that firms the meat and helps preserve its juices when it is carved. A boneless roast is easily carved for serving; holding the knife at an angle and cutting the meat diagonally across the grain will yield generous slices.

1 Trimming the loin. With a sharp knife and your fingers, remove all but a 5 mm (¼ inch) layer of fat from a boned loin. Pull away the fat and membrane strip by strip. Reserve the fat.

2 Rubbing with marinade. In a shallow dish, prepare a marinade—here, grated orange rind, chopped garlic and fresh ginger (*recipe, page 161*) and chopped sage are combined with just enough olive oil to bind the mixture into a soft paste. Place the loin in the dish and rub the marinade into it. Cover the meat with plastic film; set it aside for up to 2 hours.

4 Grilling the loin. Move the loin to the side of the rack, or reduce the heat by raising the rack 2.5 to 5 cm (1 to 2 inches) or by raking the coals to spread them out. Grill the loin for about 25 minutes, turning it after 12 minutes. The loin is done if the juices run clear when a skewer is inserted into it, or a meat thermometer registers a temperature of 75°C (170°F).

5 Grilling potatoes. Towards the end of cooking, push the loin aside to make room for skewered parboiled potatoes (*page 18*). Turning them often, grill the potatoes for about 3 minutes, or until the skins are crisp. Move the potatoes to the edge of the grill to keep them warm. Transfer the loin to a carving board and let it rest for 10 minutes.

3 **Searing the loin.** Use the reserved fat to grease a preheated grill rack set 10 to 15 cm (4 to 6 inches) above hot coals. Place the loin in the centre of the rack and sear it for about 2 minutes on each of its four long sides, turning it with tongs (*above*).

6 **Serving.** Holding the knife at a diagonal to the joint, carve the loin crosswise into slices 5 mm ($\frac{1}{4}$ inch) thick. Arrange the slices on a serving platter. Push the potatoes off the skewers and place them round the slices of pork; garnish with watercress. If you like, serve the pork and potatoes with a flavoured butter—here, olive and anchovy (*recipe, page 162*).□

Mincing Meats for Rapid Grilling

Minced meat, grilled in single servings, is easy to prepare, quick to cook and lends itself to a variety of garnishes. A favourite technique is to mould it loosely into patties or hamburgers (*right*). An unusual but appetizing alternative is kebabs made from minced meat pressed in a smooth cylinder round a skewer (*right, below; recipe, page 113*).

Hamburgers are usually made from beef, but lamb, veal or pork can be substituted or used to supplement the beef. Lean meat—including inexpensive cuts that have been trimmed of all connective tissue—is ideal. It will have a good flavour and, once minced, it will be tender.

If you like, you can include a proportion of fat with the meat—here, one part fat to four parts lean meat is used. As well as imparting flavour, fat will moisten the meat and protect it from the drying heat of the grill. However, fat must be well cooked to be digestible, so if you prefer rare hamburgers choose a lean cut of meat and add a little butter or raw beef marrow.

Make the hamburgers similar in size so that they cook through at the same rate. They should be at least 2.5 cm (1 inch) thick to cook without charring. Hamburgers can be served with almost any sauce or relish. Here, they are garnished with both a pungent chili relish and a contrasting smooth-textured sauce made from avocados.

Minced kebabs are traditionally made from lamb, spiced with aromatic flavourings such as onion, parsley, coriander and cumin. The best cuts to use are leg or shoulder. The meat must be finely minced so that it coheres well. To achieve the right consistency, first mince the meat coarsely. Then add seasonings and pass the mixture through the grinder a second and even a third time, using a fine disc.

The meat for kebabs must be well kneaded to make it close-textured, cohesive and easy to mould on the skewers. Choose skewers with flat blades to hold the meat in position while it cooks, and oil them so that you can slide the meat off for serving. Minced kebabs cook quickly—in less than 10 minutes, depending on how crisp and brown you want them. Serve them with wedges of lemon and garlic and chili sauce (*page 13*).

Making Hamburgers from Tender Beef

1 Mincing meat and fat. Trim meat—here, topside—and cut it into strips. Discard membranes and connective tissue but reserve the fat or add supplementary fat or suet. Using a meat grinder fitted with a medium blade, mince the strips of meat and fat a handful at a time (*above*).

2 Forming patties. Transfer the minced meat to a mixing bowl, season the meat with salt and pepper and toss it lightly. For each patty, scoop out a handful of the meat and shape it into a ball. Flatten the top and bottom, then place the patty on a work surface and make the edges even by rotating the patty between your two cupped hands (*above*).

Moulding Finely Minced Lamb on to Skewers

1 Assembling the ingredients. Trim fat and connective tissue from the meat—in this case, shoulder of lamb—and cut it into cubes. Chop fresh suet. Pass the meat and suet through the medium disc of a grinder. In a bowl, season the mince with salt, pepper, paprika and finely chopped onion and parsley (*above*). Add lemon juice, then combine all the ingredients.

2 Mincing a second time. Transfer the meat mixture to a tray. Fit the grinder with a fine disc and mince the mixture once or twice more. When all the ingredients have been through the grinder, use your hands to knead the mixture thoroughly to blend it and make it cohere. Cover the mixture with plastic film and refrigerate it for about 30 minutes to firm it.

3 **Grilling the hamburgers.** Use a long-handled, broad spatula to slide the patties on to an oiled grill rack 10 to 15 cm (4 to 6 inches) above medium-hot coals. Grill the hamburgers for 5 minutes. Use the spatula to lift each hamburger slightly to check that it is brown on the underside, then turn it. Grill the patties for a further 5 to 10 minutes to cook the other side.

4 **Serving.** Arrange the hamburgers on a warmed platter and present them with your choice of garnishes. In this case, grilled tomato slices are placed round the platter and parsley sprigs decorate the centre. Each hamburger is topped with a spoonful of avocado sauce (*recipe, page 163*) and chili relish (*page 12*). □

3 **Moulding the kebabs.** Brush flat-bladed skewers with olive oil. Take a handful of the meat mixture and mould it into a sausage shape roughly 15 cm (6 inches) long and 2.5 cm (1 inch) wide. Press the meat on to the skewer (*above*). Mould it with your fingers to seal the join and taper the ends smoothly round the skewer.

4 **Grilling.** Grill the kebabs on an oiled rack 10 to 15 cm (4 to 6 inches) above hot coals for 8 to 10 minutes, turning them once (*inset*). Serve with wedges of lemon and garlic and chili sauce. □

Herbed Sausages Cooked in Spirals

From mild frankfurters to spicy *chorizos*, sausages are never better than when grilled. The dry heat of the coals crisps and browns the casing, which keeps the meat inside it soft and moist.

To make your own sausages, buy casings from a butcher and stuff them with any kind of meat and flavourings you like. In this demonstration, pork is spiked with sage and garlic (*recipe, page 166*).

For pork or veal sausages, which need long cooking, the stuffing should contain 35 to 45 per cent fat. For beef or lamb, a fat content of 25 per cent is ample. You can add suet or pork back fat to lean meat—or combine a fatty cut with a lean one.

Before grilling, prick all sausages, lest they burst when their moisture turns to steam. The sausages can then be laid on the grill rack, impaled on skewers or enclosed in a hinged grilling basket. Allow 15 minutes per 2.5 cm (1 inch) of thickness for fresh pork or veal sausages, 10 minutes for others. Pre-cooked varieties, such as frankfurters, need only 5 minutes to heat through.

1 Grinding the meat. Cut meat—here, neck end and loin of pork—into strips. Leave the fat intact, but remove and discard the membranes and connective tissue. Attach a medium disc to a meat grinder and drop the strips of meat into the grinder one by one. For a smooth texture, grind the meat a second time.

2 Adding flavourings. Transfer the meat to a large bowl and season it with salt and pepper. Chop and add garlic and fresh sage leaves. Mix the ingredients well. Fry a spoonful of the mixture until all traces of pink have disappeared, about 3 minutes. Taste the cooked mixture and correct the seasoning of the raw stuffing.

Forming Links

Forming links. With your hands, roll the sausage on a flat surface to distribute the filling evenly. Form links by twisting the sausage at regular intervals of about 10 cm (4 inches). To prevent the sausage casing from unwinding, twist successive links in opposite directions.

6 Making spirals. Roll the sausages on a work surface to smooth them. Coil the sausages into tight spirals. Place them in the basket section of an oiled hinged grill or—if you prefer to cook the sausages on the grill rack—secure each spiral by inserting a skewer through it horizontally. With a skewer or knife tip, prick each sausage in several places.

7 Grilling the sausages. Close the lid of the grilling basket and clamp the handle tightly. Place the basket on a rack 10 to 15 cm (4 to 6 inches) above medium-hot coals and cook the sausages for 8 to 10 minutes on each side, or until they are golden-brown in colour.

3 **Preparing the casing.** Soak sausage casing—in this case, pig's intestines—in a bowl of tepid water acidulated with lemon until it has become soft and elastic, about 30 minutes. Using a funnel, run cold water into each piece of casing to rinse and open it. Examine the casing for holes; if you find any, cut out the torn sections and discard them.

4 **Attaching the casing.** Slide one end of casing—here, about 2 metres (6 feet) long—on to the nozzle of the sausage-stuffing attachment of a meat grinder. Gather the casing over the nozzle until only the final 15 cm (6 inches) hang free. Make a knot in the casing about 7.5 cm (3 inches) from the end.

5 **Filling the casing.** Press the stuffing into the bowl of the grinder, a handful at a time, and turn the handle at a steady pace. Smooth the casing as it fills. When the sausage is about 75 cm (30 inches) long, pull 15 cm (6 inches) of empty casing from the nozzle, cut it in the middle and knot it. Tie off the remaining casing and stuff a second sausage.

8 **Serving the sausages.** Turn the basket over so the lid is on the bottom, unclamp the handle and lift the basket section away. Slide the sausages from the lid on to a carving board. Slice across the spiral of each sausage at 2.5 cm (1 inch) intervals; then slice it at right angles to the first cuts to produce bite-sized pieces. Serve the sausages accompanied, if you like, by wedges of lime.□

The Universal Appeal of Skewered Meat

The ease and speed with which bite-sized cubes of meat can be threaded on skewers, grilled and served ensures them a special place in outdoor cookery. But the most intriguing aspect of kebabs is the diversity of effects you can create by marinating the meat in aromatic blends of herbs, spices and other ingredients. In the top demonstration, lamb is steeped in a mixture of oil, lemon juice, garlic, bay and oregano to produce kebabs with a Mediterranean flavour (*right; recipe, page 108*); in the second demonstration, beef is marinated in a thick, spicy paste to make traditional South-East Asian satay (*below; recipe, page 111*).

All types of kebab are most successful when made with meat that is tender. Suitable cuts include top or fillet end of leg of lamb, rump steak or fillet of beef.

Since the meat is lean, oil-based marinades are particularly valuable to help protect the flesh from drying out when exposed to the heat. Apart from the flavourings used here, you could combine almost any fresh or dried herbs with oil. Winter savory, marjoram, lemon thyme or rosemary complement lamb, and lemon juice, with its tenderizing properties, is always a useful addition. However, despite the preliminary moistening provided by a marinade, skewered meat must still be basted frequently while it is on the grill.

The marinade for satay contains no oil; instead, spices such as ginger, turmeric and cumin are pounded in a mortar, then mixed with fresh or dried lemon grass, which contributes a subtle tang of citrus. The addition of chopped garlic and onion and soy sauce gives the mixture pungency and binds it into a paste that will adhere to the meat both before and during cooking.

Bamboo skewers for satay can be obtained from Oriental shops; any type of thin wooden skewers would be suitable. To baste the satay while they are on the rack, peanut oil is often used, but other vegetable oils may be substituted. Satay can also be made with chicken, lamb, fish or shellfish, and with other marinades. Peanut sauce is a traditional accompaniment to meat satay.

Kebabs: Lamb Steeped in Aromatics

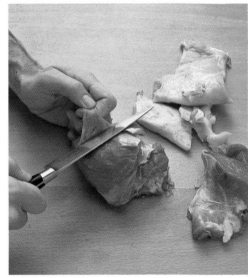

1 **Trimming meat.** Use a sharp knife to cut away fat and connective tissue from meat—in this case, fillet end of leg of lamb. Cut the trimmed meat into 2.5 cm (1 inch) strips, then cut across the strips to make cubes. Discard the trimmings.

Satay: Tender Morsels in a Spicy Coating

1 **Preparing the marinade.** Put ground cumin, turmeric, salt, pepper and a little sugar in a mortar. Add ground ginger (*above*), then pound all the ingredients thoroughly. Finely chop onion, garlic and lemon grass. Add them to the ingredients in the mortar; continue to pound until the mixture is smooth. Add soy sauce.

2 **Marinating the meat.** Cut away fat and connective tissue from the meat—here, rump steak is used. Cut the meat into 1 cm (½ inch) strips; cut across the strips to make cubes. Place the cubes of meat in a shallow dish and spoon on the marinade (*above*); use your hands to coat the cubes with the marinade. Cover the meat and leave it for at least an hour.

3 **Skewering the meat.** Thread four or five cubes of meat on each skewer (*above*); leave at least half the length of the skewer empty so that you can hold the skewer later with your fingers.

2 **Marinating the meat.** Grate onion into a wide, shallow dish. Add crushed garlic cloves, bay leaves, dried oregano, salt and pepper; pour on olive oil and the juice of a lemon. Transfer the meat to the marinade (*above*); thoroughly coat the meat, cover it with plastic film and leave it for at least an hour.

3 **Skewering the meat.** To prevent the meat from sticking to the skewers, brush the blades with olive oil. Thread each skewer with an equal number of lamb cubes. Reserve the remaining marinade for basting the meat on the grill.

4 **Grilling.** Cook the kebabs on an oiled rack set 10 to 15 cm (4 to 6 inches) above hot coals. Baste the meat and turn the skewers after about 5 minutes (*above*), then grill for a further 5 minutes. For a traditional serving, warm pitta bread briefly on the grill and serve the grilled meat in the bread with shredded lettuce and wedges of lemon.□

4 **Cooking.** Set the rack 10 to 15 cm (4 to 6 inches) above hot coals. Brush the rack with oil—here, peanut oil is used. Place the skewers on the rack. Cook them for 5 to 7 minutes on one side, basting them with more oil. Turn them; continue to baste (*above*) and grill them for a further 5 to 7 minutes to cook the other side.

5 **Serving.** To prepare traditional accompaniments, make peanut sauce (*page 15*), peel onions and cut them into narrow wedges, peel cucumber and cut it into sticks approximately 5 cm (2 inches) long. Serve the skewers piled on a warmed serving dish, with the vegetable garnishes in a bowl. Each skewer is dipped into the peanut sauce and the meat eaten straight from the skewers.□

The Special Benefits of Grilling in Caul

Cuts of offal as diverse as tender liver, delicate sweetbreads and robust heart are all suited to the rapid heat of the grill. Calf's liver will be at its most succulent grilled in a whole piece (*box, opposite page*). A mixture of offal, such as the lamb's kidneys, heart, liver and sweetbreads shown here, grills more evenly if the meat is cut into cubes for skewering.

Offal has little fat of its own; to keep it moist and to provide extra protection from the direct heat of the grill, it is wrapped in caul, the fatty membrane that surrounds a pig's stomach. Caul serves as a natural baster and, in the case of kebabs, helps to keep the meat in place.

To prepare a large piece of liver for grilling, wrap the meat before applying a light coating of oil. Kebabs of mixed offal benefit from longer marinating in oil and lemon juice to flavour them before they are skewered and wrapped. You can add herbs such as parsley or thyme or a mixture of onion, garlic and chives to the marinade. For an attractive presentation that imparts a subtle aroma, skewer the meat on rosemary branches (*Step 4, below*).

1 Soaking caul. Soften dry-salted caul in cold water for about 15 minutes. Lift it out (*above*) and pat it dry; fresh caul needs no soaking. Soak lamb's sweetbreads in several changes of cold water. Place them in a pan, cover with fresh water and bring slowly to the boil; simmer for 2 to 3 minutes. Cool them in cold water, then peel away the outer membranes.

2 Cutting up the offal. Prepare the rest of the offal—here, lamb's liver, kidneys and heart. Remove fat, connective tissue and outer membrane from the liver and the kidneys. Trim fat, fibrous tissue and tubes from the heart. Cut the sweetbreads, liver and heart into equal-sized cubes; divide the kidneys in three (*above*).

3 Marinating the offal. Put the meats in one dish and sprinkle chopped onion, garlic and chives over the meats. Pour on olive oil (*above*) and lemon juice. Use your hands to toss the pieces of meat until they are well coated; cover and leave them for at least an hour, turning them in the marinade once or twice.

4 Skewering the pieces. To make skewers, pull the leaves off 30 cm (12 inch) long branches of rosemary, leaving a tuft of leaves at the tip of each branch; sharpen the bare ends to a point. Thread the cubes of meat on to the skewers (*above*); make sure that each skewer holds a selection of all the different types of offal. Season the meat; reserve the marinade.

5 Wrapping in caul. Spread the sheet of caul out on a work surface. Lay a skewer on the edge of the sheet and roll it up until it is enclosed by a layer of caul (*above*); use a knife to cut the wrapped skewer free from the sheet of caul. Wrap all the skewers in caul—during cooking, the caul partially melts, then crisps to form a coating for the meats.

Nourishment for a Lean Cut

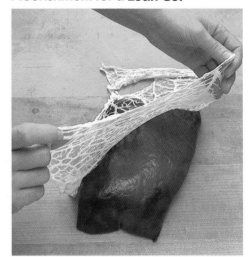

1 Wrapping in caul. Soak caul (*Step 1, opposite page*) and dry it. Cut away any fibrous connective tissue from liver—a piece of calf's liver weighing about 1 kg (2 to 2½ lb) is used here. Peel away the outer membrane. Salt the liver, then wrap it in the sheet of caul (*above*) so that it is completely enclosed.

2 Grilling. Brush the liver with olive oil; lay it on an oiled rack 10 to 15 cm (4 to 6 inches) above medium-hot coals, with the seam of the caul on the rack. Grill the liver for 10 minutes, until browned on one side. Turn it and cook it for a further 10 minutes to brown the other side. The liver is cooked when it feels firm if pressed lightly.

3 Carving the liver. Leave the cooked liver in a warm place to rest for 10 to 15 minutes—it will become firmer and will be easier to carve. Set it on a wooden board and use a long, flexible knife to carve it into thick slices (*above*).

6 Cooking and serving. Place the kebabs on an oiled rack 10 to 15 cm (4 to 6 inches) above medium-hot coals (*above*). Cook them for 15 minutes, turning them once and basting with the reserved marinade. Transfer them to a warmed dish. Serve the kebabs accompanied, if you like, by a herb pilaff (*right; recipe, page 165*). □

Roasting a Leg of Lamb on a Spit

Smoke perfumes a large roast that is cooked gently on a spit rotating over coals. Leaving the bones in place helps to keep the meat moist and compensate for juices lost where the spit and the holding forks penetrate the roast.

To rotate smoothly and thus cook evenly, the roast must be balanced well on the spit rod. With a leg of pork or lamb, as shown in this demonstration, balance is achieved by cutting out the pelvic bone and inserting the spit alongside the leg and shank bones. With a rib, shoulder or loin of pork, lamb or beef, the spit is inserted into the side of the roast near the bones at one corner and pushed diagonally through the meat to emerge close to the opposite corner. The balance then can be checked as described in Step 6, page 46.

The fat covering the roast will melt during cooking to help baste the meat, but should be trimmed to about 5 mm ($\frac{1}{4}$ inch). For flavour, the roast can be marinated with a blend of oil, seasonings and aromatics (*page 11*).

Unless the roast has been marinated, it should be liberally oiled after it is spitted. In either case, it will need frequent basting with pan drippings, leftover marinade or both to keep the meat moistened and give the roast a golden glaze. Here, the drip pan contains stock, wedges of lemon, garlic and rosemary—a mixture that blends with the fat and juices released by the meat to create a savoury basting liquid.

Roasting time will vary with the kind and size of the roast, and the degree of doneness you like. Allow 15 minutes per 500 g (1 lb) for rare, 20 minutes for medium and 25 minutes for well-done meat. Pork must always be served well done, so, to be certain the roast is cooked perfectly, test its internal temperature with a meat thermometer before removing it from the spit. The meat should reach an internal temperature of 75°C (170°F).

After roasting, the meat should be allowed to rest in a warm place for about 10 minutes to relax it, making it firmer and easier to carve. During this period, the meat will continue to cook and its temperature will rise a few degrees.

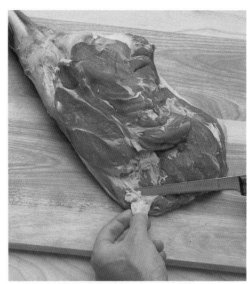

1 Trimming off fat. Ask the butcher to remove the pelvic bone from the fillet end of a leg of lamb and discard it. With a small, sharp knife, trim off any large chunks of fat from the flat inner side of the leg, but avoid cutting into the flesh.

2 Peeling off fell. Turn the leg over so the rounded side faces up. Grasp the leg at the fillet end in one hand and, with your other hand, peel back the edge of the papery fell that covers the fat. Pull the fell off at the shank end of the leg, using a small knife to free the fell where it resists. With the knife, trim the fat to a thickness of about 5 mm ($\frac{1}{4}$ inch).

6 Roasting. Rake coals from the centre of the grill and set a drip pan in the cleared space (*page 8*). Place aromatics—in this case, lemon wedges, garlic cloves and rosemary sprigs—in the drip pan and pour in stock to a depth of 1 cm ($\frac{1}{2}$ inch). Place the spitted leg over the pan.

7 Completing cooking. Baste the leg at 10-minute intervals with the liquid from the drip pan until the lamb is done to your liking. Transfer the joint to a carving board and remove the holding forks. Grasping the spit handle in one hand, press a carving fork against the sirloin end of the leg and pull the spit out. Cut off the trussing strings.

3 **Seasoning.** Slide a holding fork on to the spit rod, prongs pointing away from the spit handle. Insert the spit into the leg at the fillet end, next to the knob of the leg bone. Carefully push the spit through the leg, parallel to the bone. Salt and pepper the exposed flesh and place rosemary sprigs and garlic cloves round the knob of the leg bone.

4 **Inserting holding forks.** Fold the flap of flesh at the top of the joint over the seasonings. Holding the flap in place with one hand, push the prongs of the holding fork through it into the leg. Push one of the prongs of the second holding fork into the narrow shank end of the leg parallel to the bone. Secure the forks.

5 **Trussing.** To keep the joint compact during roasting, loop four or five pieces of kitchen string round the fillet end, knotting each loop firmly and cutting off the excess string. Rub the outside of the leg with salt and pepper.

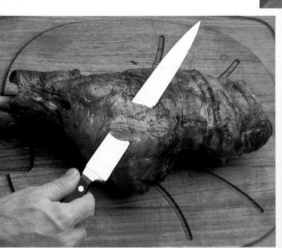

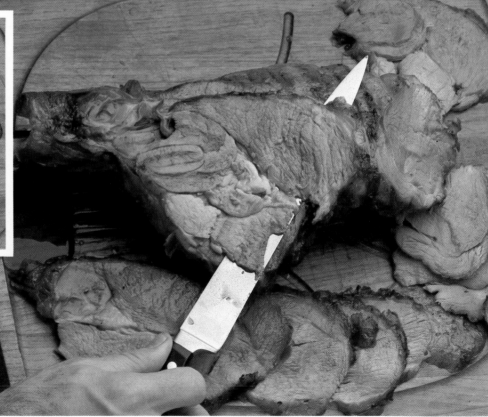

8 **Carving.** Let the roast rest for 10 minutes. If you have a *manche à gigot*—a special carving handle—screw it on to the shank bone. Alternatively, wrap a napkin round the shank bone and grasp it firmly as you cut thin slices from the rounded side of the leg (*above*). Cut away from yourself and keep the blade of the knife nearly parallel to the bone (*right*). When the first side has been carved, turn the leg over to carve the flatter, inner side. Finally, slice the meat from the shank. Serve at once.☐

Barbecued Spareribs with a Lacquered Glaze

Glazed with a tangy sauce, spareribs are welcome as either an hors d'oeuvre or a main course for a meal outdoors. Although ribs are easier to eat when cut into individual pieces, the meat will be more juicy if the rack, or side of ribs, is kept intact for cooking. Even so, the layer of meat is thin and will tend to become dry and stringy unless the rack is cooked slowly over relatively gentle heat. When grilling spareribs, constant attention is required to prevent the meat and sauce from burning. A simpler approach is to thread the entire rack on to a spit and roast it, as demonstrated here.

Because spareribs are fatty, the first step in preparing them is to trim off the excess surface fat and membrane. For grilling, the spareribs should then be parboiled for 10 minutes or so. For roasting, they can be threaded on to the spit immediately. In either case, marinating the rack in barbecue sauce for up to 2 hours will give the ribs extra flavour.

Grilling or roasting will draw out the internal fat from the spareribs, so they must always be cooked over a drip pan. To ensure that the ribs are crisp, not greasy, the rack must be grilled or roasted for 20 minutes or so before basting begins. Here, the ribs are glazed with tomato barbecue sauce (*recipe, page 164*); alternatively, you can marinate and then baste the ribs with the sweet-and-sour sauce prepared on page 12. To coat the ribs well, the sauce or marinade should be applied generously and frequently.

Like all pork, spareribs must be cooked thoroughly. Depending on the size of the ribs, allow 35 to 45 minutes for grilling them, 50 to 70 minutes for roasting. To test for doneness, prick the meat with a skewer or the tip of a knife. When the juices run clear, the spareribs are ready.

1 Trimming the spareribs. Place the rack of ribs with its meaty side up on a chopping board. Using a sharp knife, trim away surface fat and as much of the connective tissue as possible without cutting into the flesh.

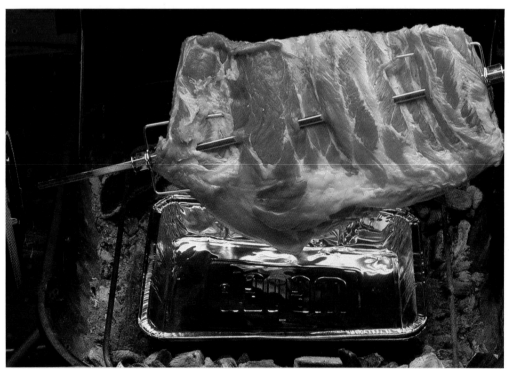

4 Positioning the spit. Balance the spit (*Step 6, page 46*). Clear a large space in the coals by raking the hot coals away from the centre (*page 8*). Set a drip pan in the cleared space. Place the spit in position over the drip pan and start to rotate the spit.

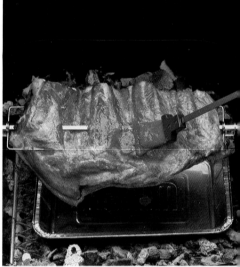

5 Roasting. Let the spareribs roast for 20 minutes, then use a long-handled brush to baste the ribs on both sides with barbecue sauce. When the coating has dried—after about 10 minutes—baste again. Continue to baste at 10-minute intervals for 30 to 45 minutes, or until the spareribs no longer exude any fat, their surfaces look crisp and the juices run clear when the meat is pricked.

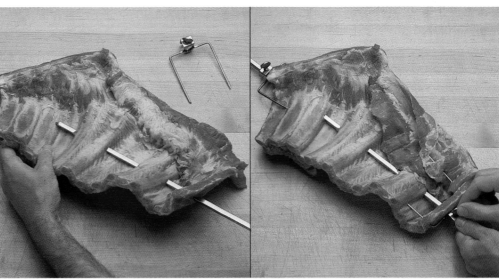

2 **Removing the membrane.** Turn the rack over and use your fingers to loosen the sheet of thin, papery membrane that covers the bones (*above*). Pull off the membrane and discard it.

3 **Spitting.** Slide a holding fork on to the spit with the prongs pointing away from the handle. Place the rack on the work surface with the bony side up. Starting at the thinner, narrower end of the rack, push the spit through the meat between the first and second ribs. Then push the tip over the next pair of ribs. Continue threading the spit over and under alternate pairs of ribs and out at the wide end of the rack (*above, left*). Slide the second fork on to the spit. Push the prongs of both forks into the rack, using one prong at the narrow end to secure the flap of meat there (*above, right*). Tighten the forks.

6 **Removing the spit.** Transfer the spareribs to a carving board and remove the holding fork nearest the tip of the spit. Pull out the prongs of the other holding fork. Remove the spit by pushing the spareribs off with the prongs of a carving fork.

7 **Separating the ribs.** First cut the rack of ribs into two pieces for easy handling. Steadying the rack with the carving fork, slice down between the ribs to separate them (*above*).

8 **Serving.** Pile the ribs on to a large plate and serve them at once, garnished with sprigs of fresh parsley. Accompany the ribs, if you like, with a spicy sauce such as a chili relish (*page 12*).□

A Self-Basting Veal Roast

Because it is boneless and cylindrical, a rolled roast balances neatly on the spit rod of a rotisserie and cooks through at a steady rate. To conserve the meat's juices and protect its surfaces from excessive drying, the joint needs to be wrapped in a thin sheet—or bard—of fat that will baste it continuously. Suitable cuts include topside and silverside of beef or neck end of pork. Even tender cuts of veal, usually considered too lean to be cooked over coals, will emerge moist and delectable.

Like the boning of the meat, its rolling and barding can be left to the butcher. But there is a bonus in doing these jobs yourself: you can place flavourings inside the roll and make them an integral part of the roast. For barding, the meat's own fat can be peeled off in layers and pounded into flat, cohesive sheets about 5 mm ($\frac{1}{4}$ inch) thick. Or you can buy slices of fresh pork back fat; these too should be pounded to form a uniform wrapping for the meat.

Before rolling the joint in the bard of fat, marinate the meat—choosing an oil and acid mixture for tougher cuts (*pages 10-11*)—or oil it thoroughly and season it with salt and pepper. Here, the inside of the joint is flavoured with a mixture of chopped fresh herbs. Other appropriate flavourings include grated lemon or orange rind, raisins, slivers of garlic or anchovy fillets that have been soaked in cold water for 30 minutes to reduce saltiness.

The timing guidelines for rolled roasts are based on weight. For rare beef or lamb, allow 15 minutes per 500 g (1 lb); for medium, 20 minutes; for well-done meat, 25 minutes. Like pork, veal is always roasted to the well-done stage; both meats should cook for 25 minutes per 500 g.

During the final hour of roasting, you can make the coals of the fire do double duty by laying foil-wrapped packets of vegetables among the coals. Small whole onions, beetroots and sweet potatoes are suitable; here, new potatoes and garlic heads are shown. When garlic heads are cooked in this way, the flesh of each clove becomes a mild-tasting purée that can be squeezed out of the papery skin and on to a slice of meat.

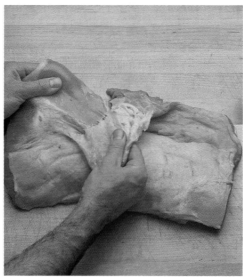

1 Removing fat. Lay the boned meat—here, loin of veal—fatty side up on a work surface. Pull off the fat in large pieces, leaving a layer no more than 5 mm ($\frac{1}{4}$ inch) thick. Use the tip of a small knife to loosen the fat where it resists, cutting parallel to the surface of the meat to avoid piercing the flesh. Set the fat aside.

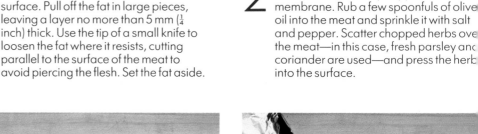

2 Flavouring. Turn the joint over and use the knife to trim away any pieces of fat or membrane. Rub a few spoonfuls of olive oil into the meat and sprinkle it with salt and pepper. Scatter chopped herbs over the meat—in this case, fresh parsley and coriander are used—and press the herbs into the surface.

6 Balancing the spit. Slide a holding fork on to the spit rod. Push the spit lengthwise through the middle of the joint. Secure the prongs of the fork in the meat; do the same with the second fork. Centre the joint on the spit. Tighten both forks. Roll the spit across your hands. If it does not rotate smoothly, reinsert the spit as close to the centre of the meat as possible.

7 Preparing garnishes. Place whole garlic heads on a large square of heavy-duty foil two layers thick. Dribble olive oil over the garlic and season with salt and pepper. Wrap the foil round the garlic and seal the edges securely. Prepare small whole potatoes in the same way.

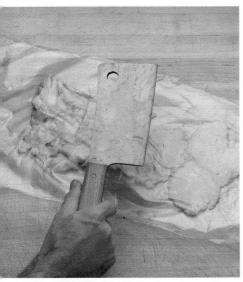

3 **Pounding the fat.** Place the reserved pieces of fat side by side on a large sheet of strong plastic film to form a rectangular layer. Cover the fat with more plastic. Use the side of a cleaver to pound the fat until the pieces cohere and form a bard about 5 mm ($\frac{1}{4}$ inch) thick.

4 **Barding the meat.** Refrigerate the fat in its wrapping for 10 minutes to firm the fat slightly. Return the bard to the work surface and peel off the top piece of plastic. Centre the meat fat-side down on the barding sheet and, starting at the thinner long edge of the joint, roll the fat and meat into a cylinder. Peel off the remaining plastic film.

5 **Tying with string.** Turn the meat so that the seam is underneath. Loop one end of a long piece of string—about 120 cm (4 feet)—once round the narrow end of the roast and knot it. Loop the string round the meat at 5 cm (2 inch) intervals, pulling it tight as you make each loop. When you reach the other end, pass the string under the joint and tie it to the first knot.

8 **Adding the vegetables.** Set a drip pan in the middle of hot coals (*page 8*). Position the spitted joint above the pan and set the spit in motion. About an hour before the end of cooking, place the vegetable packets among the coals at the edge of the fire.

9 **Serving.** When the meat is done, transfer it to a carving board and remove the spit. Let the roast rest for 10 minutes. Remove the foil packages from the coals with tongs and unwrap the vegetables. Cut the string from the roast and carve the meat crosswise into 5 mm ($\frac{1}{4}$ inch) slices. Arrange the slices on a platter surrounded by the garlic heads and the potatoes, and garnish with watercress.□

3

Poultry and Game
Diverse Techniques
for Perfect Results

Every kind of poultry—from chickens and capons to ducks, geese and turkeys—becomes a treat when cooked over glowing coals. So, too, do the fledgling pigeons called squabs, and guinea fowl, which are the size of small chickens but more assertive in taste. Hutch rabbit, distinguished by its mild flavour and tender flesh, is also suitable for the treatments that apply to poultry, as are young, tender game birds.

Poultry, game birds and rabbits can all be grilled or spit-roasted; quail—wrapped in foil—are small enough to bake in hot ashes (*page 58*). The cooking method you choose, and the size and structure of the animal, dictate the advance preparation required. To cook and brown evenly on a grill rack, birds should either be split and flattened (*page 52*), or jointed (*page 50*); rabbits can also be cut into joints for grilling (*page 56*). To cook a rabbit or a whole bird of any size on a spit, it should be securely trussed into a compact shape (*pages 54 and 56*).

Because the ambient temperature in spit-roasting is relatively low—and the cavity of a bird is broad and deep—a stuffing will not heat through in the time required to cook the meat. Instead, a whole bird can be flavoured by tucking fruits, aromatic vegetables or herbs into its cavity beforehand, and rubbing its skin with seasoned oil. A whole rabbit, however, makes an ideal candidate for stuffing: its cavity is long and narrow, so a filling will cook through in a relatively short time (*page 56*).

Another way to introduce flavour, especially for flattened birds or joints, is to steep them in a marinade. Basting during cooking nourishes the meat and crisps the skin. The basting liquid can be leftover marinade, seasoned butter or oil, barbecue sauce (*page 12*) or—for spit-roasted meat—juices from the drip pan. For ducks and geese, frequent basting with wine or cider will help to draw off excess fat (*page 54*).

Because they are naturally tender, young poultry, game birds and rabbits should be grilled or roasted just long enough to cook through. The meat is done when a skewer, inserted in thigh or hindquarter, releases clear juices, or a cooking thermometer registers 75°C (170°F). Before serving spit-roasted poultry or rabbit, let the meat rest for 10 minutes in a warm place. It will reabsorb its juices, becoming firmer and easier to carve. Small game birds, however, should be served immediately, without any rest period, to avoid the risk of overcooking.

Secured to a spit and suspended above a drip pan surrounded by hot coals, a duck is basted with cider and pan juices as it roasts (*page 54*). Apple slices are added to the pan to intensify the tanginess of the cider and counterpoint the rich flavour of the duck.

Tender Escalopes Enlivened with Spices

Chicken breasts that are boned and then halved can be pounded flat to form delicate escalopes. Capon or turkey breasts are also suitable but, because these birds are meatier than chicken, their halved breasts should be cut horizontally into slices 1 cm (½ inch) thick before they are pounded. Because pounding breaks down muscle fibres and thus further softens the tender breast meat, the escalopes will be ready to eat as soon as they are browned on both sides—after only a few minutes' grilling on the rack.

Any smooth, heavy instrument will serve for pounding the breast meat: a kitchen mallet or—as shown here—the side of a cleaver. To prevent tearing the meat, enclose each half in strong plastic film before pounding.

Flattened meat tends to dry out, so the escalopes should be liberally oiled before and during grilling. Here, they are marinated and basted with a pungent blend of oil, cardamom, cayenne pepper and black pepper (*recipe, page 160*). For milder flavour, herbs could replace the spices.

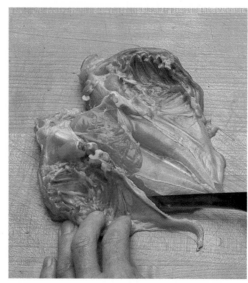

1 Pulling out the breastbone. Peel the skin from a chicken breast and place the breast with its skinned side down. Grasp it at the mid-point of the breastbone with both hands and bend the breast in half away from you until the breastbone pops up. Pull out the bone. Use the tip of a knife to free any remaining ribs (*above*).

2 Removing the collar-bones. With your fingers, free the cartilage that is attached to the narrow end of the breast. With the tip of a knife, cut through the flesh that covers the collar-bones (*above*); pull the collar-bones out.

6 Grilling. Place the escalopes on an oiled rack set 10 to 15 cm (4 to 6 inches) above medium-hot coals, and grill them for about 1 minute. Turn the escalopes over (*left*) and brush them with the remaining marinade. Turning and basting them often, grill the escalopes for 5 minutes, or until they are firm, opaque and golden-brown in colour (*below*).

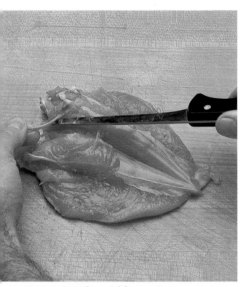

3 **Removing the wishbone.** Scrape away the flesh that surrounds the wishbone. When the entire wishbone is uncovered, grasp it by both prongs and pull it out. Then cut the breast in half along the cleft that contained the breastbone. Trim off any fat and membrane.

4 **Flattening the fillet.** Oil a large piece of heavy-duty plastic film. Lay one fillet on it, and fold the plastic over to cover the meat. With the flat side of a cleaver, beat the flesh firmly—moving from the centre outwards—until the fillet is about 8 mm ($\frac{1}{3}$ inch) thick and twice its original size. Flatten the other fillet in the same way.

5 **Marinating the escalopes.** Pour olive oil into a shallow dish and add ground cardamom, cayenne pepper and black pepper. Coat the escalopes thoroughly with the marinade. Cover and marinate the escalopes in the dish for up to 2 hours, turning them occasionally. Prepare a dish of lemon butter (*recipe, page 162*).

7 **Serving the escalopes.** Lay the grilled escalopes on a warmed platter. Here, they are garnished with watercress and halved slices of red onion (*right*). Spoon a little lemon butter on to the escalopes and serve them at once, accompanied by the remaining butter.□

Flavourings Inserted under the Skin

The most efficient way to grill a whole bird is to split it down the back and flatten it before cooking. This process transforms the bird into a neat parcel whose relatively uniform surfaces ensure that the meat cooks through swiftly and evenly. To suffuse the flattened bird with flavour and keep it moist as it cooks, you can spread finely chopped bacon or seasoned butter beneath the skin of the breast, thighs and drumsticks. In the heat of the coals, the bacon fat or butter will melt gradually, basting the bird from within.

Inserting the coating under the skin of the bird is simplicity itself. The skin is strong but supple, and attached tightly only at the backbone, drumstick tips and crest of the breastbone. Flattening the bird breaks the breastbone, loosening it from the skin. Elsewhere, the thin membranes that join the skin to the flesh are easily parted so that you can work your fingers between them.

Pigeons, quail, partridges, pheasants, poussins, guinea fowl and chickens all can be flattened and flavoured this way. In the demonstration here, a chicken is coated inside with finely chopped bacon, sage and rosemary. Butter can replace the bacon, while dill, parsley, thyme or savory make good alternatives to the sage and rosemary. In addition to herbs, you can incorporate chopped celery, shallots, garlic or *duxelles*—a mixture of sautéed chopped onions and mushrooms flavoured with lemon juice and parsley. Whatever its ingredients, the coating should be ample enough to form a layer 3 to 5 mm ($\frac{1}{4}$ to $\frac{1}{2}$ inch) thick. In this case, about 500 g (1 lb) of chopped bacon and 2 tablespoons of chopped herbs were used.

Even with this coating inside, the outer surfaces of the bird will need to be rubbed with oil before grilling, and the bird should be basted frequently while it cooks. If you wish to marinate the bird, choose an oil-based marinade (*page 11*) and season it with herbs that will complement those used in the coating.

After the bird is cooked, it needs only a simple garnish, such as grilled vegetables or fruits. Here, the chicken is accompanied by chicken-liver kebabs that are cooked quickly while the bird rests to firm its meat for carving.

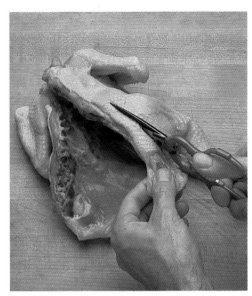

1 Cutting out the backbone. Finely chop green streaky bacon, fresh sage and rosemary leaves, then mix them together. Place the bird—here, a 1.5 kg (3 lb) chicken—on its breast and cut out the backbone with kitchen scissors (*above*).

2 Flattening the bird. Open out the bird as much as possible; place it on a work surface with its breast uppermost and legs turned inwards. With the heel of your hand, strike the bird firmly on the breast to break the breastbone, ribcage, collarbones and wishbone (*above*). Chop off the knobs at the ends of the legs.

6 Grilling. Brown the bird, skin side down, on an oiled rack 10 to 15 cm (4 to 6 inches) above medium-hot coals. Turn the bird over after 4 to 5 minutes; baste with oil and lemon juice, using a rosemary sprig. Grill for 30 minutes, basting often, until the juices run clear when a thigh is pricked. Let the bird rest on a board for 10 minutes.

3 **Coating the chicken.** Slip your fingers under the skin at the neck and loosen the skin over the breast, then over each leg. Lift the skin at the neck and push the seasoned bacon around the thighs and drumsticks of the bird. With your other hand, smooth the coating from outside. Then coat both sides of the breast.

4 **Preparing livers.** Slit the skin where each thigh meets the breast and push the ends of the legs through the slits. Rub the bird with olive oil and set it aside. Remove all bits of fat and loose membrane from fresh chicken livers. Cut the livers into halves or thirds, depending on their size.

5 **Skewering the livers.** Slice green streaky bacon 5 mm (¼ inch) thick and cut the slices into pieces about 5 mm wide and 1 cm (½ inch) long. Roll the bacon pieces in chopped rosemary. Thread the chicken livers and bacon pieces alternately on to skewers. Pour oil into a shallow dish and roll the skewers in the oil to coat the livers evenly. Set the dish aside.

7 **Serving.** Grill the liver kebabs (*above*) until firm and browned on all sides— about 5 minutes. Meanwhile, carve the chicken by first cutting off the legs at the joint where the thigh meets the body. Separate the thighs and drumsticks. Cut off the wings at the shoulder joints and halve the breast lengthwise. Reassemble the chicken pieces on a platter and, if desired, garnish with black olives, lemon wedges and rosemary sprigs. Push the livers off the skewers on to the platter.□

Ensuring Crisp Skin and Tender Flesh

Poultry and game birds can be spit-roasted to perfection above an outdoor grill (*right*) or indoors in front of an open fireplace (*box, opposite page*).

The aim of spit-roasting any bird is to conserve its succulence. To ensure crisp skin and moist, tender flesh, lean poultry and game birds should be oiled inside and out before roasting. Fatty birds, such as duck and goose, require different treatment: their skin should be lightly pierced above the thighs and under the wings, to allow the underlying fat to run out during cooking (*Step 4*).

In spit-roasting, the temperature does not rise high enough to cook a conventional stuffing, but any bird—lean or fatty—will derive extra flavour if its cavity is filled with herbs, chopped onions, garlic cloves or slices of fruit. Finally, the bird should be trussed into a compact form that will balance well on the spit.

As the bird roasts, a pan set beneath the spit will collect the drippings. For basting, you can supplement the juices in the pan with dry white wine, cider, or fruit juice such as apple, grape or orange; the resulting acidity will flavour the bird and also counterbalance any richness.

On an outdoor grill, the embers round the drip pan cook the bird; in a fireplace, the fire radiates heat as well and should be kept well stoked. Chicken, duck and goose require about 20 minutes per 500 g (1 lb), while quail and other small game birds need only about 12 to 15 minutes in all. A few minutes before the end of the cooking period, stop basting to allow the heat from the grill or fire to crisp the skin. Birds are done when a skewer pushed into the thigh produces clear juices, or when a meat thermometer registers an internal temperature of 75°C (170°F).

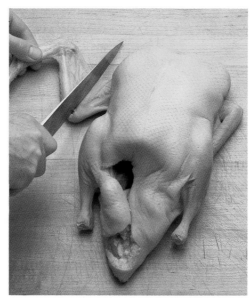

1 Preparing the bird. Lay the bird—here, a duck—on its back. Pull off and discard the solid fat around the neck and tail openings. Using a heavy, sharp knife, cut off the tip and first joint of each wing (*above*): they have little meat but can be reserved for making stock.

2 Securing the neck flap and wings. Turn the bird on its breast. Fold the flap of neck skin on to the back and secure it with a small skewer. Pull the wings behind the back and tie them together firmly with a piece of kitchen string (*above*).

5 Roasting. Add a few bay leaves to the drip pan. Place the spitted duck over the pan and set the spit in motion. Baste the duck at 10-minute intervals; after about an hour, add more cider and, for a garnish, wedges of apple. Continue to baste to build up a rich, lustrous glaze, but stop about 5 minutes before the end of cooking to allow the skin to crisp.

6 Removing the wing. When the juices run clear if a thigh is pierced with a skewer, the duck is done. Transfer it to a carving board and remove the spit. Cut away the trussing strings and let the duck rest for 10 minutes. To remove a wing, locate the shoulder joint by moving the wing bone, then, with a heavy knife, cut down firmly through the joint (*above*).

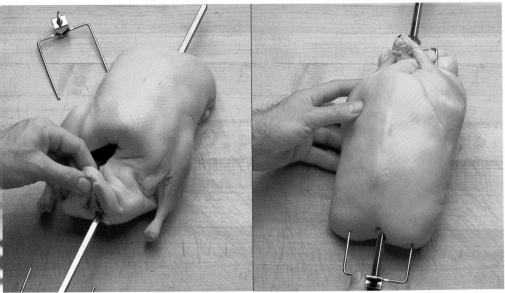

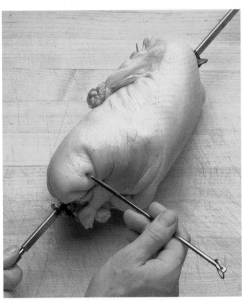

3 **Spitting the duck.** With its prongs pointing away from the handle, slide a holding fork on to the spit rod. Turn the bird on to its back; thrust the tip of the spit into the duck's tail vent and body cavity (*above, left*) and out through the flap of skin at the neck. Tie the ends of the legs together with string. Push the prongs of the holding fork deep into the legs and thighs; slide the other fork on to the spit and push the prongs into the area around the wings (*above, right*). Check that the duck is balanced evenly on the spit (*page 46, Step 6*).

4 **Piercing.** Push a skewer or a trussing needle into the fatty deposits above the thighs and beneath the wings, taking care not to pierce the flesh under the skin (*above*). Place a drip pan among the hot coals of a grill or between bricks stacked on a hearth (*page 8*). Pour cider into the pan to a depth of 1 cm ($\frac{1}{2}$ inch).

Roasting a Bird on the Hearth

7 **Removing the leg.** Slice through the duck's skin, cutting in an arc round the leg where it joins the body. Press the knife down between the thigh and the body to expose the joint, then cut through it to remove the leg (*above*).

8 **Carving the breast.** Holding the carving knife at a slight angle to the breastbone, carve the breast meat into 5 mm ($\frac{1}{4}$ inch) slices (*above*). Remove the wing and leg from the other side of the bird, and carve the remaining breast meat. Separate the legs into thighs and drumsticks.□

Basting. Pour water into a drip pan to a depth of 1 cm ($\frac{1}{2}$ inch); add black olives, lemon peel and rosemary and set the pan between bricks stacked on a hearth; rake hot coals forward from the fire. Position the spitted bird—here, a chicken rubbed with oil—over the pan and baste as it cooks (*Step 5, opposite page*).

Simple and Elaborate Treatments for Rabbit

The fine-textured, lean meat of hutch rabbits requires special handling to prevent it from drying out as it cooks. When cut into joints for grilling (*right*), rabbit must be oiled and basted frequently while it cooks; chicken joints can be grilled in the same way (*recipes, pages 126-127*). When spit-roasted whole over an outdoor grill or, as demonstrated below, at a fireplace (*page 9*), rabbit needs supplementary fat in the form of lardons—strips of pork back fat that can be rolled in herbs or spices before they are threaded into the thighs (*Step 4, below*).

For roasting or grilling, choose young rabbits; they usually weigh between 1.25 and 1.75 kg (2½ and 3½ lbs). Joints will cook quickly, in 12 to 15 minutes; a whole rabbit takes 1 to 1½ hours to roast. Unlike poultry, a rabbit can be stuffed before being roasted on the spit; its narrow body ensures that the stuffing will cook through. Here, the rabbit is stuffed with a mixture of mushrooms, bacon and herbs (*recipe, page 166*); breadcrumbs, shallots, celery, and the heart and liver of the rabbit would also be appropriate.

Grilling Herb-Scented Rabbit Joints

1 **Jointing the rabbit.** Place a skinned, gutted rabbit—here, a hutch rabbit—belly down on a work surface. Pull one foreleg away from the body and cut it off at the shoulder joint (*above*). Cut off the other foreleg. To remove the rabbit's hindquarters, cut across the body at the top of the thighs.

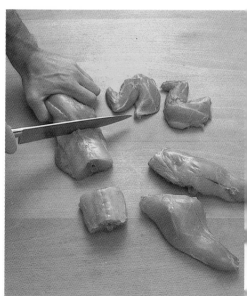

2 **Dividing the saddle.** To separate the hind legs, cut down the middle of the hindquarters. Holding the rabbit by the ribcage, cut across the body to divide the saddle into two or three pieces. Tuck the aprons of loose flesh at the sides of the saddle underneath to protect the fillets. Reserve the ribcage for stock.

Larding for Succulence

1 **Stuffing.** Sauté chopped mushrooms for 15 minutes, put them in a bowl and add lemon juice. Fry diced bacon until crisp, drain and add to the bowl with chopped savory and thyme. Cut away any fat from the cavity of a cleaned rabbit; season the cavity and fill it loosely with stuffing.

2 **Closing the cavity.** Thread a trussing needle with 45 cm (18 inches) of string. Starting at the neck end and working towards the tail, stitch at 2½ cm (1 inch) intervals, passing the string through the loop of each preceding stitch as you sew. Knot and cut off the string at the tail end.

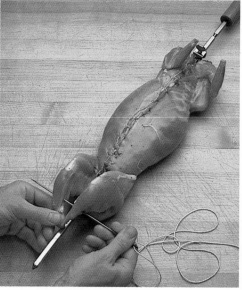

3 **Trussing.** Slide a holding fork on to a spit rod. Push the spit through the centre of the rabbit from the neck end; push the fork into the shoulders, then secure the shoulders with string. Push the second fork into the thighs. Make a stitch through the legs and tie them to the spit.

3 **Marinating.** Place the joints on a tray and pour olive oil over them; sprinkle them with mixed dried herbs, salt and pepper. Turn the joints to coat them with the marinade; cover and leave for 2 hours. To make the forelegs easier to turn on the grill, thread them on a skewer.

4 **Basting.** Place the hind legs on an oiled rack 10 to 15 cm (4 to 6 inches) above medium-hot coals. Brush them with the marinade. After 2 to 3 minutes, add the saddle joints and, 3 minutes later, the forelegs. Cook the joints for about 8 minutes more, basting frequently with leftover marinade (*above*) and turning them once.☐

4 **Larding.** Cut chilled pork fat into strips about 5 mm (¼ inch) wide. Roll them in chopped herbs—in this case, savory and thyme. Using a larding needle, insert about five lardons into each of the thighs (*above*). Trim each lardon, letting about 1 cm (½ inch) protrude at both ends.

5 **Roasting.** Set a drip pan on the hearth in front of medium-hot coals. Pour 1 cm (½ inch) of water into the pan. Baste the rabbit every 10 minutes with pan juices—here, applied with rosemary and lemon peel. Roast for 1 to 1½ hours, or until juices run clear when a thigh is pierced.

6 **Carving.** Transfer the rabbit to a board. Cut the strings, remove the spit and let the rabbit rest for 10 minutes. Use a heavy knife to slice through the joint attaching each leg to the body. Carve slices from both sides of the saddle. Slit the belly and scoop out the stuffing.☐

Providing Protection for Game Birds

Because small game birds—quail, snipe, woodcock and squab—are very lean, they must be cooked in ways that will keep their flesh moist. Two ingenious methods are shown here for protecting these birds with sufficient fat while they cook.

On the right, quail are spit-roasted on a rotisserie which can hold two spits, one above the other. The top spit, which may be stationary, is strung with lean salt pork. The quail are threaded sideways on the bottom spit, which rotates. To ensure that the spit is evenly loaded, the quail are packed tightly, head to tail, and secured with the holding forks. As the birds turn, they brush against the melting pork and receive a continuous basting.

In the second method (*below*), quail are protected by multiple layers. They are smeared with butter, wrapped in vine leaves—which impart a subtle lemony flavour—and then in bards of fat. A final covering of foil enables the birds to be baked gently in a bed of ashes. As the birds cook, the foil packages trap the juices for a remarkably succulent result.

Continuous Basting on a Double Spit

1 Trussing the birds. Rub the cavity of each quail with oil and seasoning; place fresh herbs—here, parsley and thyme—inside. Tuck the wing tips of each bird behind its back. Loop the centre of a 30 cm (12 inch) piece of string round the end of first one drumstick and then the other and tie the two together (*above, left*). Draw the two ends of string round the legs towards the wings so that the legs are pulled snugly against the body. Pass the string between the wings and body. Turn the quail over and tie the string securely at the wing tips (*above, right*). Cut off excess string. Coat the birds with oil.

Leaf-Wrapped Quail Cooked in the Ashes

1 Wrapping and barding the birds. Wash and dry vine leaves—in this case, fresh vine leaves. If using preserved ones, rinse them thoroughly to remove brine. Twist off the leaf stems. One by one, season each bird—here, quail—with salt and pepper, then smear its breast and thighs liberally with butter. Press a vine leaf over the breast (*above, left*), tucking the edges of the leaf underneath the bird. Cover the breast with two bards of pork back fat. Tie the fat in place with pieces of string (*above, right*); trim away excess string.

2 Forming packages. Cut rectangles of foil. Position a bird, breast-side up, in the centre of each rectangle, then raise the two long edges of foil (*above*). Fold and double-fold the long edges together. Fold and double-fold the short edges and tuck them under the bird to make a tightly sealed package.

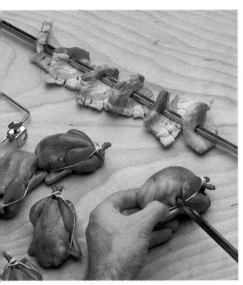

2 **Loading the spits.** Cut salt pork into 5 cm (2 inch) squares; blanch in simmering water for 5 minutes, slash the edges at 5 mm (¼ inch) intervals and thread the squares on a spit. If the birds are too small to impale on the holding forks, reverse the forks. Thread the quail sideways on a second spit, alternating them head to tail. Press the forks against the birds.

3 **Roasting.** Attach the spit of salt pork to the rotisserie motor; set drip pans beneath it. Turn the pork until it begins to drip, then move it to a higher support. Attach the spitted quail to the motor. Basting often with pan juices—applied here with thyme sprigs—roast for 15 to 20 minutes, or until juices run clear when a thigh is pricked.□

3 **Burying in ashes.** Bury the quail in a bed of hot ashes about 10 cm (4 inches) deep (*above*); the ashes must be sufficiently hot to retain heat for the duration of cooking—15 to 20 minutes. When the cooking is complete, remove the quail from the ashes—protecting your hands with a cloth or oven gloves—and transfer them to a heatproof tray.

4 **Unwrapping the quail.** Unwrap each package and cut away the pieces of string (*above*). Discard the string and the barding fat. Arrange the quail on a serving platter. If you like, add a garnish such as game chips, watercress or toast.

5 **Serving.** Allow one or two birds for each guest and add the garnish—here, game chips. The vine leaves may be eaten, if desired, or discarded. To carve each bird, steady it with a fork and use a sharp knife to cut off the thigh joints (*above*). Then slice off the breast meat.□

4
Fish and Shellfish
Preserving Natural Delicacy

Naturally tender fish and shellfish taste delectable when imbued with the smoke from a smouldering fire. Cooked outdoors, even the humblest fish acquires distinction and the fresher the seafood, the more exquisite the result. You may be fortunate enough to obtain a really fresh catch from nearby sea or river; if not, use reliable guidelines when shopping: fresh seafood has a sweet, pleasant odour; fish have bright eyes, shiny scales and glittering skins; fish fillets and steaks have moist-looking flesh; shellfish should be bought live if possible.

Seafood requires only brief grilling to firm its flesh and bring out its flavour; it must not be allowed to dry out or overcook. As a rule, the coals should never be more than medium-hot. Shellfish are protected from the heat by their shells (*page 70*). Fatty fish such as mackerel and sardines have natural oils to prevent them from drying out. Generally, however, flesh is kept succulent by basting with oil, butter or a marinade.

Another way of protecting flesh is to enclose it in foil or an edible wrapper. Oysters swathed in bacon, for example, become the delicacies known as "angels on horseback" (*page 74, above*). Wrappings of vine or lettuce leaves suit a range of fish, notably red mullet (*page 74, below*).

Since the delicate flesh of fish is easily broken when cooked, grilling baskets, which greatly facilitate handling and turning, are a feature of outdoor fish cookery. Some baskets are shaped to contain many small fish (*page 62*), others accommodate steaks (*page 66*) or single whole fish such as the fennel-filled sea bass shown on page 64.

In some cases a spit provides the answer to the problem of turning a large fish over the fire. However, since the spit rod must be securely lodged inside the fish, this method is reserved for large round fish with firm, thick flesh. A whole salmon is ample enough to be roasted with a stuffing (*page 68*); carp or salmon trout could be presented in the same way. Firm flesh is also the prerequisite for fish and shellfish that are to be grilled on skewers (*page 72*). Chunks of turbot, swordfish, tuna and eel are all suitable, as are prawns and scallops, marinated beforehand with such complementary herbs as dill, bay and parsley. Fillets of oily fish—herring, for instance—lend themselves to an unusual treatment known as planking; the fillets are nailed to a block of wood and placed near the fire so that they can slowly absorb its smoky flavour (*page 66*).

A squeeze of lemon juice lends a piquant finish to a platter of grilled seafood—lobster, oysters, prawns and clams (*page 70*). During grilling, the shells protected the delicate flesh from the heat, the lobster's flesh was bathed in melted butter and the prawns were basted with an oil-based marinade laced with garlic and parsley.

Two Strategies for Grilling Small Fish

Grilling over coals is an excellent way to bring out the natural flavour of fish. In the case of small fish—sardines, pilchards, anchovies and sprats—the process is simplicity itself. Because of their size, these varieties do not even require gutting if they are freshly caught. Their generous endowment of oil prevents them from drying out while they are on the grill, so basting can be kept to a minimum.

The distinctive flavour of the fish makes elaborate seasoning unnecessary. Often they are salted before they are cooked—a tradition rooted in the cuisine of the Northern Mediterranean. In the demonstration on the right, sardines are embedded in layers of coarse salt for several hours before being grilled. The salt counters the oiliness of the flesh, stiffens the fish slightly and dries out the skin to help it crisp during the rapid cooking. Alternatively, lightly season the fish with salt and pepper.

Like most food that is cooked directly on the grill, small fish need to be turned about half way through their cooking time. This could become a laborious task when grilling any small morsels, but fortunately there are ways of making a large batch easier to handle. One way is to use a specially designed grilling basket that is capacious enough to hold a number of fish (*right*). Another technique is to use a pair of long skewers to impale about half a dozen fish at a time (*box, opposite page*). Both methods will prevent the fish from slipping through the bars of the rack and will help to preserve the fish's shape.

The grilled fish should be served crackling hot when their skins—which will have acquired a smoky flavour from the fire—are browned and crisped. A squeeze of lemon will counteract any remaining oiliness. Crusty bread makes a welcome accompaniment for outdoor eating; the fish can be laid on the bread to saturate it with their juices.

1 **Assembling the ingredients.** Rinse fresh sardines in cold water and dry them. Sprinkle a shallow layer of coarse sea salt on to a tray that is large enough to hold all the sardines in a single layer. Arrange the fish side by side on the salt.

2 **Covering with salt.** Sprinkle over more salt, covering the exposed surfaces of the sardines completely. Transfer the tray to a cool place or the refrigerator. Leave the fish to steep in the salt for 1 to 2 hours.

3 **Loading the grilling basket.** Open a double-sided grilling basket and brush the inside with olive oil. One at a time, lift the sardines by the tail and shake off the salt; use your fingers to brush off all but a few grains from each fish. Arrange the sardines side by side on one half of the open basket (*above*), then close the basket. Discard the salt.

4 **Grilling the fish.** Place the basket on a rack 10 to 15 cm (4 to 6 inches) away from medium-hot coals. When the undersides of the fish have lightly browned—after about 5 minutes—turn the basket over. Baste the sardines with a little olive oil (*above*) and continue to grill them for a further 3 to 5 minutes, or until their skin starts to blister.

A Simple Trick with Skewers

1 **Skewering the fish.** Start by pushing a single skewer through one of the fish—in this case, salted sardines—just below its head; thread the fish along the skewer to the far end. Push another skewer through the impaled fish just above its tail, so that the fish is secured by a pair of parallel skewers. Thread the rest of the fish horizontally on to the two skewers, alternating the direction in which the heads face (*above*).

2 **Cooking and serving.** Lay the skewered fish on a rack over medium-hot coals. After 5 minutes, turn the fish, holding the loop end of one of the skewers with a cloth, and lifting the pointed end of the skewer with a spatula (*above*). Baste the fish with olive oil and continue to grill them for a further 3 to 5 minutes, or until they are done. Slide the fish off the skewers with the back of a fork, and arrange them on a warmed serving dish. Serve at once.

5 **Serving the fish.** Remove the basket from the rack and transfer the grilled sardines to a warmed serving platter (*left*). Serve at once, garnished with wedges of lemon and sprigs of parsley (*above*). □

A Large Fish Flamed with Fennel

The easiest way to handle a large fish on an outdoor grill is to enclose it in a grilling basket. Held tightly in the basket, the fish retains its shape and can be turned over without risk of breaking. In the demonstration here, a sea bass is filled with stalks of fennel and marinated in a mixture of oil, fennel leaves and seasoning. While it grills, the fish is basted with the marinade and, before serving, it is flamed with pastis—an anise-flavoured liqueur—over a bed of fennel stalks. Fish and fennel are a classic partnership but you could use dill, parsley, rosemary, thyme or bay leaves instead and replace the pastis with brandy or Armagnac.

Choose a specimen that fits snugly in the basket and does not slide about. If the fish is very large, as here, you will need to remove its head before the fish will fit; you can then gut the fish through the neck. With a smaller fish, leave the head in place and eviscerate the fish through the gills (*page 68, Step 1*). In either case, the belly will remain intact to preserve the appearance of the fish and to enclose the herb filling.

To enable the heat of the coals to penetrate the flesh, several deep slashes are made in the sides of the fish. The marinade can be rubbed into these cuts as well as over the exterior of the fish.

Before placing the fish in the basket, make sure the wires of the basket are well brushed with oil to prevent sticking. It is important to baste the fish through the basket frequently while it is on the grill and to turn it more than once so it cooks evenly and without charring. At the end of cooking, remove the basket from the rack, open the basket and use two metal spatulas to transfer the fish to the serving platter. If you intend to flame the fish, lay it on a prepared bed of herbs on the dish.

1 Scaling a fish. Wash and dry a large fish—here, a 4 kg (9 lb) sea bass. Using scissors, trim the tail and cut off the fins. To remove the scales, hold the fish firmly by the tail and draw the back of a knife or a fish scaler along the body towards the head—against the direction in which the scales lie. Turn the fish over and scale the other side in the same way.

2 Detaching the head. If the fish is too long for the basket, remove the head. Holding the head firmly, make a V-shaped cut from the point where the head and the body meet to the base of the front fin. Turn the fish over and make a similar incision on the other side, cutting all the way through the head (*above*).

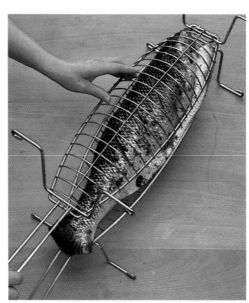

6 Using a grilling basket. Brush the inside surfaces of the basket with oil. Place the fish in the lower half of the basket and close the lid; do not worry if the tail of the fish protrudes. Reserve the marinade left on the tray. Place the basket on the grill rack 10 to 15 cm (4 to 6 inches) from medium-hot coals.

7 Basting. Grill the fish for 7 to 10 minutes. Turn the basket over and baste the fish with marinade. After a further 7 to 10 minutes, turn and baste again. Baste frequently until the fish is cooked—about 30 minutes in all. To test whether the fish is done, pierce it just behind the gills; the flesh should be opaque and just coming away from the bone.

3 **Gutting the fish.** Pull the fish's head away from the body, drawing out the viscera at the same time (*above*). Discard the head and viscera. Rinse the fish inside and out. To make sure that the fish cooks through, cut four diagonal slashes on each side of it, slitting the flesh almost to the bone.

4 **Filling the fish.** Lay the fish on a tray and place herbs—in this instance, stalks of fennel—loosely in the body cavity. The herbs will both flavour the fish and give it a plump appearance.

5 **Marinating.** Rub the fish all over with a mixture of olive oil, chopped herbs— here, fennel leaves—salt and pepper. Press the marinade gently into the slits in the flesh. Cover the fish and leave it to marinate for about 1 hour.

3 **Serving.** Remove the basket from the grill and undo the clasp. Lay a thick layer of dried fennel branches on a serving dish. Use spatulas to transfer the fish to the platter. Warm liqueur—here, pastis—in a saucepan; pour the liqueur over the fish and ignite it. When the flames have died, use a spoon and fork to serve portions of the fish with lemon wedges.□

Cooking Fish in front of the Fireplace

Any whole fish, fillet or steak that can be grilled over coals can be cooked at a fireplace. A whole round fish in a fish-shaped grill basket can simply be placed amidst the smouldering embers—the legs of the basket will keep the fish clear of the fire. Fish steaks or fillets, as well as whole flat fish, can be fitted into a rectangular basket and supported by bricks stacked on the hearth (*right*). And—in a variation on a technique American Indians used at bonfires—fillets can be planked, or nailed to a board, and propped upright in front of the fire to cook gently (*right, below*).

Such treatments are well suited to oil-rich fish—although they will still require basting, their flesh is already endowed with some protective moisture. Salmon, tuna, halibut or the swordfish shown here all yield good-sized steaks which should be cut at least 2 cm (¾ inch) thick. Fish steaks are best grilled with their central bones and outer skin left in place, to keep the flesh from breaking.

For planking, shad, mackerel or—as here—herring fillets make good choices because they will not dry out during the relatively long cooking time. The fillets should not be skinned as their skin will help to keep the flesh intact during cooking. Any sturdy hardwood board such as the chopping board shown here will serve as the plank. Avoid plywood, which ignites easily because of the adhesives it contains, and resinous woods, such as pine, which might impair the flavour of the fish. To secure the fish, use only steel, stainless-steel or aluminium nails; the coatings on galvanized nails may be toxic.

Oiling the surfaces of the fish is always a necessity and can be a means of adding flavour. Here, the swordfish steaks are marinated in an herb-laced paste (*recipe, page 161*); the herring fillets are simply brushed with melted butter.

Follow the standard rule of 10 minutes per 2.5 cm (1 inch) of thickness to grill fish. But allow anywhere from 15 to 25 minutes per 2.5 cm for planked fillets because these will cook by radiant rather than direct heat. By adding dampened hickory chips to the coals you can induce more smoke and the planked fish will gradually absorb the smoky flavour.

Swordfish Steaks Enclosed in a Basket

1 **Marinating.** Place fish steaks—in this case, swordfish—in a dish and coat them with a marinade; a mixture of chopped thyme and chervil, salt, pepper and olive oil is used here. Let the steaks marinate for 30 minutes to 1 hour. Pile bricks in two parallel stacks 18 to 20 cm (7 to 8 inches) high at the edge of the fireplace (*page 9*).

2 **Grilling the steaks.** Rake embers from the fire to form a layer about 5 cm (2 inches) deep between the two stacks of bricks. Place the steaks in an oiled hinged basket. Close the basket and fasten it. Rest the basket on the bricks. Cook the steaks until done on one side, baste them, turn the basket and baste again.

Herring Fillets Fastened to a Plank

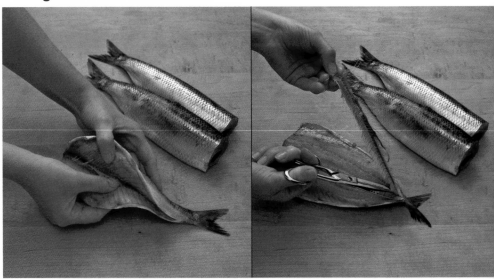

1 **Boning the fish.** With scissors, trim away the fins from the fish—in this case, herrings. Scale the fish (*page 64, Step 1*). Cut off the heads with a sharp knife. Slit open each fish along the belly, remove and discard the viscera. Hold the fish open and slip your thumb under the backbone and ribs on one side of the fish to ease the bones away from the flesh (*above, left*). Do the same with the ribs on the other side of the backbone. Lift the backbone and attached ribs free, and sever the backbone at the tail end with scissors (*above, right*). Extract any remaining small bones with tweezers.

3 **Serving.** When the steaks start to come away from the bone, place the basket on its lid next to a platter. Open the basket and slide the swordfish steaks from the lid on to the platter. Garnish the steaks with basil leaves and top each steak, if you like, with a spoonful of tomato and basil mayonnaise (*recipe, page 163*).□

2 **Brushing with melted butter.** Wash and dry the fillets; season them with salt and pepper. Choose a chopping board that is at least 2.5 cm (1 inch) thick, and made of hardwood—oak, for instance. Brush the board with oil. Using steel nails and a small hammer, nail the opened-out fish skin side down to the oiled side of the plank. Brush the fish with melted butter.

3 **Cooking.** Toss some dampened hickory chips on to the hot coals. Stand the plank at an angle of about 45 degrees against a stack of bricks on the hearth. Set the bottom of the plank inside a drip pan or on a sheet of aluminium foil. Since the fish at the bottom will cook faster than those at the top, turn the plank upside-down after 5 to 10 minutes (*above*).

4 **Serving.** Turn the plank at 10-minute intervals and baste the fish with butter. Cook the fish until it is whitish and opaque and flakes easily when tested with a fork, about 25 minutes. Lay the plank flat and remove the nails with pliers. Garnish the herrings with lemon and transfer them to plates (*above*). Serve, if you like, with sliced tomatoes sprinkled with basil.□

Roasting a Large Fish on a Spit

A large fish such as carp, salmon trout or the salmon shown on the right makes a particularly imposing presentation when its shape has been carefully preserved up to the moment of serving. One of the most successful ways of handling and cooking such a fish—especially if it has a relatively narrow body that will not fit snugly in a grilling basket—is to fill it with a stuffing and roast it on a spit. The spit supports the fish without marring its appearance, and constant rotation ensures even cooking of both the fish and the stuffing.

To avoid cutting the fish, it should be eviscerated, and then filled, through its gills (*Step 1*). If the fish is exceptionally large, you may need a long-handled spoon to reach into the belly cavity and scoop out the last of the viscera; the fish is then ready for stuffing.

Choose a stuffing that complements, rather than dominates, the fish. A mixture of chopped mushrooms, onions, parsley and garlic, when bound with egg and breadcrumbs, forms a stuffing that suits most fish, including the delicate-tasting salmon here (*recipe, page 166*). However, you could substitute parboiled, chopped spinach or sorrel for the mushrooms or, for a colourful Mediterranean stuffing that would suit sea bass or grey mullet, replace the mushrooms with chopped black olives and skinned, chopped tomatoes.

To impale the fish securely on the spit, pass the spit through the firm, thick flesh just above the backbone, rather than through the stuffed cavity. You should also secure the fish to the holding forks, for, as it cooks, the flesh contracts slightly and the spit may start to rotate inside the fish instead of turning with it. You can use a length of string, as here, or a piece of chicken wire wrapped round the fish and pinched tightly around the forks at each end of the fish.

Basting with butter will help keep the fish moist. Its skin, too, will protect it from the heat. Remove the skin to serve, and fillet the fish.

1 **Eviscerating the fish.** With scissors, trim away the fins and tail of the fish—here, a salmon. Scale the fish (*page 64, Step 1*). Hook a finger through the vent of the gills; pull out the viscera together with the gills (*above*). Reach into the cavity with your fingers or a spoon, and check that you have removed all the viscera. Rinse out the fish and dry the outside.

2 **Preparing the stuffing.** In a sauté pan, soften finely chopped onions and garlic; add finely chopped mushrooms and sauté briefly. Transfer the ingredients to a bowl. Add chopped parsley, lemon juice, an egg and fresh breadcrumbs. Mix with your hands. Season with salt, pepper and nutmeg. If the mixture feels wet, add more breadcrumbs.

5 **Cooking the fish.** Position the spit over the hot coals. Here, a fish weighing 2.25 kg (4½ lb) before stuffing is placed 15 to 20 cm (6 to 8 inches) from the coals and cooked for about 50 minutes. Allow 10 to 12 minutes per 500 g (1 lb). If the fish's skin starts to char before the flesh is cooked, move the spit further from the coals. Throughout the cooking, rotate the spit constantly and brush the fish frequently with melted butter (*above*). If the fish's tail starts to burn, protect it with foil. The fish is done when the point of a knife inserted behind the gills meets tender, opaque flesh that comes away easily.

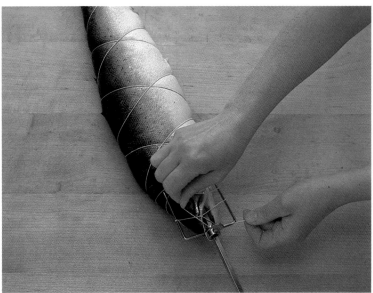

3 **Stuffing the fish.** Hold the fish by its head and push the stuffing, a little at a time, through the opening in the gills. Push the stuffing down into the belly cavity, using the handle of a wooden spoon if necessary, until the cavity is loosely filled. Slip one of the holding forks on to the spit, sliding it towards the handle. Pass the spit through the mouth of the salmon, pushing it through the flesh just above the backbone, and out through the tail. Slip on the other fork.

4 **Tying the fish.** Push the prongs of the holding forks firmly into the fish; screw down the forks tightly. Cut a piece of string about five times the length of the fish. Find the middle of the piece of string and tie it firmly to the tail fork; wind the string round the fork several times. Working towards the head, criss-cross the two ends of the string over and under the fish so that the fish's girth is encircled by loops of string. Tie the string to the head fork with a secure knot (*above*). Season the fish with salt and pepper.

6 **Skinning and filleting the fish.** Transfer the fish, still attached to the spit, to a serving dish. Cut away and discard the string. Remove the holding forks and draw out the spit carefully. Slit the salmon's skin from behind its head to its tail, making one cut along the back and another along the belly. Pull away the skin with the help of a knife (*above, left*). To divide the exposed upper flesh into two fillets, make a shallow incision along the length of the backbone (*above, right*). To free the flesh, ease it away from one side of the backbone, holding the knife at a shallow angle.

7 **Serving.** Divide each fillet into serving portions and transfer them—together with a spoonful of the stuffing and a wedge of lemon—to individual plates (*above*). When the upper fillets have been served, lift away the backbone. Divide the lower fillets into portions; lift them off the skin with a fish slice.□

Mixed Shellfish: out of the Sea and on to the Grill

Crustaceans and bivalves are in many ways marvellously well suited to outdoor grilling. Their shells, which are left in place throughout the process, shield the delicate flesh from the direct heat of the coals, keeping it tender and succulent. And the many varieties of shellfish—here, lobster, prawns, clams and oysters—can provide a magnificent medley of tastes and textures. Depending on seasonal availability, crabs, scallops and mussels might also be included.

Spared the task of removing the shells, the cook's role is chiefly confined to cleaning and trimming the seafood. Prawns should be divested of legs and intestinal veins; here, they are also steeped in an oil-based marinade that contains garlic, salt, parsley and lemon juice—a classic blend ideal for seafood (*recipe, page 161*).

Lobsters must be kept alive until the last possible moment. Choose lively specimens—they are likely to be in the best condition. The most humane way to kill a lobster is to plunge it head first into rapidly boiling water, and keep it immersed for several minutes. Once you have cut the lobster in half, remove the inedible organs (*Step 4*). The liver—the greenish to-malley—is a delicacy and should be kept intact, as should the coral, the flame-coloured undeveloped eggs often found in female lobsters. The best way to bring out lobster's flavour and succulence is to season it lightly and bathe it with melted butter, which keeps the flesh moist without masking its taste.

Bivalves should be scrubbed until absolutely clean. Tap any shells that are open. If they remain open, discard them; the creature inside is probably dead.

You may have to load the grill in stages to take account of the cooking times for different types of seafood. Here, the lobster, which takes about 15 minutes to cook, is put on the grill in advance of the prawns, clams and oysters.

Cooking times will be extended if you use wet seaweed as a barrier between the grill and the food (*box, opposite page*). This method heightens seafood's intrinsic taste and smell, whilst creating a steamy atmosphere that ensures exceptionally moist results. Seaweed suitable for cooking can be obtained from fishmongers.

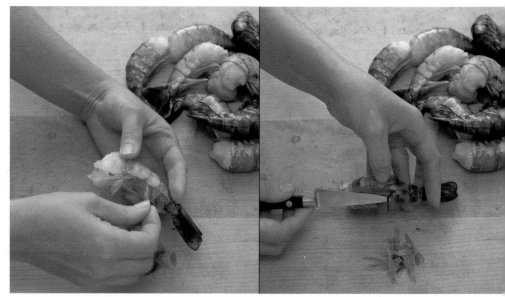

1 Preparing the prawns. With your fingers, pull the legs away from the underside of one of the prawns—here, an uncooked Pacific prawn (*above, left*). Leave the shell and the tail intact. Turn the prawn over. To remove the dark, intestinal vein—which has a bitter taste—make a shallow slit along the centre of the prawn's back, using a small, sharp knife. With the tip of the knife, prise out the black vein (*above, right*) and discard it, along with the legs. Prepare the remaining prawns in the same way.

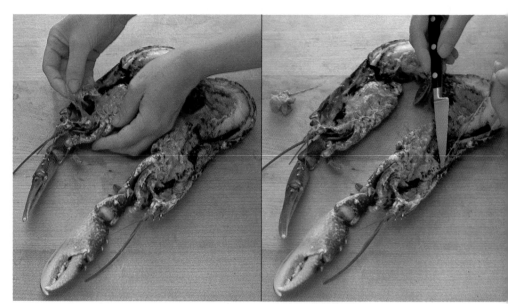

4 Preparing the lobster. Kill the lobster by plunging it head first into boiling salted water; use tongs to hold it under the surface for at least 2 minutes. During this time, the lobster will begin to turn red. Set the lobster, underside down, on a work surface; let it cool. To halve the lobster, cut it lengthwise through the centre of its head, back and tail. Lay the two sections flat on the work surface. Pull out and discard the round, whitish gravel sac near the head section of one half (*above, left*). With the tip of a small knife, detach and discard the long, thin intestinal vein (*above, right*).

Cooking on a Bed of Seaweed

Steaming seafood. Rinse some edible seaweed—such as the Bladderwrack used here or a related species—then shake off excess water. Lay the seaweed on the rack. Arrange the seafood—in this case, marinated Pacific prawns—on top. Cook the prawns for about 20 minutes, using tongs to turn them after 10 minutes (*above*). Serve the prawns at once and discard the seaweed.

2 **Making a marinade.** Put peeled garlic cloves and a little coarse salt in a mortar. Using a heavy pestle, pound the garlic and salt to a smooth paste (*above*). Add lemon juice, then gradually stir in olive oil and a handful of chopped parsley.

3 **Coating the prawns.** Place the prawns in a shallow dish and pour the marinade over them. Turn the prawns to coat them evenly with the marinade (*above*). Cover the dish with plastic film or foil, and leave it to stand for about an hour. When ready to cook the prawns, drain them and reserve the marinade for basting.

5 **Brushing with melted butter.** Melt butter in a shallow, heavy pan set over low heat. Brush the exposed flesh of the lobster halves with the butter (*above*), reserving some for basting. If you like, sprinkle the juice of half a lemon evenly over the lobster flesh, then season the lobster with salt and black pepper.

6 **Cooking.** Place the lobster halves, shell side down, on a rack set 10 to 15 cm (4 to 6 inches) above medium-hot coals; baste the flesh frequently with the melted butter. After 7 minutes, add the prawns; cook for 4 to 5 minutes, then turn them and baste them with their marinade. Add the oysters and clams. Turn the lobster halves over (*above*); cook the lobster and prawns for another 4 to 5 minutes or until the flesh is firm and opaque. When the oyster and clam shells open, the shellfish are done. Remove them from the grill and discard the upper shells. Serve with wedges of lemon.□

Skewering Firm-Fleshed Seafood

Juicy chunks of fish or small whole shell-fish make some of the most appetizing of brochettes. Protected and enhanced by complementary marinades, these morsels cook rapidly, drawing savour from the fire and remaining moist beneath a golden-brown exterior.

The fish must have firm flesh that will hold its shape during cooking and will yield 2.5 to 5 cm (1 to 2 inch) pieces. Suitable candidates include eel, large round fish such as swordfish and tuna, and thick-bodied flat fish—turbot and halibut, for instance. In the demonstration on the right, eel pieces—left unskinned for extra protection on the grill—are first steeped in an acidic marinade that balances the rich flesh. Fragrant bay leaves flavour the eel as it cooks.

Removed from their shells, mussels, clams, oysters and prawns seem tailor-made for brochettes. Below, marinated scallops are skewered with pieces of cucumber (*recipe, page 156*). Some of the scallops' coral is beaten into an accompanying butter (*page 14*).

Eel Segments Interspersed with Bay Leaves

1 **Preparing the eels.** Cut off the heads of freshly killed eels, slicing just behind the gills with a heavy knife. Slit open the belly of each eel about half way along the eel's length; pull out the greyish-white viscera (*above*) and discard them along with the heads. Chop the eels into 5 cm (2 inch) segments and put them in a dish.

2 **Marinating and skewering.** Sprinkle the eel pieces with a little wine vinegar, lemon juice and olive oil, and turn the segments in the liquid. Cover the dish and leave the eel to marinate. After about 2 hours, thread the eel segments on to skewers with bay leaves; start and finish with a bay leaf, and make sure that the leaves touch the eel pieces.

Brochettes of Scallops and Cucumber

1 **Preparing the cucumbers.** Peel cucumbers with a vegetable peeler; cut them in half lengthwise. Remove the seeds by running your thumb down the middle of each half (*above*). Discard the seeds and peel. Slice the cucumber halves crosswise into 1 cm (½ inch) pieces. Plunge the cucumber pieces into boiling, salted water for about a minute, then drain them in a sieve. Set the sieve over a bowl, so that the cucumbers continue to drain.

2 **Halving scallops.** Remove scallops from their shells (*page 14*). Wash and dry the large white muscle and the orange coral of each scallop and discard the rest of the shell contents. If you like, reserve the coral from a few scallops to flavour an accompanying butter. Cut large scallops in half, slicing across the grain (*above*); leave small scallops whole. Put the scallops in a dish containing a marinade—here, olive oil, lemon juice, salt, pepper and finely chopped fresh dill. Add the cucumber pieces.

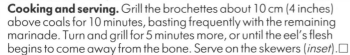

3 **Cooking and serving.** Grill the brochettes about 10 cm (4 inches) above coals for 10 minutes, basting frequently with the remaining marinade. Turn and grill for 5 minutes more, or until the eel's flesh begins to come away from the bone. Serve on the skewers (*inset*). □

3 **Filling the skewers.** Mix the ingredients in the marinade. Cover and leave for about 1 hour, then thread the scallops and the cucumbers alternately on to skewers. Skewer the scallops against the grain so that they hold together. To avoid splitting the cucumber pieces, thread them on to the skewers with a gentle twisting action. Reserve the marinade.

4 **Serving the brochettes.** Grill the brochettes about 10 cm (4 inches) above medium-hot coals for 8 to 10 minutes, turning the skewers after 4 minutes and basting frequently with the reserved marinade. You can serve the brochettes just as they are, or accompany them, as here, with a coral-flavoured butter. □

Wrappings that Flavour and Protect

Basting is not the only way to keep fish and shellfish succulent on the grill; you can achieve the same results by enclosing the seafood in a wrapping. Vine leaves, lettuce and bacon are all good choices because they impart a complementary flavour to the seafood as well as providing moisture and protection.

Oysters, for instance, wrapped in bacon rashers and grilled over coals in a hinged basket, retain their juices and acquire a superb smoky flavour (*right*). The melting bacon fat bastes the oysters as they grill and, at the end of cooking, the bacon's crispness counterpoints the tender texture of the oysters.

Oysters, which are bought live, must first be checked to see that their shells are shut; discard any that gape because the oyster inside will probably be dead. Scrub the shells, then use a small, sharp knife, or an oyster knife, to open the shells and free the flesh. Available at kitchenware shops, an oyster knife has a strong, short blade and a pointed tip to pierce the shell's thick hinge and force it open.

The shucked oysters should be quickly wrapped in the bacon and grilled. Here, a small basil leaf and a square of grilled sweet red pepper are tucked inside each package; other flavourings—thyme and pieces of spring onion, for instance— might be used instead. Similar packages could be assembled using shucked mussels, clams and scallops.

Leaves also make valuable wrappers. In the demonstration on the right, red mullet are encased in vine leaves, which give the fish a pleasantly sharp flavour. At the end of cooking, the mullet's liver— prized as a delicacy—is incorporated into a vinaigrette to make a delectable sauce to accompany the fish.

Apart from possessing a tangy flavour, vine leaves are firm-textured and do not shrivel in the heat of the grill. However, several layers of lettuce leaves make a sturdy enough alternative, and their mild flavour goes well with trout, salmon, and swordfish (*recipe, page 143*). You can, of course, use foil to wrap a wide range of lean-fleshed fish; and if garnishes such as mushrooms and onions are incorporated into the packages, their flavours intermingle with delicious results.

Crisp Coverings for Tender Oysters

1 **Opening oysters.** Scrub oysters under cold running water. Place one oyster at a time on a folded napkin with its flatter shell uppermost and the hinged end towards you. Grasp the broad end of the oyster with the cloth; insert the tip of an oyster knife into the hinge and twist the blade to force the shells apart.

2 **Severing the muscles.** Slide the knife along the inside surface of the top shell to cut the muscle that attaches the shell to the flesh. Discard the top shell. Slide the knife under the oyster to release the flesh from the bottom shell. Use the tip of the knife to clean out any bits of shell. Empty the oyster and its juices into a dish.

Small Fish Encased in Leaves

1 **Gutting the fish.** Cut off the fins and scale the fish (*page 64, Step 1*)—here, red mullet. To eviscerate the fish, slit the belly open and locate the reddish-brown liver situated just behind the head. Leaving the liver in place, pull out and discard the rest of the viscera (*above*).

2 **Marinating and wrapping.** Chop dill, as here, or fennel and scatter over the fish. Pour olive oil over the fish and leave them to marinate for an hour. Rinse vine leaves and blot them dry. Lay each fish across the underside of a leaf and roll it up (*above*), using a second leaf if necessary to enclose the fish completely.

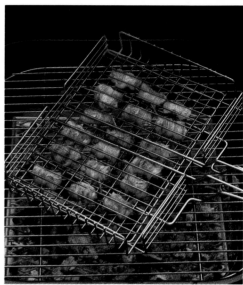

3 **Wrapping the oysters.** Grill, seed and peel a sweet red pepper (*page 19*); cut it into small squares. Pull the small leaves from sprigs of fresh basil. Halve bacon rashers crosswise. For each assembly, place an oyster at one end of a bacon slice. Lay a basil leaf and pepper square on the oyster. Roll the oyster in the bacon.

4 **Securing the bacon.** Insert a wooden toothpick that has been soaked in water for 10 minutes into the overlapping end of the bacon. Press the pick diagonally through the roll until its point emerges on the opposite side. Wrap the remaining oysters in bacon in the same way.

5 **Grilling the oysters.** Place the bacon-wrapped oysters side by side in an oiled, hinged grilling basket. Close the basket and set it on a rack 10 to 15 cm (4 to 6 inches) away from medium-hot coals. Turning the basket frequently, grill the oysters for about 6 minutes, or until the bacon is crisp and brown on all sides.□

3 **Grilling.** Lay the wrapped fish on an oiled rack with the loose ends of the leaves underneath to prevent them from unrolling. Grill the fish over medium-hot coals for about 5 minutes, until the leaves begin to char and the exposed heads and tails of the fish become crisp; turn the fish (*above*) and grill them for a further 5 minutes. Transfer each fish to a plate.

4 **Removing the liver.** Use a knife to peel away the leaves—the fish's skin should come away at the same time. With a fork and the tip of the knife, remove the fish's liver (*above*) and reserve it. Extend the slit in the belly as far as the tail, then slit along the backbone. Lift away the top fillet. Grasp the tail of the fish and pull away the backbone and head; discard them.

5 **Making a sauce.** In a small bowl, mix olive oil, vinegar and salt and pepper to make a vinaigrette (*recipe, page 163*). Place the reserved fish liver in a dish; use a fork to mash it and mix it smoothly with a little of the vinaigrette (*above*). Serve the liver and vinaigrette mixture as a pungent sauce to accompany the fillets.□

5
Special Presentations
Surprises and Celebrations

Varied roles for cheese
How to handle a whole pig
A pit for steaming seafood
Using a smoker

Outdoors or at a fireplace, an adventurous approach to ingredients and methods can be highly rewarding. With a little improvisation, you can apply the techniques demonstrated in the previous chapters to produce outdoor feasts of epic dimensions, serving up to a hundred people. Or, on a smaller scale, you can bring the unique savour of fire and smoke to ingredients not usually considered to be barbecue food.

Cheese, for example, might seem an improbable candidate for the outdoor grill. Yet hard and soft cheeses alike can be transformed into epicurean delights if their melting is controlled by a protective coating pressed on to their surfaces (*opposite*), or by a wrapper of leaves (*page 78*). And a large wedge of cheese becomes the classic Swiss dish known as *raclette* if it is simply set beside the fireplace and scraped off as it melts.

Almost any ingredient assumes an entirely new character if it is cooked in a smoker (*pages 6-7*), a covered grill that allows the aromatic smoke from dampened wood to permeate the food. Because the ambient temperature inside the smoker is low and the atmosphere steamy, the food cooks gently, becoming tender and succulent and taking on a smoky flavour and a burnished finish. The wide variety of foods that lend themselves to this treatment—fish, poultry, game, meat, offal and even vegetables—can either be cooked together as a mixed grill (*page 86*), or singly, like the smoked turkey shown on page 88.

Even a whole large animal such as a lamb, goat or pig (*pages 80-83*) can be spit-roasted by adapting the principles of cooking on a rotisserie shown in Chapters 2 and 3. The tactics of marinating and trussing the animal, then turning and basting it as it cooks, remain the same. Only the scale changes: a length of steel rod is used for a spit, and its supports are stacks of hollow concrete blocks. Instead of a modest mound of fuel, you will need a bonfire of kindling and enough coals to cook the meat for 5 to 7 hours.

A good fire is also the secret of success for another favourite outdoor banquet, a traditional American clambake—usually held on the beach. A fire of wood, driftwood or coals is laid in a pit lined with smooth stones (*page 84*); when the stones are hot, the fire is raked out and the food placed in the pit to cook between layers of seaweed. Besides clams, other shellfish such as lobsters and crabs can be baked in this manner, as can fish fillets, poultry joints and vegetables such as sweetcorn and potatoes.

Slices of grilled goat's cheese, coated with breadcrumbs and ground walnuts (*page 79*) await serving with toast, tossed green salad and walnut halves. The cheese was grilled until soft in a basket over glowing coals. As well as preventing the melting cheese from dripping on to the fire, the crisp coating contrasts with the creamy softness of the cheese.

77

The Multiple Pleasures of Melted Cheese

Cheese is delicious when served bubbling from an outdoor grill. It needs only gentle heating to give it a soft, melting texture and to bring out its flavour. As demonstrated here, the tactics for accomplishing this vary according to the character of the cheese that is used.

Soft cheeses, with their high moisture content, will hold together in the brief time they are on the grill if they are provided with a protective coating. The soft goat's cheese shown on the opposite page, for example, is sliced thickly and dipped in a crunchy mixture of breadcrumbs and nuts. The cheese will heat through in 8 to 10 minutes but it must be turned frequently. A hinged basket allows you to turn the cheese during cooking without disturbing the coating. Suitable cheeses for this treatment include *feta, mozzarella* and any variety of goat's cheese.

Most hard cheeses are too dry for a coating to adhere well but they melt readily when exposed to the heat of a grill. The best way to deal with these cheeses is to enclose them in a wrapping that will contain the melting cheese safely and prevent it from dripping on to the coals. Foil, of course, may be used for the packages, but vine leaves (*below*) offer an attractive alternative and give a tangy flavour to the cheese. Any good melting cheese—whether hard or soft—may be grilled in this way: Bel Paese, Gruyere, *fontina*, Emmenthal, Lancashire, Brie and Camembert are among the possibilities.

Large wedges of firm cheese form the base for the Swiss speciality known as *raclette*, from the French verb *racler*, "to scrape". *Raclette* cheese is available from speciality cheese shops or delicatessens. The cheese is placed on the hearth before the fire and, as its exposed edge melts, it is scraped off on to warm plates (*box, right*) and quickly eaten. The traditional accompaniments for *raclette* cheese are small potatoes boiled in their jackets, gherkins and pickled onions.

Raclette: a Fireside Speciality

Serving raclette. Place a half or quarter *raclette* cheese on a board, with the cut edge about 15 cm (6 inches) from a hot fire. After about 30 seconds, when the cut surface is bubbling, remove the cheese from the fire. Using a broad-bladed knife or spatula, scrape the melted cheese on to a warmed plate (*above*). Season with pepper and serve with boiled potatoes.

Vine Leaf Packets with a Creamy Filling

1 **Wrapping the cheese.** Prepare vine leaves (*page 58*). Cut firm cheese—in this case, Bel Paese and Gruyère—into slices about 1 cm (½ inch) thick and about 5 cm (2 inches) in length. Place a slice of cheese in the centre of a vine leaf, on the leaf's prominently veined underside. Fold the base of the leaf over the cheese (*above, left*) and wrap the rest of the leaf tightly round it. Place the package on a second vine leaf and wrap it again (*above, right*). Wrap the remaining cheese slices in the same way.

2 **Grilling.** Place the cheese packages on an oiled rack about 10 cm (4 inches) above medium-hot coals. Cook them for 5 minutes on one side; use tongs to turn each package over (*above*). Grill for a further 5 minutes, or until the packages feel soft when pressed with the tongs.

Walnut Coating for Goat's Cheese

1 **Cutting the cheese.** With a sharp knife or a cheese wire, cut soft cheese—here, *chèvre*—into 1 cm (½ inch) slices (*above*). Using a processor or a mortar and pestle, finely grind nuts—walnuts, in this case. Mix the nuts with half their weight of stale white breadcrumbs. Spread the mixture on a plate or shallow tray.

2 **Filling the basket.** Lay each slice of cheese—halved, if you like, as here—on the nut and breadcrumb mixture and press the coating into the cheese. Turn the slice over and coat the other side. With your fingers, press the coating into the cut edges and rind of the cheese. Coat all the slices in the same way and place them in a grilling basket (*above*).

3 **Serving.** Grill the cheese about 10 cm (4 inches) from medium-hot coals for 8 to 10 minutes, turning often. Towards the end of cooking, toast fresh bread slices on the rack for 1 minute on each side, or until golden-brown. Serve the cheese on the hot toast, accompanied, if you like, by a salad—here, endive with walnut pieces, tossed in a walnut oil vinaigrette. □

3 **Serving.** Transfer the packages to a serving platter and then to individual plates. Using a knife and your fingertips, peel away the vine leaves to reveal the cheese (*left*). Spread the hot cheese on to pieces of fresh bread (*above*); the inner leaves may be eaten or discarded with the charred outer leaves. □

Spit-Roasting on a Grand Scale

The most spectacular centrepiece for an outdoor feast is a whole animal roasted on a spit over coals. Calves are too large for an amateur cook to handle, but pigs, lambs and goats are of manageable size.

Producing such a treat for a large gathering requires careful planning. The animal must be ordered well in advance from a butcher. Since only the smallest suckling pig will fit on to the spit of a rotisserie, the roasting apparatus must usually be improvised. In the demonstration here and overleaf, a steel rod supported by hollow concrete blocks serves as a spit.

The dressed weight of lambs and goats ranges from 5 to 22.5 kg (11 to 50 lb), that of pigs from 3.5 to 68 kg (8 to 150 lb). However, an animal weighing 31.5 kg (70 lb)—such as the pig shown here—is about the largest size practicable. A whole carcass may only be available frozen, in which case ask the butcher to defrost it.

Several days in advance, buy a 1 cm ($\frac{1}{2}$ inch) cold-rolled or stainless-steel rod about 120 cm (4 feet) longer than the animal's length when its legs are extended. (Avoid galvanized steel; its coating may be toxic.) Ask a blacksmith or welder to make two right-angle bends at one end of the rod to produce a handle in an L-shape, and drill a 3 mm ($\frac{1}{8}$ inch) hole near each end of the rod to secure the wires that will hold the animal's feet (*Step 7*). You will also need a piece of chicken wire large enough to enclose the animal, several metres of 16-gauge steel wire, pliers and hollow concrete blocks to support the spit. Erect the concrete block supports with a broad base for stability and high enough to raise the spitted animal about 75 cm (2$\frac{1}{2}$ feet) above the fire.

Start the fire about 2 hours before you plan to roast the animal. During roasting, keep the fire stoked so that the temperature at spit level will be constant.

Allow 3 hours for the heat to penetrate any animal. An animal weighing up to 6.75 kg (15 lb) may be fully cooked at this stage. Roast a larger animal about 1 hour longer for each additional 6.75 kg. When the estimated time has almost elapsed, test with a meat thermometer (*Step 14*) to ensure well-done pork—and lamb or goat that is cooked to the degree you prefer.

1 Starting the fire. Build two parallel graduated stacks of hollow concrete blocks about 90 cm (3 feet) high and 120 cm (4 feet) apart. Top each stack with a halved block. Midway between the stacks, form a pyramid of kindling round a wad of crumpled newspaper. Ignite the paper and, when the kindling is burning well, begin to add charcoal gradually—using a total of about 13.5 kg (30 lb) of charcoal. When all the charcoal is burning, use a metal rake to spread it into a layer 20 cm (8 inches) deep.

5 Spitting the pig. When you have sewn up the body cavity, knot the string and cut off the excess. Using another piece of string, close the neck cavity with a few stitches. Lay the pig on its side and push the spit—in this case, a length of 1 cm ($\frac{1}{2}$ inch) cold-rolled steel rod—through the tail end into the body cavity. Pushing gently, guide the spit so that it emerges through the mouth of the pig. Wrap the pig's ears with foil to prevent them from burning.

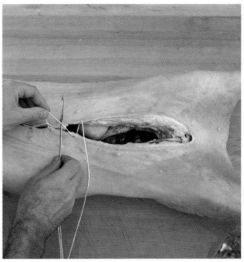

2 **Preparing the marinade.** To flavour the pig, make a marinade—here, a lime, orange and garlic mixture (*recipe, page 161*). Chop the cloves of several garlic heads and place them in a large bowl. Add bay leaves. Squeeze limes and oranges and strain the juice into the bowl. Reserve the peel. Stir in olive oil, coarse salt and black pepper.

3 **Marinating the pig.** Rub the marinade into the body cavity and the skin of the pig, making sure it is thoroughly coated. Alternatively, place the pig in a large tub and pour the marinade over it. Let the pig marinate for up to 2 hours, brushing marinade over its skin occasionally.

4 **Closing the cavity.** Brush the garlic and bay leaves from the pig's skin and place them in the body cavity with the lime and orange peel and a handful of coarse salt. Thread a trussing needle with 90 cm (3 feet) of string. Starting at the chest, make stitches across the body cavity at 5 cm (2 inch) intervals; pass the string through the preceding stitch each time (*above*).

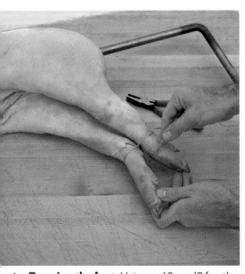

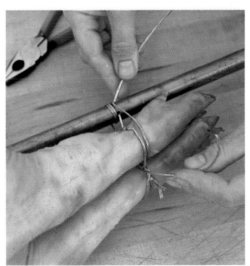

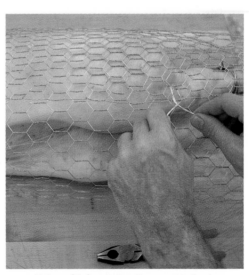

6 **Trussing the feet.** Using a 60 cm (2 foot) length of 16-gauge stainless-steel wire, make a loop round one of the pig's hind feet. Tighten the loop with pliers, then pass the wire round the other hind foot and draw it close to the first. Twist the two ends of the wire together tightly and cut off any excess. Truss the front feet of the pig in the same way.

7 **Binding the feet to the spit.** Wrap the middle section of another 60 cm (2 foot) piece of wire round the spit several times next to the hole drilled in the spit rod. Twist tightly with the pliers, then pass the wire through the hole. Pull the hind feet close to the spit and loop the wire round them several times. Twist the ends of the wire together and cut off the excess. Do the same with the front feet.

8 **Tying chicken wire.** To provide further support for the pig, place it on a piece of chicken wire large enough to wrap round it loosely. Pull the edges of the chicken wire over the pig. Join the overlapping portions with pieces of wire (*above*), twisting their ends together. ▶

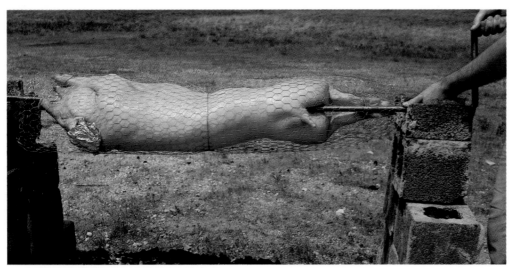

9 **Setting the spit in place.** When the charcoal is covered with white ash—after about 2 hours—rake the embers into two parallel banks almost as long as the spit and about 45 cm (18 inches) apart. Restoke the fire if necessary. With the aid of a helper, lift the spitted pig into position between the banks of coals, resting the ends of the spit in the upturned hollows of the split concrete blocks. To hold the pig steady, brace the handle of the spit with a wooden stake wedged against an extra concrete block placed on the ground.

10 **Basting.** Strain the leftover marinade and set it aside in a convenient place. When fat begins to drip from the pig—after about 20 minutes of roasting—baste it with the marinade. Then rotate the spit to give the pig a quarter turn. Continue to baste and turn the pig every 20 minutes.

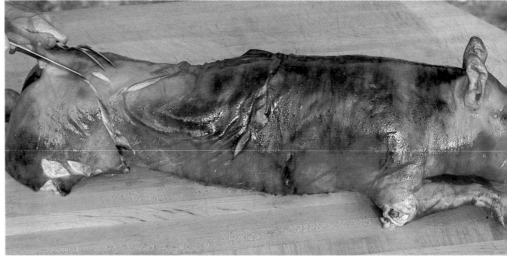

14 **Testing for doneness.** After the pig has roasted on the spit rod for the estimated time—in this instance, 6½ hours—insert a meat thermometer into the thickest part of one hind leg. When the thermometer registers 75°C (170°F), take the spitted pig off the fire with the aid of a helper; wear heatproof gloves to handle the spit.

15 **Removing the legs.** Lay the pig on a large table or board and pull out the spit. To facilitate carving, let the pig rest for 15 to 20 minutes. Then, steadying the pig with a carving fork, use a sharp, heavy knife to cut off a hind leg, slicing from the front of the haunch towards the tail (*above*). To remove the foreleg, cut into the shoulder where it joins the leg. Slice behind the shoulder blade to within a few centimetres of the ear, then cut straight down to sever the leg.

11 **Removing the wire cage.** After about an hour of roasting, the flesh of the pig will be firm on the spit and you can remove the chicken-wire cage. Wearing heatproof gloves to protect your hands, cut the wire ties with pliers (*above*). Then carefully unfold the chicken wire and lift it away.

12 **Rearranging coals.** As the pig roasts, some parts may brown more quickly than others. If this happens, rearrange the coals so that less heat reaches those parts. In this instance, the coals have been raked into banks parallel to the concrete supports.

13 **Wrapping the pig in foil.** For further protection, wrap the browned parts of the pig in heavy-duty aluminium foil— the chest and middle of the pig are covered here. Leave the foil in position until the pig is almost done. During cooking, periodically add charcoal to the fire to maintain a constant temperature at spit level.

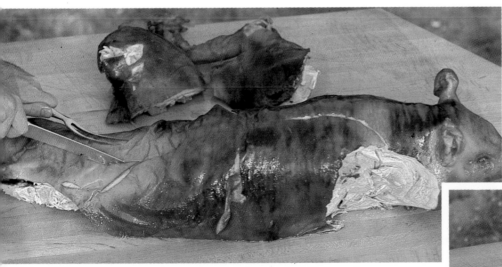

16 **Carving the loin.** Make an incision the length of the spine, pressing the knife down to the bone (*above*). Press the back of the carving fork against the loin and slice down, keeping the knife blade against the ribs, to detach the loin in one piece. Carve the loin crosswise into pieces about 7.5 cm (3 inches) wide. Cut through the knee joint to divide the leg in two (*right*), then carve the thigh into thin slices, holding the knife parallel to the bone. Carve the other side of the pig in the same fashion.□

The Clambake: a Seaside Feast

A traditional American clambake is one of the true extravaganzas of outdoor cooking. Despite its name, a clambake does not involve baking: the food is covered with seaweed and steamed in a pit lined with hot stones. Preparation and cooking may take up to 6 hours, but the quantity of food produced is likely to be enough for a feast.

The ingredients are usually diverse as well as abundant. As well as clams, all manner of other shellfish, fish, vegetables, poultry and meats can be included. The menu shown here consists of clams, lobsters, sea bass, potatoes and sweetcorn—in amounts to serve 12 generously.

For any clambake, finding a suitable site is the first requirement. Landlocked chefs may dig their pit in earth, but a sandy beach is traditional. Be sure to obtain permission from the local authority or landowner before you begin to dig.

To line the pit, you will need hundreds of smooth, dry, regularly sized large stones. The firewood, too, must be dry—and sufficient to maintain a fire over the entire pit for about 2 hours in order to heat the stones. The seaweed—gathered on the beach or obtained from a fishmonger—must be washed and wet. To cover the seaweed and hold in the heat, you will also need a sheet of tarpaulin or heavy-duty canvas cloth.

Preparing the food is comparatively simple. Clams and other bivalves should be scrubbed, then added to the pit to steam in their shells. If you are planning to cook lobsters or crabs, keep them alive until just before you add them to the pit. Kill lobsters by piercing the shell in the centre of the cross-shaped mark behind the head with the tip of a heavy knife; or plunge lobsters and crabs briefly into boiling water (*page 70, Step 4*). Fish, meats and poultry need to be wrapped in foil. Ears of sweetcorn should have the silk removed before being rewrapped in the husks (*page 22*). Potatoes are left in their skins.

The critical stage of a clambake occurs when you add the food. To keep the stones hot, you must work quickly to rake out the embers, lay the seaweed, distribute the food and cover it with more seaweed and, finally, with tarpaulin. After that, you simply wait for about 3 hours as the ingredients gently steam until cooked.

1 Digging and raking the pit. Drive four sticks into a level stretch of sand or earth to mark out a rectangle about 1.5 by 1.75 metres (5 by 8 feet). Dig out the sand or earth to a depth of about 45 cm (18 inches), then rake the bottom of the pit to smooth it (*above*). If you are digging in sand, stand well back to avoid breaking down the edges of the pit; if in earth, bank the earth round the sides of the pit.

2 Lining the pit. Line the bottom and sides of the pit with smooth, dry stones from a nearby pebbly beach or from a garden centre. Alternatively, line the pit with bricks; ordinary bricks will do, though they may crumble slightly when heated.

6 Spreading seaweed. Working as quickly as possible so as to conserve the heat of the stones, spread well-washed, wet seaweed evenly over the bottom of the pit. Continue to spread the seaweed until you have formed an even layer about 15 cm (6 inches) deep.

7 Distributing the food. Lay the prepared food in a single layer on top of the seaweed. To simplify serving, arrange the food in rows according to type. In this case, ears of sweetcorn are followed by potatoes, sea bass fillets wrapped in foil with butter, seasoning and lemon slices, then lobsters and clams.

3 Laying the fire. Remove the sticks used as markers for digging the pit. Place a pile of crumpled newspaper in the centre of the pit; then, starting with small twigs and finishing with larger sticks and branches, build a pyramid of kindling on top of the newspaper (*above*).

4 Lighting the fire. Ignite the newspaper with a match or lighter. When the kindling has begun to burn, gradually add logs to the fire until it fills the entire pit (*above*). Keep the fire stoked for at least an hour, then let it burn down for another hour to ensure that the stones lining the pit are heated thoroughly.

5 Removing the embers. Let the wood burn until only glowing embers remain. With the back of the rake, carefully pull the embers out of the pit without disturbing the stones beneath (*above*). Once all the embers have been raked from the pit, extinguish them with a thick layer of sand, or douse them with water.

8 Covering with seaweed. Still working as quickly as possible to conserve heat, spread a 15 cm (6 inch) layer of wet seaweed evenly over the food (*above*). Make sure all the food is completely covered by the seaweed.

9 Covering the pit. With the aid of helpers, cover the pit with a tarpaulin that extends at least 30 cm (1 foot) beyond each of the sides of the pit. Weight the corners of the cover with stones. Let the food cook undisturbed for about 3 hours. Lift off the tarpaulin. Wearing heatproof gloves, remove enough seaweed to check that each type of food is done.

10 Serving. When cooked, the clams will be open and the lobsters' legs will pull away easily. The unwrapped fish and the potatoes will offer no resistance to a fork. The sweetcorn will steam when the husks are pulled off. Place the food on plates. Butter the potatoes and sweetcorn; serve lemon and melted butter with the lobsters and clams.□

A Medley of Meats Transformed in the Smoker

In a smoker, the aroma of smouldering wood penetrates meat to give it a marvellous flavour. Although charcoal is the primary fuel, most of the smoke is produced by small logs or wood chips that are placed on the coals when these have reached the white-ash stage.

Use only hard wood, which burns evenly and releases a pleasant fragrance. Wood chips are usually obtainable where fuel is sold and fruit farms may supply logs; some of the types available are apple, beech, hickory, oak and cherry. To keep the wood smouldering throughout the cooking process, choose freshly cut logs, or soak chips and dry logs in water for at least half an hour before using them. Do not use soft wood such as pine, which would give meats a resinous taste.

The liquid in the water pan above the fire can also impart aroma as it evaporates if it contains flavourings such as the garlic and chili peppers used here. The water can be replaced by stock, beer, wine, cider or citrus juice. Red wine or beer suits beef; cider goes well with pork or ham; and citrus juice, white wine or stock will enhance fish, chicken or veal.

Because the steam rising from the water pan provides moisture that will tenderize meats, almost any cut—including such firm offal as heart or tongue—can be smoked. The only essential preparation is to trim away fat. You may, however, marinate the meat or coat it with sauce beforehand.

Depending on the time available, the meats can be either cooked or simply flavoured in the smoker. At the prevailing temperature of 100°C (212°F), cuts weighing up to 1.5 kg (3 lb) will need 3 hours in the smoker to cook and develop flavour. For larger cuts of meat allow a total cooking time of 1 hour per 500 g (1 lb).

To speed the process, either pre-cook meats and use the smoker to flavour them, or smoke meats for 2 to 3 hours and finish their cooking in the oven or on a spit or grill. Here, ox tongue, pork spareribs, a 1 kg (2 lb) piece of beef brisket and an 800 g (1¾ lb) piece of beef skirt are parboiled and set on the lower rack for smoking. Stuffed sweet peppers, pork sausages and frankfurters are placed on the upper rack to cook through without charring in the gentler heat at the top of the smoker.

1 **Stuffing sweet peppers.** If you are cooking tongue, soak it in cold water for several hours. Prepare a filling for sweet peppers—here, a pilaff (*recipe, page 165*) flavoured with chopped parsley. Set the stuffing aside to cool. Choose firm sweet red or green peppers. Slice off their tops, leaving the stalks intact. Pull out and discard the seeds and pith from inside the peppers. Parboil the sweet peppers and their tops for 3 to 4 minutes, then drain them. Fill each pepper with stuffing (*above*) and replace the top.

5 **Adding water.** Place aromatics—here, whole dried chili peppers and unpeeled garlic cloves—in the bottom of the water pan. Still protecting your hands with the fireproof gloves, set the pan in position above the fire. Fill the water pan to its brim with boiling water (*above*).

6 **Adding the food.** Place the grill rack on the brackets just above the water pan. Arrange the parboiled, sauced meats in a single layer on the rack (*above*). Leave space between the meats to allow the smoke to circulate freely.

2 **Preparing tongue.** Place the tongue in a pan of fresh water and bring to the boil to draw out impurities; rinse the tongue. Simmer it in fresh water with carrots, onions and seasonings for 1½ hours. Let the tongue cool in the liquid, then drain it. Trim away fat, gristle and bones from its base; loosen the skin with the tip of a knife and peel it off (*above*).

3 **Saucing the meats.** Simmer boned beef brisket and skirt in water with carrots, onions and a bouquet garni for about 45 minutes. Remove the skirt; simmer the brisket for a further 45 minutes. Parboil the rack of spareribs with aromatics for 1 hour. Drain the meats and cut the rack into ribs. Brush the meats and tongue with barbecue sauce (*page 12*).

4 **Preparing the fire.** Build a small mound of charcoal in the charcoal pan of the smoker, then place odourless firelighters among the charcoal. Wearing fireproof gloves, light the fire. When the coals are covered with white ash, use tongs to lay water-soaked wood—here, applewood logs—on top of the coals.

7 **Loading the upper rack.** Set the second grill rack on the upper brackets and arrange sausages, frankfurters and the stuffed sweet peppers on the rack (*above, left*). Place the lid on the smoker and let the meats and peppers smoke undisturbed for about 1¾ hours (*above, right*). Use tongs to transfer the sausages, frankfurters and peppers to a wooden board. Lift out the upper rack. Transfer the tongue, brisket, skirt and spareribs to the board.

8 **Carving the meats.** To slice the tongue, turn it on its side and steady it with a carving fork. Cut the tongue crosswise into thin slices. Carve the beef brisket (*above*) and the skirt across the grain, as thinly as you like.□

Suffusing a Bird with the Flavour of Wood Smoke

Roasted in the gentle, moist heat of a smoker, poultry and game birds emerge juicy and flavourful without requiring any basting at all. During cooking, the smoker must be kept covered to hold in the smoke and maintain an average temperature of 100°C (212°F), so the lid should be removed only if necessary to replenish fuel or water. Even so, the process is a lengthy one. The 4.5 kg (10 lb) turkey used in this demonstration requires 8 hours of smoking, and a 9 kg (20 lb) bird needs 12 hours. A 2.5 kg (5 lb) chicken or duck needs at least 6 hours, and a 1 kg (2 lb) pheasant or guinea fowl about 4 hours.

For faster results, you can smoke the bird for 2 hours or so and then transfer it to an oven preheated to 180°C (350°F or Mark 4) to finish cooking. Smoking will impart a pinkish colour to the meat even when it is fully cooked, so it is important to test for doneness by piercing the bird's thigh with a skewer. The juices will run clear, not pink, when the bird is cooked.

1 Adding flavourings. Start the fire in the smoker (*page 87, Step 4*). Rub the cavity of the bird—here, a 4.5 kg (10 lb) turkey—with oil, season it, and add flavourings such as halved onions, strips of orange peel and sprigs of mint (*above*). Coat the skin with oil—here, olive oil flavoured with sprigs of rosemary.

2 Placing the bird in the smoker. Tuck the tips of the wings behind the bird's back. Leave the legs untrussed so that smoke and steam can circulate freely round them. Wearing fireproof gloves, lower the water pan into the smoker. Fill the pan with hot water. Oil the rack, set it in place and put the turkey on it.

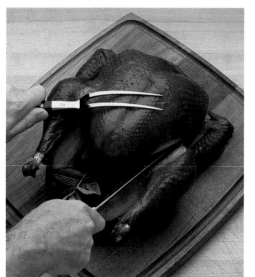

3 Smoking the turkey. Cover the smoker and leave the turkey to cook for about 8 hours, or until the juices run clear when a thigh is pricked with a skewer. Lift the rack and the turkey out of the smoker (*above*). Transfer the turkey to a carving board and let it rest for 10 minutes.

4 Removing a leg. Remove the aromatics from the cavity of the bird and discard them. Steadying the turkey with a carving fork, cut through the skin between the thigh and the breast. Push the thigh down to expose the hip joint. Cut through the joint, severing the leg, and separate the drumstick from the thigh.

5 Slicing the breast. Cut off the wing at the shoulder joint. To carve the breast meat, steady the turkey with the fork and cut down at an angle to the breastbone to produce uniform slices (*above*). Then carve the opposite side of the turkey in the same manner. □

Anthology
of Recipes

The 227 recipes in the Anthology that follows have been selected by the Editors and consultants from the cooking literature of 29 countries. The 124 authors whose work is represented include cooks, restaurateurs and collectors of regional and national recipes, who have recorded the culinary traditions of countries as diverse as Spain, Yugoslavia, Russia and those of the Middle and Far East. The choice of recipes includes simply grilled fish and meat, spicy South-East Asian satays and Indian tandoori dishes, American barbecued seafood and the numerous lamb dishes of Arab cookery. A number of these recipes have never before been published in English. What they all have in common is authenticity and an emphasis on the meticulous preparation of fresh, high-quality ingredients which are suitable for cooking outdoors or indoors at a fireplace.

To preserve the character of the original and to create a true anthology, the authors' texts have been changed as little as possible. Where appropriate, introductory notes in italics have been provided by the Editors and, in some cases, quantities or cooking times have been judiciously added. Some instructions have necessarily been expanded, but in cases where the cooking directions seem somewhat abrupt, the reader need only turn to the appropriate demonstration in the front of the book to find the technique in question explained in words and pictures. In particular, the reader is recommended to refer to pages 8-9 for information on preparing the fire, as detailed instructions for this step have not been included in the recipes. Cooking terms and ingredients that may be unfamiliar are explained in the combined General Index and Glossary at the end of the book.

For ease of use, the recipes in the Anthology have been organized into sections according to their main ingredient. Recipes for standard preparations such as marinades, sauces and stuffings can be found at the end of the Anthology.

Following the main ingredient, recipe ingredients are listed in order of use. Metric and imperial measurements for each ingredient are listed in separate columns. The two sets of figures are not exact equivalents, but are consistent for each recipe. Working from either metric or imperial measurements will produce equally good results, but the two systems should not be mixed for the same recipe. All spoon measures are level. The serving suggestions included in some recipes are, of course, optional.

Vegetables and Fruits

Grilled Artichokes

Alcachofas Asadas

To serve 4

4	large globe artichokes, stalks cut off	4
	salt	
	olive oil	
	vinegar	

Open up the artichokes by separating the leaves gently, taking care not to break them. Sprinkle with salt and pour oil and vinegar over them, ensuring that the dressing runs down between the leaves.

Place the artichokes on a rack and cook them over coals. The heat should be gentle, so that the artichokes cook through without burning. When done, after about 30 minutes, discard the charred outer leaves and serve with grilled chops.

VICTORIA SERRA
TIA VICTORIA'S SPANISH KITCHEN

Grilled Red Chicory

This is an excellent accompaniment to mixed grilled fish.

To serve 4

800 g	red chicory, leaves separated	1¾ lb
¼ litre	oil	8 fl oz
	salt and pepper	

Brush each leaf with oil, then place the leaves over a hot rack and cook for 5 minutes only, turning them frequently. They should still be slightly crisp. Season the leaves with salt and pepper and serve.

GIULIANA BONOMO
LA BUONA CUCINA

Roasted Plantain

Platano Asado

To serve 1

1	ripe plantain	1
	butter	

Cut a slit in the skin of the plantain from end to end. Place the plantain on a rack over charcoal embers and bake for 15 to 20 minutes, turning the plantain several times to be sure it bakes on all sides. A skewer inserted in the slit should meet no resistance when the plantain is done. Take off the skin quickly and serve the plantain garnished with butter.

ST. MARY'S CATHEDRAL LADIES GUILD, CARACAS (EDITORS)
BUEN PROVECHO

Campfire Corn Roast

To serve 4

4	ears young sweetcorn, silk removed, husks twisted closed again	4
	salt	
	butter	

Bury the ears of corn in the hot ashes of the fire. Leave them for 30 minutes, or until the kernels are tender. Remove the husks and add salt and butter to the corn.

Alternatively, husk the corn and fix each ear on to a long sharpened stick or skewer. Hold the corn directly over the heat to roast for about 15 minutes.

FERNE SHELTON (EDITOR)
PIONEER COOKBOOK

Grilled Corn on the Cob

To serve 6

6	ears young sweetcorn, husks and silk removed	6
125 to 175 g	butter, softened	4 to 6 oz
	salt	
60 g	Cheddar cheese, grated	2 oz

Spread the sweetcorn with the butter, season them with salt to taste and sprinkle them with the grated cheese. Wrap each ear of corn in a double thickness of aluminium foil. Grill the packets 15 to 20 cm (6 to 8 inches) from the coals, turning every 3 to 4 minutes, until the corn is roasted and the cheese has melted—15 to 20 minutes.

NANCY FAIR MCINTYRE
IT'S A PICNIC!

Potatoes Baked in the Ashes

Ziemniaki Pieczone w Popiele

To serve 4

4	large potatoes, scrubbed but unpeeled	4
	salt	
	butter	

When the fire dies down, put the potatoes into the edge of the fire. Cover them first with hot ashes, then with embers. Bake for about 25 to 35 minutes, or until they are soft when pierced with a skewer. Remove the potatoes with wooden skewers and blow off the coating of ash. Serve with salt and butter.

MARIA LEMNIS AND HENRYK VITRY
KSIAZKA KUCHARSKA

Potatoes with Bacon

Prażonka

This classic peasant dish can be varied by adding sliced ham or sausage, or fresh wild mushrooms. Pickled gherkins or fresh cucumbers are a good accompaniment.

To serve 4 to 6

1 kg	potatoes, thickly sliced	2 to 2½ lb
500 g	thin rashers smoked bacon	1 lb
3 or 4	large onions, sliced	3 or 4
	salt and pepper	
1	large cabbage leaf	1

Line the bottom of a heavy, enamelled cast-iron casserole with rashers of bacon. Put in a thick layer of potatoes, then a layer of onion. Sprinkle with salt, and with pepper if you wish. Repeat the layers in the same sequence until the casserole is filled to within about 7.5 cm (3 inches) of the top. The top layer should be potatoes. Cover with the cabbage leaf, then with a sheet of greaseproof paper greased with lard or butter and somewhat larger than the top of the casserole.

Cut a circle of turf and fit it on to the casserole on top of the paper, making sure that it seals the casserole completely.

Bury the casserole in the glowing embers of a fire, avoiding direct contact with flames. Leave, adding bits of firewood as necessary, for 40 minutes to 1 hour. The casserole is done when the aroma of the contents is perceptible. The top layer of potatoes should be very soft.

MARIA LEMNIS AND HENRYK VITRY
KSIAZKA KUCHARSKA

Grilled Potatoes with Caraway

Grillkartoffeln

To serve 1

1 or 2	medium-sized potatoes, scrubbed but unpeeled	1 or 2
	salt	
	caraway seeds	
	butter, salt, soured cream or herb butter (*page 162*)	

Prick the potatoes several times with a knife tip. Cut extra strong aluminium foil into pieces large enough to enclose one potato, and spread each piece of foil thinly with oil or butter. Place a potato on each piece of foil, sprinkle on salt and caraway seeds, then wrap the foil tightly round the potato and seal the foil carefully. Place the potatoes close together on the red-hot charcoal and leave them to cook for 30 to 40 minutes. Serve them with a little butter or some salt, or with soured cream or herb butter.

FRISCH VOM GRILL

Cheese Potatoes in a Parcel

Käsekartoffeln im Paket

Serve with small grilled sausages or cutlets, hard-boiled eggs and a side salad.

To serve 4

1 kg	potatoes, sliced	2 to 2½ lb
200 g	cheese, cubed	7 oz
	salt and pepper	
	paprika	
One 200 g	piece streaky bacon, cubed	One 7 oz
2	onions, very thinly sliced into rings	2
60 g	butter	2 oz

Brush four large pieces of double-thickness aluminium foil with oil. Distribute the potato slices evenly among the pieces of foil and sprinkle them with a pinch each of salt, pepper and paprika. Scatter the bacon, onion rings and cheese evenly over the potatoes and put flecks of butter on top. Fold the foil into parcels and close the edges very carefully.

Cook the cheese potatoes over a charcoal grill for 50 minutes. Turn the parcels repeatedly during cooking, but take care that the foil does not open anywhere.

ANNETTE WOLTER
DAS PRAKTISCHE GRILLBUCH

Baked Onion and Potato Salad from Huesca

Ensalada de Cebollas y Patatas

To serve 4

4	onions, unpeeled	4
4	potatoes, scrubbed but unpeeled	4
8 cl	oil	3 fl oz
2 tbsp	white wine vinegar	2 tbsp
	salt	

Place the onions and potatoes in the embers of a fire to bake. When they are tender, after about 45 minutes, remove the skins and eat them while they are still warm, dressed with oil and vinegar, and seasoned with salt.

COCINA REGIONAL ESPAÑOLA

Barbecued Herbed Onions

Substitute dried herbs if fresh ones are not available, but use only half the amount—dried herbs are more potent.

To serve 4

4	large onions, slashed into quarters but not cut completely apart	4
60 g	butter, softened	2 oz
1 tbsp	finely chopped parsley	1 tbsp
1 tbsp	finely chopped chives	1 tbsp
1 tbsp	finely chopped tarragon leaves	1 tbsp

Mix the butter and herbs together well. Stuff equal portions of the herb mixture into each onion. Wrap the onions in pieces of aluminium foil and roast them over hot coals for 20 to 30 minutes, or until tender.

LOIS M. BURROWS AND LAURA G. MYERS
TOO MANY TOMATOES, SQUASH, BEANS AND OTHER GOOD THINGS

Small Bean and Bacon Rolls

Bohnen-Speck-Röllchen

To serve 4

500 g	green beans	1 lb
250 g	rashers streaky bacon, rind removed	8 oz
½ tsp	salt	½ tsp

In a large saucepan, bring plenty of salted water to the boil. Put a handful of beans into a sieve or basket and blanch them for 5 minutes from the time the water returns to the boil. After blanching, dry the beans with kitchen paper. Repeat with the remaining beans.

Lay flat two rashers of bacon, one overlapping the other slightly. Put a small bundle of beans crosswise on top and roll the beans up in the bacon. Wrap each small bacon roll in aluminium foil, folding the edges together well.

Cook the rolls at the edge of the charcoal fire, placing the parcels either directly on the coals, or on a very hot rack. Leave for about 20 minutes, or until the bacon is well cooked, turning the parcels repeatedly with tongs.

ANNETTE WOLTER
DAS PRAKTISCHE GRILLBUCH

Courgette Parcels

To serve 4

4	medium-sized courgettes	4
½ tsp	oregano	½ tsp
4	tomatoes, skinned, seeded and chopped	4
	salt and freshly ground black pepper	
90 g	butter, divided into 4 equal pieces	3 oz

Parboil the courgettes for about 4 minutes in salted water to which the oregano has been added. Drain the courgettes and slice each one into quarters. Place each quartered courgette on a sheet of heavy-duty aluminium foil. Add a chopped tomato, salt and pepper and a pat of butter. Wrap the foil securely round the food and cook the parcels over medium-hot coals for about 15 minutes, turning once.

JAMES F. MARKS
BARBECUES

Courgette and Tomato Kebabs

To serve 2

2	medium-sized courgettes, parboiled for 5 minutes in boiling salted water, each cut into 4 pieces	2
8	cherry tomatoes	8
	melted butter	
30 g	Parmesan cheese, grated	1 oz
½ tsp	oregano	½ tsp
	salt and pepper	

Thread the pieces of courgette alternately with the tomatoes on two small skewers. Baste with melted butter and cook 20 cm (8 inches) above hot coals for about 10 minutes. Turn and baste the vegetables frequently. Sprinkle them with the grated cheese, oregano and salt and pepper before serving.

ED CALLAHAN
CHARCOAL COOKBOOK

Barbecued Aubergine

Courgettes can be prepared in the same way, but they are not peeled. Both courgettes and aubergines go well with barbecued meat, fowl or fish.

To serve 4

2	aubergines, peeled and sliced into 1 cm (½ inch) pieces	2
3 tbsp	oil	3 tbsp
½	garlic clove, finely chopped	½
½ tsp	paprika	½ tsp
4	peppercorns, crushed	4
¼ tsp	finely chopped oregano	¼ tsp
	salt	

Mix together the oil, garlic, paprika, peppercorns and oregano, and add salt to taste. Place the aubergine slices in this marinade for about 10 minutes. Grill the aubergine slices over a slow charcoal fire for about 7 minutes on each side, or until they are well browned.

THE BROWN DERBY COOKBOOK

Grilled Aubergine

To serve 6

1	large aubergine, cut lengthwise into 6 slices	1
1	garlic clove	1
2 tsp	salt	2 tsp
	dried oregano	
4 tbsp	olive oil	4 tbsp
1 tbsp	red wine vinegar (optional)	1 tbsp

Crush the garlic in a mortar with the salt. Add a pinch of oregano, the olive oil and the red wine vinegar, if using. Paint the slices of aubergine with this mixture and grill them, slowly, over embers until the cut surfaces are brown and tender, about 30 minutes.

HELEN EVANS BROWN
HELEN BROWN'S WEST COAST COOK BOOK

Stuffed Aubergines

Gefüllte Auberginen

To serve 4

4	small aubergines, ends cut off, halved lengthwise	4
	salt	
1	lemon, juice strained	1
	oil or melted butter	
Mushroom rice stuffing		
350 g	cooked rice	12 oz
175 g	mushrooms, chopped	6 oz
1	large onion, finely chopped	1
4 tbsp	finely chopped parsley	4 tbsp
2 tbsp	single cream	2 tbsp
1	egg	1
2 tbsp	melted butter	2 tbsp
	salt and pepper	

Salt the aubergines lightly, sprinkle with lemon juice, and leave for 30 minutes. Pour off any liquid that has formed, and scrape out and chop the pulp.

Combine all the stuffing ingredients, seasoning to taste. Mix with the aubergine pulp. Stuff the aubergines with this mixture, brush with oil or melted butter, and grill for about 10 minutes or until browned and cooked through.

THEODOR BOTTIGER
DAS GRILL-BUCH

Aubergine and Pepper Salad

Escalivada Gironina

	To serve 4	
2	aubergines	2
2	sweet red or green peppers	2
4 tbsp	oil	4 tbsp
	salt	
1	garlic clove, chopped	1
3 tbsp	chopped parsley	3 tbsp

Cook the aubergines and peppers over a wood fire for 15 minutes, turning often, until the skins are charred and the flesh is soft. When they are well cooked, skin them, split them lengthwise and remove the seeds from the sweet peppers. Cut them into long strips and arrange them on a serving dish. Season them with the oil and with salt, and sprinkle over the garlic and parsley.

M. DEL CARME NICOLAU
CUINA CATALANA

Poor Man's Caviare

Zelen Hayver

	To serve 6 to 8	
550 g	aubergines	1 lb 2 oz
150 g	sweet green peppers	5 oz
4 or 5	garlic cloves	4 or 5
	salt and pepper	
1¼ tbsp	wine vinegar	1¼ tbsp
1 tbsp	finely chopped parsley	1 tbsp
4 tbsp	vegetable oil	4 tbsp
	Garnish	
50 g	tomatoes, skinned, seeded and sliced into rounds	2 oz
	black olives	
	parsley sprigs	

Roast the aubergines and the peppers directly over glowing charcoal. Turn them over from time to time until they are soft and their skins have charred and blistered—about 20 minutes. Cover the sweet peppers with a cloth and keep them on one side until cool. Peel and finely chop the aubergines while still hot, then peel, seed and finely chop the cooled peppers.

Pound the garlic with a little salt in a mortar. Add the chopped aubergines and peppers and continue pounding until the vegetables are reduced to a pulp. Using a wooden spoon, stir in the vinegar, chopped parsley and oil. Continue stirring until the mixture has absorbed the oil and is smooth. Adjust the seasoning to taste. Turn the purée into a serving dish and decorate it with the tomatoes, black olives and parsley sprigs.

M. TSOLOVA, V. STOILOVA AND SN. EKIMOVA
IZPOLZOUVANE NA ZELENCHOUTSITE I PLODOVETE V DOMAKINSTVOTO

Marinated Mushrooms

	To serve 6 to 8	
1 kg	small mushrooms	2 lb
	Marinade	
12.5 cl	white wine vinegar	4 fl oz
15 cl	olive oil	¼ pint
1 tbsp	finely chopped parsley	1 tbsp
½ tsp	sugar	½ tsp
1 tbsp	lemon juice	1 tbsp
½ tsp	pepper	½ tsp
½ tsp	salt	½ tsp
1	garlic clove, finely chopped	1

In a large jar, combine all the marinade ingredients. Shake vigorously. Add the mushrooms and refrigerate for 24 hours. Drain off the marinade, thread the mushrooms on skewers and grill them, turning frequently, until they are golden-brown—about 5 minutes.

ED CALLAHAN
CHARCOAL COOKBOOK

Mushroom Kebabs Tyrolean-Style

Pilzspiesschen Tiroler Art

If possible, use a mixture of mushrooms such as ceps, morels and chanterelles, as well as large field mushrooms, for these kebabs. Plum tomatoes are occasionally available during the summer, but small, sweet round tomatoes may be substituted. All the pieces of mushroom, tomato, onion, bacon and sweet pepper should be of similar size.

To serve 4

750 g	mushrooms, cut into thick slices	1½ lb
40 g	butter	1½ oz
2	plum tomatoes, seeded and cut into pieces	2
½ tsp	ground dried basil	½ tsp
2	onions, cut into large pieces	2
125 g	piece smoked streaky bacon, cubed	4 oz
1	sweet red pepper, seeded and cut into squares	1
	salt and freshly ground black pepper	
2 tbsp	oil	2 tbsp
15 g	parsley, finely chopped	½ oz

Heat the butter and braise the mushroom slices in it for 5 to 8 minutes, or until the mushroom liquid has evaporated. Sprinkle both sides of each tomato piece with the basil.

Take the mushrooms out of the butter and thread them, with the tomato, onion, bacon and sweet red pepper, on to four skewers. Season with salt and pepper and baste with oil. Grill over a very low heat for about 10 minutes. Serve, sprinkled with the chopped parsley.

MECHTHILD PIEPENBROCK
GRILL VERGNÜGEN

Ceps with Herb Butter

To serve 4

8	medium-sized ceps, stems removed, underside of caps slashed	8
80 g	butter	3 oz
1 tbsp	chopped parsley	1 tbsp
1 tsp	lemon juice	1 tsp
	salt and white pepper	
	oil	

First, prepare the herb butter. Knead the butter with the parsley and lemon juice, and season with salt and pepper. Roll it into eight balls, wrap them in foil, and refrigerate.

Pour a little oil over each mushroom, season with salt and pepper, and place on a preheated grill rack. Cook over medium-hot coals for 10 minutes, or until cooked through.

Arrange the mushrooms on a heated serving dish, place a ball of herb butter in each one, and serve immediately.

GIULIANA BONOMO
LA BUONA COCINA

Grilled Vegetables

Verdure alla Griglia

To serve 8

4	large potatoes, unpeeled	4
2	aubergines	2
4	sweet green or red peppers	4
4	large ripe tomatoes, halved	4
500 g	large ceps, stems removed	1 lb
	salt	
	olive oil	
	lemon juice	

Salt the potatoes lightly. Steam them over boiling water in a tightly covered pan until they are just tender, about 30 minutes. Cool slightly, peel, cut into thick slices and brush with oil. Slice the aubergines thickly, salt them and leave them to drain for 30 minutes before cooking. Rinse them under cold water and pat them dry with kitchen paper.

Brush the peppers and the aubergine slices with oil and grill them over hot charcoal for about 20 minutes, turning often. Oil the tomatoes and place them, cut side up, on the rack 5 minutes after the peppers. Sprinkle them with salt. Rub the mushrooms with lemon juice, brush them with oil and grill them for about 10 minutes, turning them half way through the cooking. Salt them after cooking. Grill the potato slices on one side only, until they are toasted.

When the peppers are cooked, peel and halve them and remove the seeds. Sprinkle them with salt. Season the aubergines with salt, oil and lemon juice.

ANNA BASLINI ROSSELLI
100 RICETTE PER LA COLAZIONE SULL'ERBA

Pumpkin Kebabs

Kürbis-Kebab

To serve 4

250 g	pumpkin flesh, cut into 4 cm (1½ inch) cubes	8 oz
4	small tomatoes, halved	4
250 g	waxy potatoes, parboiled, cut into 4 cm (1½ inch) cubes	8 oz
	oil	

Thread the pumpkin cubes on to skewers, alternating them with tomato halves and cubes of half-cooked potato. Brush with oil and cook on the grill for 15 minutes, or until cooked thoroughly and browned.

THEODOR BOTTIGER
DAS GRILL-BUCH

Stuffed Pepper Kebabs

Saté Pedis

Lemon grass (sereh) and the large red chili peppers called lomboks *may be found in Oriental food shops. The minced meat may be replaced by minced peeled shrimps.*

To serve 4

16	large, unblemished red *lomboks*, cut open lengthwise down one side, and seeded	16
1 tbsp	powdered lemon grass	1 tbsp
6	slices fresh ginger root	6
4 tsp	ground coriander	4 tsp
2 tsp	ground cumin	2 tsp
8	small red onions, finely chopped	8
6	garlic cloves, crushed	6
	salt and pepper	
500 g	minced beef or veal	1 lb
2 tbsp	finely chopped leek	2 tbsp
1½ tbsp	finely chopped parsley	1½ tbsp
3 or 4	eggs, yolks separated from whites	3 or 4
	lemon juice	
2 tbsp	salad oil	2 tbsp

Pound the lemon grass, ginger, coriander, cumin, onions, garlic, and a little salt and pepper together in a mortar to make a smooth paste. Mix this into the meat with the leek, parsley, egg yolks and a little lemon juice. Fill the *lomboks* with the mixture and press them closed. Thread the stuffed *lomboks* lengthwise on skewers. Beat together the egg whites and oil and brush the *lomboks* with this mixture. Grill gently, turning frequently until the meat filling is browned and cooked through, about 10 minutes.

HUGH JANS
VRIJ NEDERLAND

Bananas in Their Skins

Bananes en Robe

To serve 8

8	bananas, barely ripe	8
8 tsp	sugar	8 tsp
10 cl	kirsch	3½ fl oz

With a sharp knife, cut the skin of the bananas lengthwise and carefully remove half of the skin, making sure not to damage the flesh.

Place the bananas, skin side down, on a rack over coals that are not too hot. Cook for about 5 minutes. When the flesh is soft, sprinkle with sugar and cook for another 5 minutes, or until the skin has blackened.

Remove the bananas from the grill; heat the kirsch, pour it over the bananas and set it alight. Serve immediately.

MYRETTE TIANO
LES MEILLEURES RECETTES: PIQUES-NIQUES, BARBECUES

Geraldine's Apple Slices

Apfelscheiben Geraldine

To serve 4

2	large apples, peeled, cored and cut into slices about 2 cm (¾ inch) thick	2
1	lemon, juice strained	1
45 g	butter, melted	1½ oz
About 2 tbsp	sugar	About 2 tbsp
1 tbsp	ground cinnamon	1 tbsp

Sprinkle the apple slices with lemon juice and let any excess juice drain off. Spread a large piece of aluminium foil with some of the melted butter and place the apple slices on it in a single layer. Brush them with some more of the butter. Place the foil over a charcoal grill and cook the apples for 3 to 4 minutes. Meanwhile, mix together the sugar and the ground cinnamon. Lightly sprinkle a little of the mixture over the apple slices. Turn the slices on the foil and cook them for another 3 to 4 minutes, or until they are tender, brushing them with the remaining butter and sprinkling them lightly with a little more cinnamon sugar.

Before serving, dip the cooked apple slices into any remaining cinnamon sugar, or serve the sugar separately.

ANNETTE WOLTER
DAS PRAKTISCHE GRILLBUCH

Glazed Pineapple Rings

Serve these pineapple rings with barbecued sausages.

To serve 6 to 8

6 to 8	rings pineapple	6 to 8
12.5 cl	honey, melted	4 fl oz
1 tbsp	French mustard	1 tbsp

Mix the honey and mustard together. Cook the pineapple over medium-hot coals for 5 to 7 minutes or until lightly browned, basting frequently with the honey and mustard glaze during the cooking, and turning the rings once.

ELIZABETH SEWELL
BARBECUE COOKBOOK

Fruit Kebabs

Brochettes de Fruits

The fruits can be macerated for up to 30 minutes in the rum.
The technique of cooking fruit kebabs is shown on page 24.

To serve 6

3	bananas, quartered	3
2	oranges, cut into thick wedges	2
1	lemon, cut into thick wedges	1
1	small pineapple, thickly sliced and cut into large pieces	1
2 tbsp	rum	2 tbsp
150 g	castor sugar	5 oz
1	loaf white sandwich bread, cut into 2 cm (¾ inch) slices, crusts removed	1
100 g	butter, melted	3½ oz

Macerate the fruits for a few minutes in the rum and 2 tablespoons of the castor sugar.

Cut each slice of bread into eight rectangles. Brush the pieces of bread with the melted butter and roll them in sugar.

Thread all the ingredients on to skewers, alternating bread and fruits. Cook over coals for about 10 minutes or until the surface is caramelized, sprinkling with sugar during the cooking without allowing the sugar to fall on the coals. Serve the fruit kebabs immediately.

MYRETTE TIANO
LES MEILLEURES RECETTES: PIQUES-NIQUES, BARBECUES

Mixed Fruit Skewers

The author suggests using a selection of the following fruits: quartered peaches, halved apricots, unripe bananas cut into 2.5 cm (1 inch) slices, chunks of pineapple, orange segments, wedges of apple and pear sprinkled with lemon juice so that they do not darken, stoned plums or cherries.

A very attractive alternative to the caramel is to brush the skewers frequently with a mixture of 125 g (4 oz) of melted butter, 1 tablespoon of sugar and 1 teaspoon of cinnamon or powdered ginger or the seeds from a cardamom pod. Or squeeze lemon or orange juice into the melted butter. Serve the skewers with some basting sauce poured over them.

To serve 4

750 g	mixed fresh fruits	1½ lb
60 g	sugar	2 oz

Thread the fruits on to skewers. Cook them over a medium-hot fire, turning often, for 5 to 10 minutes. Then sprinkle them with the sugar and let it caramelize over the fire.

CLAUDIA RODEN
PICNIC

Meats

Barbecued Steak

Churrasco

In this great speciality of Argentina, Uruguay and parts of southern Brazil, the steaks are typically cooked on special leaning grids over a wood fire that has burnt down to vivid coals; charcoal can be used.

To serve 6

One 3 kg	beef sirloin steak or two 1.75 to 2 kg (3½ to 4 lb) sirloin steaks, cut 7.5 cm (3 inches) thick, excess fat trimmed off	One 7 lb

Barbecue sauce

350 g	spring onions, chopped, or 275 g (9 oz) onions, finely chopped	12 oz
275 g	butter	9 oz
½ tsp	crumbled dried rosemary or oregano, or a mixture of both	½ tsp
1½ tsp	salt	1½ tsp
1 tbsp	freshly ground black pepper	1 tbsp
¼ litre	dry white wine	8 fl oz
12.5 cl	white wine vinegar or cider vinegar	4 fl oz

To make the sauce, sauté the spring onions or onions in 250 g (8 oz) of the butter, stirring often. Add the rosemary and/or the oregano, salt, pepper, wine and vinegar. Bring to the boil, lower the heat and simmer for 5 minutes, stirring constantly. Remove the sauce from the heat, correct the seasoning and add the remaining butter.

Grill the steak or steaks over hot charcoal until done to taste—for the large steak about 30 minutes on each side for rare, 40 minutes for medium and 60 minutes for well done. Halve the times for the smaller steaks. To serve, carve the steak and pour the sauce over the slices.

ALEX D. HAWKES
THE FLAVORS OF THE CARIBBEAN AND LATIN AMERICA

Florentine Steak

Fiorentina

A Florentine steak is a rib steak with the fillet attached, cut from young beef or even veal.

	To serve 6	
2 or 3	large rib steaks	2 or 3
8 cl	olive oil	3 fl oz
	salt and freshly ground black pepper	

Several minutes before cooking the steaks, moisten them liberally with the olive oil and spread with plenty of pepper. Grill over hot coals for 8 to 10 minutes, making sure that the outside does not darken too much and that the meat remains pink inside. Salt sparingly before serving.

VINCENZO BUONASSISI
CUCINA ALL'ARIA APERTA

Entrecote Gipsy-Style

Entrecôte auf Zigeunerart

	To serve 4	
Four 200 to 250 g	entrecote steaks	Four 7 to 8 oz
2 tbsp	red wine vinegar	2 tbsp
2 tbsp	hot mustard	2 tbsp
1	onion, chopped	1
4	garlic cloves, crushed	4
1	small sweet red pepper, finely chopped	1
½ tsp	dried thyme	½ tsp
	salt and pepper	
125 g	lemon butter (page 162)	4 oz

Remove most of the outer fat from the steaks. With a sharp knife, make slits in the remaining border of fat at about 3 cm (1¼ inch) intervals, cutting right through to the meat. Mix together the vinegar, mustard, onion, garlic, sweet red pepper, and thyme. Spread the steaks thickly with this mixture, wrap them in foil and leave them to marinate for several hours. Then scrape off the marinade and reserve it. Pat the steaks dry and cook them on a hot grill for 3 to 5 minutes on each side, or until browned on the outside but still pink in the middle. Remove the steaks from the grill and season them. Heat the reserved marinade and spread it on the steaks, place a piece of lemon butter on each one and serve.

ULRIKE HORNBERG
SCHLEMMEREIEN VOM GRILL

Beef Marinated Malay-Style

Panggang Perchik

	To serve 4	
750 g	sirloin steak, cut into thin 10 cm (4 inch) long pieces	1½ lb
4	fresh chili peppers	4
2	dried chili peppers	2
2	small onions	2
1	fresh ginger root	1
15 g	tamarind	½ oz
1 tbsp	soft brown sugar	1 tbsp
	powdered saffron	
35 cl	coconut milk (page 167)	12 fl oz
	salt	

Crush the fresh and dried chili peppers, the onions, ginger root and tamarind to a paste. Add the sugar, a pinch of saffron and the coconut milk.

Season the pieces of steak with salt. In an earthenware dish, marinate the meat in the spice and coconut mixture. Leave for at least 2 hours, turning the meat frequently.

Grill the steak pieces over hot coals, brushing them frequently with the marinade, for 3 to 4 minutes on each side. When the steaks are cooked, heat the remaining marinade and pour it over the meat.

MARIA KOZSLIK DONOVAN
THE FAR EASTERN EPICURE

Peter Hyun's Barbecued Korean Beef

Bul-Kogi

To serve 4

1 kg	beef (sirloin, rib steak or skirt)	2 lb
3	spring onions, finely chopped	3
4	garlic cloves, crushed	4
5 tbsp	soy sauce	5 tbsp
2 tbsp	sesame seed oil	2 tbsp
1 tbsp	sesame seeds	1 tbsp
60 g	sugar	2 oz
2 tbsp	sherry	2 tbsp
$\frac{1}{8}$ tsp	black pepper	$\frac{1}{8}$ tsp

Slice the beef very thinly across the grain, diagonally from top to bottom. Score each piece lightly with a cross. Combine the remaining ingredients in a bowl and mix this marinade well. Add the meat to the marinade, turning it so that it is well coated on all sides. If possible, it is best to marinate the meat for at least 2 hours. Grill the meat over hot charcoal for 10 minutes, turning once.

NIKA HAZELTON
THE PICNIC BOOK

The Qodban of Tangier

Fillet of beef may be used for these kebabs, but less expensive cuts are often more flavoursome.

To serve 6 to 8

1 kg	boneless beef, lamb or liver, cut into 4 cm (1$\frac{1}{2}$ inch) cubes	2 to 2$\frac{1}{2}$ lb
About 125 g	beef or lamb fat, cut into small squares	About 4 oz
1	large onion, finely chopped	1
2 tbsp	finely chopped parsley	2 tbsp
2 tsp each	salt and freshly ground pepper	2 tsp each
2 tsp	crushed cumin seeds	2 tsp

Mix all the ingredients together with your hands in order to incorporate the flavourings. Marinate at room temperature for 2 hours. Thread the meat on to skewers, putting a small piece of fat between each piece of meat. Grill the skewers over hot coals, turning them to brown the meat evenly, for about 10 minutes, or until the meat is brown on the outside but still pink in the centre.

MAGGIE WALDRON
FIRE AND SMOKE

Coated Skewered Beef

Tsitsinga

Ablemanu, the roasted cornmeal used in this recipe, can be bought from shops that sell West African food. If it is not available, cut the kernels from fresh sweetcorn and roast them in a preheated 180° C (350° F or Mark 4) oven, stirring them frequently, until they are dry to the touch—about 15 minutes. Grind the roasted kernels in a blender or processor until they are the consistency of cornmeal. Alternatively, toast cornmeal in a preheated 150° C (300° F or Mark 2) oven for 20 minutes.

To serve 4 to 6

500 g	beef rump steak, cut into 2.5 cm (1 inch) cubes	1 lb
$\frac{1}{2}$ litre	vegetable oil	16 fl oz
2 tbsp	vinegar	2 tbsp
	salt	
2	tomatoes, skinned	2
$\frac{1}{2}$	onion	$\frac{1}{2}$
1 tbsp	chopped fresh ginger root	1 tbsp
3	fresh chili peppers or $\frac{1}{2}$ to 1 tbsp chili powder, or $\frac{1}{2}$ to 1 tsp cayenne pepper	3
60 g	roasted cornmeal	2 oz

Combine $\frac{1}{4}$ litre (8 fl oz) of the oil with the vinegar, add salt to taste and leave the meat in this mixture to marinate for at least 1 hour. Thread the meat on skewers and grill it over charcoal until it is half done, about 5 minutes. Remove the meat from the skewers.

Mince or blend the tomatoes, onion, ginger and chili peppers. (If you are using chili powder or cayenne pepper, add it after mincing the vegetables and ginger.) Coat the meat well with the vegetable mixture, then thread it on skewers again and roll it in the roasted cornmeal. Dab the coated meat generously with the remaining oil and return it to the grill until done, about 5 minutes more.

HARVA HACHTEN
KITCHEN SAFARI

Five-Flavoured Kebabs

Spiedini dei Cinque Sapori

To serve 4

400 g	fillet of beef	14 oz
200 g	streaky bacon, in one piece	7 oz
	salt and pepper	
4	tomatoes, halved, or 8 very small tomatoes	4
2	onions, quartered	2
8	stuffed green olives	8
	olive oil	

Cut the beef into eight cubes and the bacon into eight small blocks. Sprinkle the cut sides of the tomatoes with salt and leave them to drain, cut sides down.

Thread the ingredients on to four skewers in the following order: tomato, bacon, onion, beef, olive, bacon, onion, beef, olive, tomato. Brush the kebabs with oil and cook for about 8 minutes over a hot grill, turning them half way through the cooking time. Season with salt and pepper and serve at once.

ANNA BASLINI ROSSELLI
100 RICETTE PER LA COLAZIONE SULL'ERBA

Kebabs from Anguilla

To serve 4

1 kg	top sirloin of beef, cut into twelve 3.5 cm (1½ inch) cubes	2 lb
6 tbsp	pineapple juice	6 tbsp
3 tbsp	distilled white vinegar	3 tbsp
2 tbsp	molasses or black treacle	2 tbsp
2 tsp	salt	2 tsp
	freshly ground pepper	
12	small white onions, parboiled for 5 minutes and skinned	12
12	small tomatoes	12
2	medium-sized sweet green peppers, seeded and cut into 3.5 cm (1½ inch) squares	2
½	pineapple, cut into twelve 2.5 cm (1 inch) cubes	½

Combine the pineapple juice, vinegar, molasses or treacle, salt and several grinds of pepper. Add the cubes of beef and marinate them at room temperature for 1 hour. Drain the meat and reserve the marinade to use as a basting sauce.

Thread the meat, onions, tomatoes, peppers and pineapple

in sequence on to four 30 to 35 cm (12 to 14 inch) skewers. Brush with the marinade. Cook the kebabs over a preheated charcoal grill, about 10 cm (4 inches) from the heat, turning every 3 minutes, for about 10 minutes, or until the beef is cooked to the required degree. Baste with marinade each time the kebabs are turned. Serve with plain boiled white rice and pour any remaining marinade over the kebabs.

ELISABETH LAMBERT ORTIZ
CARIBBEAN COOKING

Spicy Barbecued Meat with Peanut Satay Sauce

Saté Bumbú

This recipe, from the former Netherlands Antilles, shows the influence of the cuisine of another former Dutch colony, Indonesia. For a more strongly flavoured peanut sauce, substitute 125 g (4 oz) of raw peanuts for the peanut butter; brown the peanuts in a very little oil over a medium heat, then grind them roughly in a mortar.

To serve 6

650 g	rump steak, cut into 2.5 cm (1 inch) cubes	1½ lb
4	small white onions	4
2	garlic cloves	2
¼ tsp	cayenne pepper or Tabasco sauce	¼ tsp
1 tbsp	dark brown sugar	1 tbsp
1 tsp	lime juice	1 tsp
1½ tsp	curry powder	1½ tsp
2	cloves	2
½ tsp	grated fresh ginger root	½ tsp
3 tbsp	warm water	3 tbsp
3 tbsp	soy sauce	3 tbsp
	Peanut sauce	
2 tbsp	olive oil	2 tbsp
2 tbsp	grated onion	2 tbsp
1 tbsp	dark brown sugar	1 tbsp
About 1 tsp	lime juice	About 1 tsp
⅛ tsp	salt	⅛ tsp
60 g	peanut butter	2 oz
¼ litre	coconut milk (*page 167*)	8 fl oz

Grind together the onions and garlic, using the fine blade of a food mill or processor. Place the mixture in a bowl with the cayenne pepper or Tabasco sauce, the brown sugar, lime juice, curry powder, cloves and ginger, then blend in the water and the soy sauce. Add the meat cubes, toss, and marinate in the refrigerator for 6 hours.

To make the peanut sauce, lightly heat the olive oil and fry the onion for 5 minutes without allowing it to brown. Add the brown sugar, lime juice, salt and peanut butter, blending well. Add the coconut milk gradually, stirring all the time, and cook until the sauce is thick and smooth.

Reserving the marinade, thread the meat on to skewers and grill them 7.5 cm (3 inches) from coals for 15 to 20 minutes. Brush the meat with the reserved marinade and turn the skewers often. Serve them with the peanut sauce.

ALEX D. HAWKES
THE FLAVORS OF THE CARIBBEAN AND LATIN AMERICA

Skewered Spiced Meat Grill

Satay

If red onions are unavailable, substitute one large Spanish onion. Spanish onions are moister than red onions, so, before grinding, squeeze the quartered onion in your hands to press out as much excess moisture as possible; otherwise the spice paste will be too wet to fry properly.

Tamarind is a ripened fibrous pod which is sold as tamarind pulp in Oriental food shops. Tamarind is generally used in cooking for its acidic effect; lemon juice or vinegar can be substituted for the tamarind water.

To serve 4

175 g	lean beef or mutton, cut along the grain into 2.5 by 5 cm (1 by 2 inch) strips	6 oz
1 tbsp	coriander seeds	1 tbsp
1 tsp	aniseeds	1 tsp
1/4 tsp	poppy seeds	1/4 tsp
1	garlic clove	1
4	dried red chili peppers	4
4	small red onions, quartered	4
2.5 cm	lemon grass	1 inch
2	macadamia nuts (optional)	2
2	white peppercorns	2
1 cm	fresh ginger root	1/2 inch
4 tbsp	thick coconut milk *(page 167)*	4 tbsp
	coconut oil	
1 tsp	tamarind pulp soaked in 4 tbsp water, liquid strained and reserved, pulp discarded	1 tsp
	sugar	
	salt	
1 tbsp	peanuts, roasted, skinned and lightly pounded	1 tbsp

Garnish		
1/4	cucumber, peeled and cut into chunks	1/4
1	tomato, cut into 8 segments	1
1	large onion, cut into segments	1

Grind together the coriander, aniseeds, poppy seeds, garlic, chili peppers, onions, lemon grass, macadamia nuts, if used, white peppercorns and fresh ginger to a paste. Rub each strip of meat with some of this paste and then soak the meat in the coconut milk to soften it.

Heat 2 tablespoons of coconut oil in a saucepan until it is smoking and fry the rest of the spice paste in the oil until it separates. Add the tamarind water and sugar and salt to taste. Bring to the boil. Reduce the heat and simmer, uncovered, until the sauce is thick enough to coat the back of a spoon and the flavours are well blended. Stir in the peanuts and the coconut milk and simmer to thicken. Pour the sauce into a bowl and leave it to cool.

Thread the meat on to satay sticks, leaving 2.5 cm (1 inch) free at one end and 12.5 cm (5 inches) at the other. Brush the meat evenly with oil and cook the skewers on a well-greased rack over a glowing charcoal fire. Turn the skewers frequently until the meat is tender and the coating is well puffed up, 10 to 15 minutes.

Serve the meat on the satay sticks with the cold sauce and garnish each serving with cucumber, tomato and onion.

LILIAN LANE
MALAYAN COOKERY RECIPES

Spit-Roasted Beef Fillet

Filetbraten Natur

The author suggests serving the fillet with herb butter (recipe, page 162), chips or potato croquettes and peas. You can vary the dish by using different herbs in the herb butter, or by serving it with a sauce such as a béarnaise (recipe, page 164).

To serve 6

One 1 to 1.5 kg	fillet of beef, membrane removed	One 2 to 3 lb
	oil	
	salt and freshly ground pepper	

Brush the fillet of beef all over with oil and season it with pepper. Wrap it in aluminium foil and leave it for at least 2 hours and preferably overnight.

Unwrap the fillet, pat it dry lightly and thread it on to a rotating spit. Cook it for 20 to 25 minutes, then remove the fillet from the spit, salt it lightly and leave it for 5 minutes before carving it into slices about 2.5 cm (1 inch) thick.

ULRIKE HORNBERG
SCHLEMMEREIEN VOM GRILL

Roast Sirloin Done on a Spit

Pieczeń z Rożna

To serve 6 to 8

1.5 to 2 kg	sirloin of beef, in one piece	3 to 4 lb
2 to 3 tbsp	olive oil	2 to 3 tbsp
$\frac{1}{2}$	lemon, juice strained	$\frac{1}{2}$
3 or 4	onions, sliced	3 or 4
	salt and pepper	
	melted butter	
1 tbsp	flour	1 tbsp

Rub the meat with the olive oil and sprinkle it with the lemon juice. Place half the onion slices in a dish, put the beef on top and cover it with the remaining onion slices. Leave the meat to stand for 3 hours. An hour before cooking, season the meat with salt and pepper.

Fix the meat on to a spit and roast it over a preheated grill at a very high temperature, brushing it frequently with melted butter. Place a drip pan beneath the spit to catch all the juices. When the meat is well browned, after about 20 minutes, dust it with the flour, allow the flour to dry out, and again brush it with melted butter. The roast should be ready in 35 to 50 minutes, depending on its size and how well done you prefer your meat to be.

Slice the meat thinly and serve it with potatoes and vegetables. Skim the fat from the roasting juices in the pan and serve them with the meat.

MARJA OCHOROWICZ-MONATOWA
POLISH COOKERY

Grilled Tongue with Tarragon

To pre-cook a fresh ox tongue, first soak it in cold water for several hours to remove blood. Place it in a pan and cover with cold water; bring to the boil, then discard the water and rinse the tongue. Transfer it to a clean pan of warm water and add an onion, a bouquet garni containing a bay leaf, parsley and thyme and a celery stick, and some salt. Bring the water to a simmer—do not let it boil—and cook the tongue for at least 2 hours or until tender. Leave it in its cooking liquid until it is

cool then remove it from the pan, trim off any fat or gristle at the base, remove any bones and peel off the skin gently. Reserve 12.5 cl (4 fl oz) of the cooking liquid for use in the recipe.

To serve 6 to 8

One 1.5 kg	fresh ox tongue, pre-cooked and skinned	One 3 lb
2	garlic cloves, crushed	2
3 tbsp	chopped fresh tarragon leaves or $1\frac{1}{2}$ tbsp dried tarragon	3 tbsp
1 tbsp	mustard	1 tbsp
2 tbsp	tarragon vinegar	2 tbsp
$\frac{1}{2}$ tbsp	salt	$\frac{1}{2}$ tbsp
12.5 cl	reserved tongue cooking liquid	4 fl oz
45 g	butter, melted	$1\frac{1}{2}$ oz

Make a paste with the garlic, tarragon, mustard, 1 tablespoon of the vinegar and the salt. Rub half of this over the tongue. To the remainder add the tongue cooking liquid, butter and the rest of the vinegar. Arrange the tongue on a spit, from tip to base, fasten and balance it, then grill over a moderate heat for about 45 minutes, turning constantly. While it roasts, baste the tongue with the sauce. The tongue should be brown and crusty on the outside, tender and juicy within.

JAMES A. BEARD AND HELEN EVANS BROWN
THE COMPLETE BOOK OF OUTDOOR COOKERY

Smoked Rarified Brisket

The technique of smoking meat is demonstrated on page 86. The author suggests using this smoked brisket in sandwiches made from sourdough bread (i.e., bread that has been made from a natural yeast culture).

To serve 8

2 to 2.5 kg	boned beef brisket, trimmed of fat	4 to 5 lb
2	thick slices bacon, chopped	2
15 g	parsley, chopped	$\frac{1}{2}$ oz
3	garlic cloves, slivered	3
	paprika	
	crumbled dried thyme	
	salt and freshly ground black pepper	

Mix together the bacon pieces and the chopped parsley. Cut gashes in the meat and poke in a sliver of garlic and a little bacon and parsley. Dust the meat generously on both sides with paprika, thyme, salt and pepper. Set the meat in a smoker and cook for 35 to 45 minutes per 500 g (1 lb), or until a meat thermometer inserted into the centre of the meat registers 65°C (150°F). Slice the meat on the diagonal to serve.

MAGGIE WALDRON
FIRE AND SMOKE

Tangy Barbecued Beef

The technique of smoking is shown on page 86. The authors
suggest that you use the drippings in the water pan to make a
gravy, and serve the beef with potatoes or boiled rice.

To serve 6 to 8

2 kg	boneless beef chuck, in one piece	4 lb
5 tbsp	red wine vinegar	5 tbsp
4 tbsp	tomato ketchup (*page 165*)	4 tbsp
4 tbsp	soy sauce	4 tbsp
2 tbsp	oil	2 tbsp
1 tbsp	Worcestershire sauce	1 tbsp
1 tsp	salt	1 tsp
½ tsp	dry mustard	½ tsp
¼ tsp	freshly ground black pepper	¼ tsp
1	garlic clove, crushed	1

Put the meat in a baking dish or heavy-duty plastic bag.
Combine all the remaining ingredients in a small mixing
bowl and pour this marinade over the meat. Turn the meat so
that it is completely coated with marinade. Cover the dish
with plastic film or close the bag securely. Leave the meat to
marinate in the refrigerator overnight.

About 6 hours before serving, remove the meat from the
refrigerator. Put two or three chunks of wood or a handful of
wood chips to soak. Fill the fire pan of the smoker with
charcoal and start the fire. When the coals turn grey, drain
the wood pieces and add them to the coals. Put the water pan in
place and fill it almost full with hot water. Put the cooking
rack in place. Lift the meat from the marinade and put it in
the centre of the cooking rack. Pour the marinade into the
water pan. Cover the smoker and smoke-cook the beef for
about 5 hours or until it is firm to the touch. After about 4
hours you may need to check the water pan and add about 1
litre (1¾ pints) of hot water. Slice the beef thinly to serve.

THE EDITORS OF CONSUMER GUIDE PUBLICATIONS
SMOKE COOKERY

Cutlets for the Village Festival

Costelles de Fiesta Mayor

This is a Catalan regional dish from Rupiá, Gerona.

To serve 6

6	veal cutlets	6
12.5 cl	vinegar	4 fl oz
3	truffles, diced	3
100 g	ham, cubed	3½ oz
1 tbsp	flour	1 tbsp
	lemon juice	

Marinade		
15 cl	dry white wine	¼ pint
1 tsp	black peppercorns	1 tsp
	salt	
1	lemon, juice strained	1

Combine the marinade ingredients and marinate the veal
cutlets for 2 hours. Remove the cutlets from the marinade, dry
them with a cloth and grill them over hot coals for 12 to 15
minutes, turning once.

Place the vinegar, truffles, ham and flour in a saucepan
and strain in the remaining marinade. Bring to the boil and
let the sauce thicken—about 5 minutes. Add a little lemon
juice to taste. Arrange the veal cutlets in a serving dish and
pour the sauce over them.

COCINA REGIONAL ESPAÑOLA

Veal or Lamb Chops

To serve 3

6	veal or lamb chops, about 4 cm (1½ inches) thick	6
1 tsp	finely chopped thyme or ½ tsp dried thyme	1 tsp
½ tsp	ground cumin	½ tsp
1 tsp	finely chopped oregano leaves or ½ tsp dried oregano	1tsp
1 tsp	chili powder	1 tsp
1 tsp	salt	1 tsp
100 g	onion, finely chopped	3½ oz
5 tbsp	red wine	5 tbsp
4 tbsp	olive oil	4 tbsp
12.5 cl	tomato purée (*page 164*)	4 fl oz
1	garlic clove, crushed	1
1 tsp	lime or lemon juice	1 tsp

Combine the thyme, cumin, oregano, chili powder, salt,
onion, wine, olive oil, tomato purée, garlic and lime or lemon
juice. Marinate the chops in this mixture for at least 4 hours.
Grill the chops over charcoal for 8 to 10 minutes on each side,
basting them frequently with the marinade.

RONALD JOHNSON
THE AFICIONADO'S SOUTHWESTERN COOKING

Veal Olives on Skewers

Quagliette di Vitello

Serve the skewers on a dish of white rice. Those who find the scent of sage overpowering can replace it with mint or basil, or simply sprinkle the meat with marjoram or thyme before cooking it. This dish can also be made with pork or lamb.

	To serve 4	
4	thinly cut veal escalopes, cut into 10 cm (4 inch) squares	4
	salt and pepper	
	lemon juice	
125 g	thinly cut cooked ham, cut into 10 cm (4 inch) squares	4 oz
125 g	streaky bacon, thinly sliced	4 oz
2	onions, sliced	2
	sage leaves	
125 g	stale white bread, cut into 1 cm (½ inch) cubes	4 oz
	melted bacon fat or dripping	

Season the pieces of veal with salt, pepper and lemon juice. On each slice lay a piece of ham. Roll them up, and round each little roll place a very thin piece of bacon. Thread the rolls on to small skewers, alternating each roll with a slice of onion, a sage leaf and a cube of stale bread. Pour over the skewers a little melted bacon fat or dripping and grill them for 7 to 8 minutes, or until they are cooked through, turning them over and basting them two or three times.

ELIZABETH DAVID
ITALIAN FOOD

Skewered Sweetbreads with Devil Sauce

Brochettes de Ris de Veau à la Diable

	To serve 2	
1	pair calf's sweetbreads, soaked in several changes of cold water, blanched in boiling water for 3 to 5 minutes, refreshed in cold water and patted dry	1
45 g	butter	1½ oz
1	large sweet red pepper, roasted and skinned, cut into squares	1
125 g	thickly sliced lean green bacon, cut into squares, blanched in boiling water for 2 minutes, refreshed in cold water and patted dry	4 oz

	Devil sauce	
1 tbsp	chopped shallots or spring onions	1 tbsp
30 g	butter	1 oz
1 tbsp	cognac	1 tbsp
1 tbsp	tomato purée (*page 164*)	1 tbsp
4 tbsp	*glace de viande* (*page 167*)	4 tbsp
	salt	
2 to 3 tbsp	Worcestershire sauce	2 to 3 tbsp
	cayenne pepper	

Trim the sweetbreads by peeling off the thin membrane, fat and tubes that cover them. Place them between two boards, put weights on the upper board and leave for at least 1½ hours.

Heat the butter in a straight-sided saucepan, put in the sweetbreads, cover the pan and cook slowly for 10 to 15 minutes, basting and turning the sweetbreads from time to time. Remove the sweetbreads and cut them into 4 cm (1½ inch) pieces. Thread them on to metal skewers, alternating them with pieces of sweet pepper and bacon.

To make the devil sauce, lightly brown the shallots or spring onions in the butter. Add the cognac and reduce the liquid by about half, then add the tomato purée and the *glace de viande*. Simmer the sauce, uncovered, for 5 minutes. Season with salt, Worcestershire sauce and cayenne pepper to taste. Whisk the sauce to combine the ingredients and strain it through a wire sieve.

Place the skewered sweetbreads over a hot grill and cook them for about 5 minutes, turning the skewers so that the meat browns evenly. Do not let the sweetbreads become dry. Serve them coated with 2 tablespoons of sauce, and pass the remaining sauce separately.

LOUISETTE BERTHOLLE (EDITOR)
SECRETS OF THE GREAT FRENCH RESTAURANTS

Grilled Calf's Liver Florentine-Style

Fegato alla Griglia

	To serve 4	
Four 100 g	slices calf's liver, 1 cm (½ inch) thick	Four 3½ oz
	salt and freshly ground black pepper	
2 tbsp	olive oil	2 tbsp
	lemon wedges	

Place the rack over the fire and sprinkle it with 2 to 3 teaspoons of salt. When the rack is very hot, put on one slice of liver and cook it for about 45 seconds on each side or until it is browned on the outside. Remove it to a serving dish and keep it warm. Repeat the procedure with the other three slices of liver. When they are cooked, the slices should be light pink inside and very tender and soft. The longer you cook liver, the tougher it becomes.

Sprinkle the liver with a little pepper and with olive oil. Garnish with lemon wedges and serve immediately.

GIULIANO BUGIALLI
THE FINE ART OF ITALIAN COOKING

Kidney Kebabs with Prunes

To serve 4

2	calf's kidneys	2
2 tbsp	vinegar	2 tbsp
16	prunes	16
16	thin slices smoked bacon	16
	salt	
¼ litre	double cream	8 fl oz
3 tbsp	Dijon mustard	3 tbsp

Halve the kidneys and remove the core of fat. Place the kidneys in a bowl of water, add the vinegar, and leave for 5 minutes. Rinse the kidneys and dry them with kitchen paper. Cut them into 24 equal-sized pieces.

Soak the prunes in warm water for 20 minutes. Remove the stones, and wrap each prune in a slice of bacon. Thread the kidney pieces and the prunes on to eight small skewers, beginning and ending with a piece of kidney.

Cook the kebabs on a hot grill for 15 minutes or until well done. Salt them at the end of cooking, off the heat, and serve on heated plates. Whisk the cream and mustard together and serve separately as a sauce.

GIULIANA BONOMO
LA BUONA COCINA

Small Tripe Kebabs

Serve this dish with grilled tomatoes and baked potatoes.

To serve 4

500 g	calf's tripe	1 lb
1	lemon, juice strained	1
	salt and pepper	
200 g	mushrooms, stems removed	7 oz
200 g	smoked bacon	7 oz
	melted butter	
	dry breadcrumbs	

	Madeira sauce	
50 g	butter	2 oz
25 g	flour	1 oz
¼ litre	veal stock (*page 167*)	8 fl oz
4 tbsp	Madeira	4 tbsp
	salt and pepper	

First prepare the sauce. Melt the butter, stir in the flour, and cook until foamy. Pour in the stock. Simmer the sauce gently for about 10 minutes or until smooth and thick. Add the Madeira and season with salt and pepper. Remove the sauce from the heat and keep it warm.

Soak the tripe for 10 minutes in a bowl of water with the lemon juice, and a little salt and pepper. Remove the tripe and rinse it well. Soak the mushrooms for 5 minutes in the same water. Cut the tripe and bacon into 5 cm (2 inch) squares.

Thread the mushrooms and the pieces of tripe and bacon, one after another, on to skewers. Brush them with melted butter and dip in breadcrumbs. Grill the kebabs, turning them frequently, for about 10 minutes or until crisp and browned. Serve with the Madeira sauce.

GIULIANA BONOMO
LA BUONA COCINA

Brewer's Kebabs

Kebab auf Brauer-Art

Veal sausages can be bought in shops specializing in German food. Wild hops are sometimes found growing in hedgerows in hop-growing areas. Otherwise, they can be obtained from hop farmers in the late summer at hop-picking time.

To serve 4

500 g	veal sausages, sliced	1 lb
16	sprigs fresh hops	16
	melted butter	

Thread the hop sprigs and sausage slices alternately on to skewers. Brush them with melted butter and grill for 10 to 15 minutes, turning several times.

THEODOR BOTTIGER
DAS GRILL-BUCH

Veal Sausages in a Cloak

Kalbsbratwürste im Mantel

Veal sausages can be bought in shops specializing in German food. The author suggests serving this dish with tartare sauce (recipe, page 163), salted potatoes and salad.

	To serve 4	
4	veal sausages	4
1 tsp	paprika	1 tsp
4	very thin slices raw gammon	4

Skin the sausages, dust them all over with paprika and wrap them in the gammon slices. Fasten the gammon with a toothpick. Place the parcels on a rack over a hot grill and cook them for 4 to 5 minutes on each side.

ULRIKE HORNBERG
SCHLEMMEREIEN VOM GRILL

Lamb Cutlets to Burn Your Fingers

Cotolette d'Abbacchio a "Scottadito"

The author specifies cutlets from lamb that is only 20 to 30 days old, but cutlets from more mature, but still young and tender, lamb can be cooked in the same way.

Serve a mixed seasonal salad to accompany the cutlets. If you are dextrous enough, use your fingers rather than a fork to turn the cutlets on the grill and to eat them. But be careful not to burn them too much.

	To serve 4	
1 kg	milk lamb cutlets	2 to 2½ lb
	lard	
	salt and pepper	

Remove a little fat from the cutlets if there is a great deal. Beat the cutlets out lightly and rub them with lard. Grill them over a hot fire for about 8 minutes, turning them half-way through the cooking time. Season the cutlets with salt and pepper and serve at once.

ANNA BASLINI ROSSELLI
100 RICETTE PER LA COLAZIONE SULL'ERBA

Grilled Lamb Chops

Kotlety Baranie z Rusztu

	To serve 4	
8	lamb chops, boned and lightly pounded	8
	salt and pepper	
1	garlic clove, crushed	1
About 4 tbsp oil		About 4 tbsp

Dust the chops lightly with pepper and rub with salt and garlic. Brush them with oil. Place the chops on a very hot grill and cook them for 2 to 3 minutes on each side. They should be slightly pink inside.

HELENA HAWLICZKOWA
KUCHNIA POLSKA

Lamb Chops with Mustard Butter

Lamskarbonades met Mosterdboter

	To serve 4	
4	double rib lamb chops, 6 cm (2½ inches) thick	4
2 tbsp	olive oil	2 tbsp
1 or 2	garlic cloves, crushed	1 or 2
2 tbsp	lemon juice	2 tbsp
	salt and pepper	
	Mustard butter	
1 tbsp	Dijon mustard	1 tbsp
½ tsp	lemon juice	½ tsp
1	garlic clove, crushed	1
125 g	butter, softened	4 oz
	salt and pepper	

Brush the lamb chops with the olive oil, crushed garlic and lemon juice; season with salt and pepper. Set aside for 2 hours.

To make the mustard butter, work the mustard, lemon juice and garlic into the butter, season with salt and pepper and set aside at room temperature.

Grill the lamb chops for 7 minutes on each side, 10 cm (4 inches) from the heat source. Serve immediately, with the mustard butter beside them.

HUGH JANS
VRIJ NEDERLAND

Milk Lamb Cutlets, Peasant-Style

Costillas de Cordero Lechal a la Campesina

A milk lamb is an unweaned lamb, killed before it is eight weeks old. It is usually available only in late winter or spring. Cutlets from more mature lamb can also be cooked in this way.

	To serve 4	
8	milk lamb cutlets	8
3	sprigs thyme	3
3	sprigs fennel	3
3	sprigs rosemary	3
	salt and pepper	
8 cl	oil	3 fl oz

Place the sprigs of thyme, fennel and rosemary on a flat metal sheet or baking sheet over medium coals. Place a rack on top of this and let it get very hot. Salt the lamb cutlets, rub them with oil and season them with pepper. Place them on the rack and cook them for about 5 minutes, turning once. They will absorb the aroma of the herbs.

MANUEL VAZQUEZ MONTALBAN
LA COCINA CATALANA

Chops in Breadcrumbs

Chuletas con Pan Rallado

	To serve 4	
4	lamb double loin chops, bones removed, meat flattened	4
15 cl	oil	¼ pint
1 or 2	garlic cloves, crushed	1 or 2
1	lemon, juice strained	1
60 g	dry white breadcrumbs	2 oz
1	sprig parsley	1

Make a marinade with the oil, garlic and lemon juice. Place the chops in a dish with the marinade and leave to soak for about 1 hour, or until they are needed for cooking.

When the chops have been well steeped in the marinade, take them out and dust them all over with breadcrumbs. Pat the crumbs gently so that they adhere. Place the chops on a rack over glowing charcoal. Cook them for about 15 minutes, turning them several times and basting them with the marinade, using the parsley sprig to brush it on.

LUIS RIPOLL
NUESTRA COCINA

Chops Roasted on a Tile

Chuletas Asadas "a la Teja"

Old-fashioned Spanish roof tiles are usually very thick and will not crack if placed over glowing embers. A large, fireproof earthenware dish, or an unglazed quarry tile, could be substituted. Rosemary branches may be used instead of the cistus (Spanish rock rose) for the fire and for turning.

	To serve 4	
8	lamb or 4 veal chops	8
	salt	
	thyme	

Make a fire from pine wood, dry cistus and pine needles. Salt the chops. Clean the tile and rub it with thyme. Place it between two large stones in the burning embers of the fire and allow it to get very hot. Place the chops on the tile and cook them for about 20 minutes, turning them once. Use a cistus stem to turn them over. When they are done, serve the chops directly from the tile.

ANTONIO ARAGONES SUBERO
GASTRONOMIA DE GUADALAJARA

Barbecued Liver and Bacon

	To serve 4 to 6	
750 g	lamb's liver in one piece, soaked in water for 1 hour, skin and tubes removed, cut diagonally into 1 cm (½ inch) thick slices	1½ lb
4 to 6	rashers bacon, rinds removed	4 to 6
	Marinade	
5 tbsp	olive oil	5 tbsp
1	lemon, juice strained	1
	salt and freshly ground pepper	
1 tbsp	finely chopped parsley	1 tbsp

Combine the olive oil, lemon juice, salt, pepper and parsley and mix together thoroughly. Place the slices of liver in a shallow dish and pour the marinade mixture over them. Cover the dish and leave for 1 hour.

Drain the liver, reserving the marinade liquid. Grill the slices of liver over medium-hot coals for 10 to 12 minutes, turning once. Grill the bacon until it is crisp and brown. Heat the reserved marinade and serve it with the liver and bacon.

ELIZABETH SEWELL
BARBECUE COOKBOOK

Lamb Kebabs

The author suggests that, for a more spicy dish, you can substitute a marinade made by mixing together 1 teaspoon of ground coriander, 1 teaspoon of ground cumin, 60 cl (1 pint) of yogurt and the juice of 1 lemon. Season with salt and pepper.

To serve 6 to 8		
500 g to 1 kg	boned lean shoulder or leg of lamb	1 to 2 lb
	Marinade	
2	garlic cloves, crushed	2
2	bay leaves, crushed	2
1 tsp	dried oregano	1 tsp
1	onion, finely grated, or juice only, extracted with a garlic press	1
1	lemon, juice strained	1
3 tbsp	olive oil	3 tbsp
	salt and pepper	

Trim the lamb to remove most of the fat. Cut the meat into 2.5 cm (1 inch) cubes and put into a dish or bowl. Mix together the ingredients for the marinade, season it with salt and pepper, and pour it over the meat. Leave to marinate for a minimum of 1 hour—longer if convenient.

Drain the meat and thread it on to metal skewers or kebab sticks. Cook over a glowing charcoal or wood fire for 7 to 10 minutes, depending on how rare you like your meat. Turn the kebabs as they cook, so that they cook evenly, and baste them with the marinade to keep them really moist. Serve them on a bed of rice, or with pitta bread, which can be warmed through as you cook the kebabs.

HENRIETTA GREEN
THE MARINADE COOKBOOK

Grilled Lamb on Skewers

Souvlakia

The author suggests serving this dish with pilaff (recipe, page 165) or with fried potatoes and tomato salad.

To serve 6		
1	leg of lamb, boned and cut into 2.5 cm (1 inch) cubes	1
12.5 cl	olive oil	4 fl oz
4 tbsp	lemon juice	4 tbsp
1 tsp	salt	1 tsp
	pepper	
	chopped oregano	

Mix together the oil, lemon juice and salt, and add a little pepper. Marinate the lamb in this mixture for about 1 hour. Thread the cubes on to metal skewers. Grill the meat over glowing coals for about 15 minutes, turning the skewers once. Sprinkle with oregano before serving.

CHRISSA PARADISSIS
THE BEST BOOK OF GREEK COOKERY

Skewered Lamb

Brochettes d'Agneau de Pré Salé

The author suggests that the skewers should be served on a bed of rice, surrounded by halved tomatoes which have been sprinkled with herbs and grilled, and accompanied by lightly boiled green beans.

To serve 8		
One 2.5 to 3 kg	leg of lamb, boned, trimmed and cut into 2 cm (¾ inch) cubes	One 5½ to 6 lb
250 g	very thinly sliced bacon, cut crosswise into 2.5 cm (1 inch) wide strips	8 oz
4	sweet green peppers, seeded and cut into squares	4
	groundnut oil	
4 tbsp	mixed dried herbs (thyme, bay leaf, sage, rosemary and savory)	4 tbsp
16	very thin slices prosciutto	16

Thread the lamb cubes on to 16 metal skewers, alternating them with the bacon pieces and squares of sweet green pepper. Brush the skewers with oil and roll them in the dried herbs. Cook the skewers over hot coals for about 10 minutes on each side, turning once.

Meanwhile, grill the prosciutto for 1 to 2 minutes. To serve, wrap one slice of prosciutto on the bias round each skewer.

LOUISETTE BERTHOLLE (EDITOR)
SECRETS OF THE GREAT FRENCH RESTAURANTS

Moroccan Skewered Mutton

To serve 4 to 6

1 kg	lean boneless mutton or lamb, cut into 2.5 cm (1 inch) cubes	2 to 2½ lb
125 g	suet, cut into 2.5 cm (1 inch) cubes	4 oz
175 g	onions, finely chopped	6 oz
30 g	parsley, finely chopped	1 oz
1 tbsp	salt	1 tbsp
1 tsp	ground black pepper	1 tsp

Pound the onion, parsley, salt and pepper to a paste in a mortar. Blend this paste with the meat and suet and leave to marinate for 15 minutes. Then spit the cubes of meat and suet alternately on skewers. Grill the meat over hot coals of wood or charcoal for 3 to 5 minutes on each side.

IRENE F. DAY
KITCHEN IN THE KASBAH

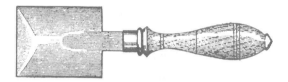

Skewers of Lamb, Pineapple, Peppers and Other Things

To serve 4

1 kg	lean boneless shoulder of lamb, cut into 4 cm (1½ inch) cubes	2 lb
16	4 cm (1½ inch) cubes fresh pineapple	16
3	sweet green peppers, seeded and cut into 5 cm (2 inch) squares	3
10	small onions, parboiled for 5 minutes	10
10	cherry tomatoes	10
12.5 cl	soy sauce	4 fl oz
2 tbsp	olive oil	2 tbsp
2	garlic cloves, each cut crosswise into 4 pieces	2
1 tsp	chopped basil leaves or ½ tsp dried basil	1 tsp
1 tbsp	grated fresh ginger root or ½ tsp ground ginger	1 tbsp
	freshly ground pepper	

Mix all the ingredients together in a large ceramic or glass bowl, adding the lamb cubes last, and marinate in the refrigerator overnight. (This is an important step; the time for marination should be from 12 to 24 hours.) Remove the bowl from the refrigerator to allow the contents to come to room temperature before grilling. This will take about 2 hours.

Thread the lamb cubes, pineapple, sweet peppers, onions and tomatoes on to 25 cm (10 inch) skewers. Reserve the marinade. Place the skewers over hot charcoal, about 10 cm (4 inches) from the coals. Cook for 15 minutes, or until the lamb is done to your taste, turning the skewers often and brushing the ingredients frequently with the reserved marinade.

JOE FAMULARO AND LOUISE IMPERIALE
THE FESTIVE FAMULARO KITCHEN

Shish Kebabs

To serve 6

1 kg	lean boneless lamb, cut into cubes	2 lb
12.5 cl	lemon juice	4 fl oz
4 tbsp	olive oil	4 tbsp
3	spring onions, finely chopped	3
1 tsp	ground ginger	1 tsp
1 tsp	ground coriander	1 tsp
1	garlic clove, finely chopped	1
2 tsp	curry powder	2 tsp
2 tsp	salt	2 tsp
2	courgettes, cut into 2.5 cm (1 inch) thick slices	2
2	sweet green peppers, seeded and cut into squares	2
2	ears sweetcorn, husks and silk removed, cut into 2.5 cm (1 inch) thick slices	2
8	small pickling onions	8
12	cherry tomatoes	12
60 g	button mushroom caps	2 oz

Combine the lemon juice, olive oil, spring onions, ginger, coriander, garlic, curry powder and salt to make a marinade. Add the cubed lamb to the marinade and leave to marinate at room temperature for 2 to 8 hours.

Drain the lamb and reserve the marinade. Thread the lamb cubes, courgette pieces, squares of sweet pepper, pieces of sweetcorn and onions on to skewers, alternating each piece of vegetable with a piece of meat. Thread the tomatoes and mushroom caps alternately on to separate skewers.

Grill the lamb skewers over hot charcoal for 10 minutes. Then place the tomato and mushroom skewers over the grill and grill everything for 5 more minutes. Baste all the skewers with marinade occasionally and turn them often.

LOIS M. BURROWS AND LAURA G. MYERS
TOO MANY TOMATOES, SQUASH, BEANS AND OTHER GOOD THINGS

Meat-Cheese Sandwich on Skewers

Kabab Puksand Paneeri

To make Indian cheese, boil 1.5 litres (2½ pints) of milk. Remove the milk from the heat and stir in 1 teaspoon of powdered alum (available from chemists). Return to the heat and stir until the milk curdles and the liquid has separated completely. Drain off the liquid through a fine-meshed sieve. Place the cheese in a muslin bag and squeeze out all moisture. You now have a crumbly cheese.

To serve 4

500 g	lean, boneless lamb, cut into 5 cm (2 inch) squares, 5 mm (¼ inch) thick	1 lb
500 g	Indian cheese, cut into squares a bit thinner than the meat	1 lb
1 tbsp	cumin seeds	1 tbsp
4	limes, juice strained	4
60 g	fresh ginger root, grated	2 oz
1	onion, finely chopped	1
15 cl	thick yogurt	¼ pint
12.5 cl	double cream	4 fl oz
90 g	*ghee*, melted	3 oz
125 g	blanched almonds, ground	4 oz
1 tbsp	finely ground pomegranate seeds	1 tbsp
½ tsp	powdered saffron	½ tsp

Grind the cumin seeds with a few drops of the lime juice. Make a thick infusion of the ginger with half the remaining lime juice and a similar infusion of onion with the other half of the lime juice. Combine the yogurt and the cream with half the melted *ghee* and the ground almonds.

Prick the surface of the meat with a sharp fork and rub in the ginger infusion. Dip the cheese in the onion infusion. Spread the meat with a little of the cream and almond mixture, the ground pomegranate seeds, a very light sprinkling of saffron and the rest of the onion infusion.

Place a piece of cheese on each piece of meat and tie them together with thread. Run a long, oiled skewer through four or five of these "open sandwiches" at a time. Place over the grill. When the meat becomes dry, baste with the remaining almond marinade. Cook until the meat is a perfect russet-brown on all sides, about 15 minutes. Then rub with the remaining saffron mixed with the remaining *ghee*. Crisp the meat for another few seconds only, remove the meat from the skewers, untie the threads and serve.

DHARAMJIT SINGH
INDIAN COOKERY

Russian Lamb Kebab

Shashlyk

Herbs can be thrown on to the charcoal while the meat is cooking, to add perfume and flavour.

To serve 4

1 to 1.5 kg	boneless lamb in one piece	2 to 3 lb
60 cl	water	1 pint
60 cl	vinegar	1 pint
2½ tsp	pickling spice	2½ tsp
	salt	
2	garlic cloves, cut into slivers	2
12.5 to 15 cl	brandy (optional)	4 to 5 fl oz
2	onions, chopped	2
4	sprigs parsley, finely chopped	4
4	lamb kidneys, fat and membrane removed, quartered and cored	4
500 g	cherry tomatoes	1 lb

Boil the water, vinegar and pickling spice together and allow to cool. Salt the meat all over and then lard it with slivers of garlic. Place it in an earthenware bowl, pour on the brandy (if used) and sprinkle over it the chopped onion and parsley. Pour on the cold vinegar and spice mixture, cover the bowl with a cloth and leave it to marinate in a cool place for several hours, turning the lamb frequently.

Remove the meat from the marinade, cut it into 2.5 cm (1 inch) cubes and thread these on to skewers, interspersing the meat with quarters of kidney and whole tomatoes. Cook the skewers over hot charcoal, basting frequently with the marinade and turning often, for 15 minutes or until the meat is browned on the outside and still slightly pink in the middle.

SOFKA SKIPWITH
EAT RUSSIAN

Indian Lamb Kebab

Boti Kabab

To serve 8

1 kg	lean, boned loin or leg of lamb, cut into 4 cm (1½ inch) pieces	2 lb
2	limes, juice strained	2
5	garlic cloves, crushed	5
2 tsp	poppy seeds	2 tsp
1 tsp	ground ginger	1 tsp
2 tsp	turmeric	2 tsp
4 tsp	ground coriander	4 tsp
¼ tsp	cayenne pepper	¼ tsp
1 tsp	mustard seeds	1 tsp
12.5 cl	yogurt	4 fl oz
125 g	butter, melted	4 oz

Grind together the juice of one lime, the garlic, poppy seeds, ginger, turmeric, coriander, cayenne pepper, mustard seeds and yogurt to form a paste. Prick the pieces of meat with a fork and cover them with the paste. Marinate them for 2 hours.

Thread the meat pieces on skewers and grill them, turning them frequently and basting them with a mixture of the melted butter and the remaining lime juice, for 15 minutes, or until the meat is well done and glazed. If the meat is grilled too rare, the spices will have a raw taste.

MOHAN CHABLANI AND BRAHM N. DIXIT
THE BENGAL LANCERS INDIAN COOKBOOK

Lamb Satay

Saté Kambing

To serve 4

750 g	lean lamb, cubed	1½ lb
	salt and pepper	
½	lemon, juice strained	½
15 cl	soy sauce	¼ pint
2	garlic cloves, crushed	2
2	onions, sliced	2

Season the meat with salt and pepper. Leave it to marinate for about 1 hour in a sauce made from the lemon juice, 12.5 cl (4 fl oz) of the soy sauce and the garlic. Thread the meat on to skewers and grill it over hot charcoal until it is cooked—about 15 minutes—turning several times. Serve the skewers of meat sprinkled with the remaining soy sauce and garnished with the sliced raw onion.

OMA KEASBERRY
OMA'S INDISCHE KEUKENGEHEIMEN

Malaysian Meat Satay

The recipe comes from the Sateh Pantai Timor (satay stall) in Kuala Lumpur, Malaysia. Lemon grass can be bought from Oriental food shops.

To serve 4

500 g	mutton or beef, cut into 1 cm (½ inch) cubes	1 lb
4	small red onions, chopped	4
2	garlic cloves, chopped	2
3	stalks lemon grass, chopped	3
1 tsp each	ground cumin and ginger	1 tsp each
1 tbsp	turmeric powder	1 tbsp
½ tsp each	black pepper and salt	½ tsp each
1 tsp	sugar	1 tsp
3 tbsp	light soy sauce	3 tbsp
	peanut oil	

Satay sauce

6	small red onions, finely chopped	6
3	garlic cloves, finely chopped	3
3	stalks lemon grass, finely chopped	3
3 tbsp	peanut oil	3 tbsp
2.5 cm	stick cinnamon	1 inch
1 tsp	chili powder	1 tsp
2 tbsp	sugar	2 tbsp
	salt	
2 tbsp	lime juice	2 tbsp
125 g	ground peanuts	4 oz
3 tbsp	thick coconut milk (*page 167*)	3 tbsp
15 cl	water	¼ pint

Garnish

	onion slices	
	cucumber wedges	

Pound together the onions, garlic, lemon grass, spices, salt, sugar and soy sauce. Mix together the meat and the spice mixture thoroughly and leave it to stand for at least 1 hour. Thread the meat on to skewers (about four or five pieces on each skewer) and cook the skewers over charcoal for about 15 minutes, turning and basting them with oil frequently.

To make the sauce, fry the onions, garlic and lemon grass in the oil for 5 minutes. Add all the other ingredients and bring to the boil. Lower the heat and simmer for 15 to 20 minutes.

Serve the meat with the garnish and satay sauce.

KENNETH MITCHELL (EDITOR)
THE FLAVOUR OF MALAYSIA

Lamb Offal Skewers

Brochettes d'Abats d'Agneau

The author suggests that a saffron and tomato pilaff (recipe, page 165) would make a perfect accompaniment to this dish.

Sharpened rosemary branches, a tuft of leaves left at the unsharpened end, may replace metal skewers, affording much the prettiest and most appetizing presentation.

	To serve 4	
4	lamb's kidneys, surface membrane removed, each cut crosswise into 3 pieces, or 1 veal kidney, membrane removed, split lengthwise, interior fat cut out, each half cut crosswise into slices 2 to 2.5 cm ($\frac{3}{4}$ to 1 inch) thick	4
3	lamb's hearts, pared free of fat and of the tough tubes and vessels at the top, halved lengthwise, each half cut into 3 pieces	3
125 g	bacon or lean, parboiled salt pork, cubed (optional)	4 oz
175 g	lamb's sweetbreads, parboiled, pared, pressed and sliced (optional)	6 oz
175 g	lamb's liver, cubed (optional)	6 oz
175 g	fillet of lamb, cubed (optional)	6 oz
175 g	button mushrooms, stems finely chopped	6 oz
1 or 2	medium-sized onions, half finely chopped, half cut into sections (optional)	1 or 2
2	small courgettes, sliced (optional)	2
1	large sweet red or green pepper, cut into 2.5 to 4 cm (1 to 1$\frac{1}{2}$ inch) squares	1
2 tbsp	finely chopped parsley	2 tbsp
1 tsp	finely crumbled mixed dried herbs	1 tsp
1	large garlic clove, crushed	1
About 8 cl	olive oil	About 3 fl oz
	salt and pepper	

Combine all the ingredients, except for the salt and pepper, in a large mixing bowl, mixing thoroughly but gently so that all the meat and vegetable pieces are uniformly coated with oil, herbs and chopped vegetables. Marinate for 2 hours, if you like, turning the elements around two or three times.

Pierce the meats and vegetables in sequence on four skewers, salt and pepper all sides, and grill over hot coals for 12 to 15 minutes, turning the skewers every 3 to 4 minutes and brushing the just-grilled surface lightly with marinade (supplemented with more olive oil if necessary) after each turn.

RICHARD OLNEY
SIMPLE FRENCH FOOD

Shepherd's Lamb Kebab Roasted on a Spit

Agneshki Shish Kebap po Karakachanski

This dish is traditionally cooked on a long thin spit of hard wood such as cornelian cherry wood, which gives a special flavour to the meat. Milk lamb is lamb that is slaughtered at less than eight weeks old. Meat from more mature lamb may be successfully used instead.

Serve the kebab straight from the spit, accompanied by salads or cooked vegetables.

	To serve 7 or 8	
1 kg	boned leg of milk lamb, cut into 4 cm (1$\frac{1}{2}$ inch) pieces	2 to 2$\frac{1}{2}$ lb
1	whole lamb's liver, sliced thickly and cut into 4 cm (1$\frac{1}{2}$ inch) squares	1
2	lamb's kidneys, cleaned and cut into 2.5 cm (1 inch) cubes	2
1	lamb's heart, cleaned and cut into 4 cm (1$\frac{1}{2}$ inch) pieces	1
2	lamb's sweetbreads, cleaned and cut into pieces	2
	salt and black pepper	
	paprika	
125 g	caul	4 oz
About 2 metres	lamb's intestines, washed thoroughly inside and out	About 2$\frac{1}{4}$ yards
150 g	butter, melted	5 oz

Start a good fire of well-dried wood. Season the leg of lamb pieces, the liver, kidneys, heart and sweetbreads generously with salt and pepper, then dust them lightly with paprika. Thread the meat on to a spit, alternating each cube of leg meat with pieces of liver, kidney, heart and sweetbreads, in that order. When all the meat is on the spit, wrap the caul closely round the meat and tie it securely by winding the intestines tightly round the spit.

Wait until the embers of the fire are glowing all over. Then brush the wrapped spit on all sides with the melted butter, and place it over the embers. Cook, turning the spit slowly and continuously, until the kebab is well browned and cooked through, about 15 minutes.

NATSKO SOTIROV
SUVREMENNA KOUHNYA

Grilled Meat Balls

Koubba Machwiyya

In Arab countries, the salted fat called for in this recipe would be lamb fat that has been salted and smoked in the same way as bacon. Bacon fat or speck (smoked pork fat, available from shops specializing in German food) can be substituted.

Instead of forming the meat into balls, you can shape it into flat cakes. In that case you will need to put a slightly larger quantity of fat inside.

To serve 4

300 g	lean lamb, minced	10 oz
150 g	fine *burghul*, soaked in cold water for 10 minutes, drained, excess water squeezed out	5 oz
100 g	onions, sliced	3½ oz
100 g	lamb fat, minced	3½ oz
50 g	powdered dried mint	2 oz
	salt	
2 tsp	freshly ground black pepper	2 tsp
100 g	salted fat	3½ oz

Place the minced lamb meat, *burghul* and onions in a mixing bowl and knead them together, rubbing them vigorously against the sides of the bowl. Then add the lamb fat and mix it in well. Sprinkle on the dried mint, add salt to taste and knead the mixture again.

Sprinkle the pepper over the salted fat, knead the fat and divide it into small pieces about 1.5 cm (⅔ inch) square. Take small portions of the lamb and *burghul* paste and form them into balls, leaving an opening in the top. Cupping each ball in the hollow of your half-closed hand, place a piece of salted fat inside, then close the opening. Dip your fingers in a little water, dampen your palms and roll the ball between your palms to make it into a perfect sphere.

When all the paste has been formed into balls in this way, place the balls on a rack over a charcoal fire and grill them for 15 minutes, turning them often so that they brown evenly all over. Serve the meat balls hot.

RENÉ R. KHAWAM
LA CUISINE ARABE

Moroccan Minced Meat on Skewers

L'Kifta Mtoona

The technique of moulding minced meat on to skewers is shown on page 34. To preserve lemons, cut each lemon almost, but not completely, into quarters, ending each cut about 1 cm (½ inch) above the base of the lemon. Stuff the cuts with coarse salt. Place a layer of salt in a preserving jar and add a layer of lemons. Press them down so that they release their juice. Add a bay leaf and spices such as coriander, a cinnamon stick, cloves and black peppercorns. Cover with more layers of salt, lemons and spices, ending with salt. Pour on just enough lemon juice to cover the lemons, then seal the jars and keep them in a cool dark place for at least one month.

To serve 6

1 kg	lean boneless lamb, mutton, beef or veal, coarsely chopped	2 to 2½ lb
250 g	suet	8 oz
½	onion, finely chopped	½
30 g	parsley, finely chopped	1 oz
1 tsp	freshly ground black pepper	1 tsp
1 tsp	paprika	1 tsp
1	lemon, juice strained	1
1 tbsp	salt	1 tbsp
Garlic and chili sauce		
1 tsp	cumin seeds, crushed	1 tsp
1 tsp	chili powder	1 tsp
1 tsp	paprika	1 tsp
1	head garlic, cloves separated	1
5 tbsp	finely chopped parsley	5 tbsp
12.5 cl	lemon juice or white wine vinegar	4 fl oz
4 tbsp	olive oil	4 tbsp
½ litre	water	16 fl oz
	salt	
1	preserved lemon or fresh lemon, including rind, finely diced	1
125 g	black or green olives, stoned	4 oz

To make the sauce, pound the cumin, chili powder and paprika in a mortar; add the garlic cloves and parsley, and pound to a paste. Blend together the lemon juice or vinegar, oil, water, salt to taste and the diced preserved or fresh lemon. Combine the garlic paste with the mixture of liquids, toss in the olives and stir well. Set the sauce aside.

Pass the meat and suet through the medium disc of a grinder, then pass this mixture through the grinder again, together with the onion, parsley, black pepper, paprika, lemon juice and salt, using the fine disc. Blend the mixture thoroughly. Wet your hands and mould the meat mixture lengthwise on to metal skewers to form sausage shapes about 2.5 cm (1 inch) in diameter. Barbecue the skewers over hot smokeless coals of wood or charcoal for 8 to 10 minutes, turning several times. Do not allow the flames to scorch the meat. Serve the skewers with the sauce.

IRENE F. DAY
KITCHEN IN THE KASBAH

Indian Minced Lamb Kebabs

Seekh Kebab

The technique of shaping minced meat on skewers is demonstrated on page 34.

Use lamb or mutton free from skin and tendons, but with a good amount of fat to keep the kebabs moist and juicy.

To serve 6

1 kg	lamb or mutton, minced twice and worked to a paste with the hands, or put through a food processor	2 to 2½ lb
1 tbsp	coriander seeds, roasted and ground	1 tbsp
1 tsp	cumin, roasted and ground	1 tsp
2 tsp	ground cinnamon	2 tsp
	grated nutmeg	
	ground mace	
	ground cloves	
1 tsp	*garam masala*	1 tsp
3	cardamom pods, husks removed	3
1	large onion, grated	1
2.5 cm	fresh ginger root, crushed	1 inch
3	garlic cloves, crushed	3
	lemon juice	
3 tbsp	yogurt	3 tbsp
3 or 4	sprigs fresh coriander leaves, chopped	3 or 4
3 or 4	mint leaves, chopped	3 or 4
3 or 4	sprigs parsley, chopped	3 or 4
1 or 2	green chili peppers, finely chopped, or ½ tsp or more cayenne pepper	1 or 2
	salt and black pepper	
	oil or clarified butter (optional)	

	Garnish	
6	lemon wedges	6
2	onions, thinly sliced, sprinkled with salt and left for 30 minutes to soften	2

Mix the meat with the coriander, cumin, cinnamon, a good pinch each of nutmeg, mace and cloves, the *garam masala*, cardamom seeds, onion, ginger, garlic, a little lemon juice, the yogurt, fresh herbs, chili peppers and salt and pepper. Leave to stand in a cool place, covered, for 2 to 3 hours.

Take lumps of meat and press them into sausage shapes about 2.5 cm (1 inch) in diameter round skewers that have a wide flat blade (so that the meat does not slide). Place on a rack over a medium heat. Cook gently for about 20 minutes, turning over once and basting with oil or clarified butter if there is not enough of the meat's own fat. The kebabs should be brown but still tender and juicy inside. Garnish with the lemon wedges and onion slices before serving.

CLAUDIA RODEN
PICNIC

Gigot of Lamb on the Spit

Parcha Seekhi

The author suggests that this dish can also be made with veal.

To serve 6

One 1.5 kg	boned leg of lamb	One 3 lb
60 g	fresh ginger root, pounded	2 oz
1¼ tsp	salt	1¼ tsp
150 g	*ghee*	5 oz
250 g	onions, grated	8 oz
2 tbsp	ground coriander	2 tbsp
15 cl	yogurt, whipped	¼ pint
2 tbsp	cumin seeds, lightly roasted	2 tbsp
9	cloves, ground	9
5 cm	stick cinnamon, ground	2 inch
9	cardamom pods, ground	9

Remove as much fat, sinew, gristle and connecting tissue as possible from the boned meat. Wipe the meat with a damp cloth, then dry it and prick it all over with a sharp knife. Rub it well with the ginger and salt. Reserve for the moment.

Heat 30 g (1 oz) of the *ghee* and fry the onions with the coriander until the onions are dark gold, about 15 minutes. Add about 5 tablespoons of water and cook until the mixture is dry. Place this mixture in the centre of the meat and roll the meat up, securing it with string. Place the meat on a greased revolving spit above a drip pan and cook over a hot fire until browned, about 15 minutes, then let the heat die down to medium. As soon as the flesh looks dry, baste at once with the remaining *ghee* mixed with the yogurt, cumin, cloves, cinnamon and cardamom.

The *parcha* should be cooked after about 1¼ hours. Test by inserting a sharp skewer; the juices should be clear. Mix the drippings with a little water and reduce this mixture to a paste over a medium heat. Serve this as a sauce with the meat.

DHARAMJIT SINGH
INDIAN COOKERY

Leg of Lamb Kebab

Kabab-e Ran-e Bareh

To serve 8

1	leg of lamb, boned	1
2	large onions, chopped	2
45 g	butter	1½ oz
10 to 15	chicken livers, halved	10 to 15
2 tbsp	tomato purée (*page 164*)	2 tbsp
12.5 cl	hot water	4 fl oz
2 tsp	lemon juice	2 tsp
60 g	almonds, slivered	2 oz
60 g	pistachio nuts, slivered	2 oz
45 g	candied orange peel, cut into thin slices	1½ oz
200 g	rice, boiled in salted water for 15 minutes, then drained	7 oz
2 or 3	garlic cloves, slivered	2 or 3

Sauté the onions in the butter until golden-brown. Add the chicken livers and sauté them until brown. Dilute the tomato purée with the hot water and pour it over the livers. Add the lemon juice, slivered almonds and pistachio nuts, and the slices of candied orange peel. Cover the pan and simmer gently for 15 minutes. Stir in the boiled rice.

Fill the boned leg of lamb with this stuffing, roll it up and truss it well with string. Secure the ends well so that the stuffing will not spill out. Prick the outer skin in several fatty places and insert slivers of garlic under the skin. Spit-roast the lamb over a charcoal fire for about 2 hours. Remove the slivers of garlic just before serving.

NESTA RAMAZANI
PERSIAN COOKING

Spit-Roasted Leg of Mutton

Hammelkeule Pumpota

The technique of spitting a leg of lamb is shown on page 42.

To serve 6 to 8

One 2 to 2.5 kg	leg of mutton or lamb	One 4 to 5 lb
1	small onion, chopped	1
1	garlic clove, chopped	1
6 tbsp	oil	6 tbsp
1 tsp	lemon juice	1 tsp
1 tbsp	finely chopped parsley	1 tbsp
	dried sage	
	salt and pepper	

Trim the leg of mutton or lamb of excess fat and skin, but leave the white skin that covers the leg. Purée the onion and garlic with 1 tablespoon of the oil in a blender. Little by little add 3 more tablespoons of the oil, the lemon juice, parsley, a pinch of sage and some salt and pepper. Mix well and rub the mixture thoroughly into the leg of mutton on all sides. Place the leg on a sheet of aluminium foil, pour any remaining marinade over it and close up the foil loosely but securely. Leave the leg of mutton in the refrigerator overnight.

Heat the grill at least 1 hour before it is needed. Take the leg of mutton out of the foil and pat it dry thoroughly with kitchen paper so that none of the marinade remains. Place the leg on a rotating spit, making sure it is evenly balanced.

Grill the joint on the spit over a fierce heat until it is crisp and brown on all sides, about 20 minutes. Move the spit farther from the coals and continue to cook for another 2½ to 3 hours, basting now and then with the rest of the oil. If you use a meat thermometer, the meat is ready when the thermometer reads about 80°C (176°F).

After grilling, remove the leg from the spit and leave it to rest for 10 minutes before carving.

ANNETTE WOLTER
DAS PRAKTISCHE GRILLBUCH

Spit-Roasted Lamb

Arni sti Soúvla

To judge when the lamb is cooked through, insert a meat thermometer into the thickest part, avoiding the bone. Lamb is medium-rare at an internal temperature of 60°C (140°F), medium to well done at 63° to 80°C (145° to 176°F). Greek roast lamb is traditionally very well cooked.

If the fire is in a pit, prop sheets of corrugated iron on each side of the fire to deflect the heat on to the lamb.

	To serve 40 to 50	
1	lamb, weighing about 23 kg (50 lb)	1
3	lemons, 1 halved, juice of 2 strained	3
	salt and freshly ground black pepper	
	large fresh thyme, oregano and rosemary sprigs	
35 cl	olive oil	12 fl oz
3 or 4	garlic cloves, crushed	3 or 4

Wipe the lamb inside and out with a damp cloth. Rub the cavity well with the lemon halves and with salt and pepper. Put a few sprigs of herbs in the cavity and close it with skewers. Rub the outer surfaces of the lamb with the lemon halves, salt and pepper.

Set the lamb on its stomach and push the spit through the centre, from between the back legs, along the spine and through the neck. Pull the forelegs forward and tie them securely on to the spit with wire. Press the back legs along the spit and cross them above it, again securing them with wire.

Mix together the lemon juice, olive oil and garlic, and salt and pepper to taste. Wrap sprigs of thyme, oregano and rosemary in muslin and tack the package to the end of a long rod. Set the package of herbs in the oil and lemon mixture until it is required for basting.

Set a wood fire in a pit or a halved fuel drum and let it burn until the flames die down. Add a layer of charcoal and put the spitted lamb in position. Turn the lamb slowly over the fire. Begin with the spit well away from the fire, if possible, then lower it closer to the fire half way through the cooking. Baste the lamb occasionally with the soaked package of herbs. Roast the lamb for 6 to 7 hours over the glowing coals, adding more charcoal as needed.

TESS MALLOS
GREEK COOKBOOK

Spit-Roasted Kid

Jare na Ražnju

The technique for fixing a whole animal to a spit is demonstrated on pages 80-83.

Young mountain kid roasted over vine prunings is considered an excellent Serbian dish. Serve with a variety of salads.

To make the fire, dig a rectangular pit and fill it with vine branches at least 20 cm (8 inches) above the level of the soil. Ignite the wood and, as soon as the flames have died down, add more branches until you have an even layer of wood embers about 20 cm (8 inches) thick.

	To serve 8 to 10	
1	kid (about 3 weeks old), skinned and gutted	1
	salt	
250 g	lard, melted	8 oz

Season the kid with salt and thrust a spit lengthwise through the carcass. Roast the kid over the embers of the fire, rotating the spit slowly and evenly all the time. A second person should brush the meat quite frequently with water and the melted lard. When the kid is well cooked and browned all over, in 3 to 4 hours, remove it from the fire and serve at once.

SPASENIJA-PATA MARKOVIĆ (EDITOR)
VELIKI NARODNI KUVAR

Smoked Stuffed Lamb Shoulder

The technique of smoking meat is shown on page 86.

	To serve 6 to 8	
One 2 to 2.5 kg	shoulder of lamb, boned	One 4 to 5 lb
750 g	pork sausage-meat (*page 166*)	1½ lb
1	medium-sized onion, chopped	1
1	garlic clove, finely chopped	1
1 tbsp	finely chopped parsley	1 tbsp

Combine the sausage-meat, onion, garlic and parsley, and mix well. Flatten the meat and spread the sausage-meat mixture over the lamb. Roll up the meat tightly and secure it with string or skewers. Place the meat in a smoker and cook it for 8 to 10 hours or until a meat thermometer inserted into the centre of the meat registers 75°C (170°F). Let the meat stand for 20 minutes before slicing it.

ROSE CANTRELL
CREATIVE OUTDOOR COOKING

Leg of Lamb in Foil

Arni ala Pallakari

The author recommends that you use black olives from Kala-mata, in southern Greece, as they are particularly large and well flavoured. They are available from Greek food shops.

To serve 4 or 5

One 2 to 2.5 kg	leg of lamb	One 4 to 5 lb
	salt and pepper	
2	garlic cloves, finely chopped	2
165 g	butter	5½ oz
1 kg	pearl onions, parboiled for 5 minutes	2 lb
2 tbsp	chopped parsley	2 tbsp
2 tbsp	chopped fresh mint	2 tbsp
¼ litre	dry white wine	8 fl oz
12.5 cl	olive oil	4 fl oz
2	lemons, juice strained	2
1 tbsp	chopped fresh oregano	1 tbsp
1	bunch watercress	1
250 g	tomatoes, halved	8 oz
12	black olives, stoned	12

Rub the lamb with salt, pepper and the garlic. Melt 125 g (4 oz) of the butter in a deep pan and brown the lamb gently until it is crisp on all sides. Remove the lamb and strain and reserve the butter. Brush a large double sheet of aluminium foil with butter and place the lamb in the centre. Meanwhile, sauté the parboiled onions until golden-brown in the remaining butter with the parsley, mint, salt and pepper.

Surround the lamb with the onions and brush the pan juices from the onions and the reserved butter over the leg. Pour the wine, oil and lemon juice over the lamb; sprinkle with the oregano. Fold the foil round the lamb and seal tightly. Place the sealed foil parcel on a rack over the charcoal and roast for about 3 hours or until the lamb is cooked to your liking. Serve the lamb in its foil on a platter surrounded by the watercress and the tomato halves topped with the olives.

EVA ZANE
GREEK COOKING FOR THE GODS

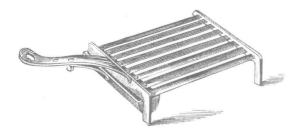

Grilled Marinated Pork Chops

To serve 4

4	pork rib or loin chops, 2.5 cm (1 inch) thick, trimmed of fat	4
12.5 cl	olive oil	4 fl oz
12.5 cl	white wine vinegar	4 fl oz
1	garlic clove, finely chopped	1
1	bay leaf, crumbled	1
2	black peppercorns, coarsely crushed	2
¼ tsp	dry mustard	¼ tsp
½ tsp	salt	½ tsp
⅓ tsp	pepper	⅓ tsp

Place the chops in a shallow dish. Combine all the other ingredients and pour the mixture over the chops. Cover the dish and marinate the chops in the refrigerator overnight or all day, turning them occasionally.

When you are ready to use the chops, drain them and place them on a grill over hot charcoal. Cook them, turning once, until they are tender, about 15 minutes. Serve immediately.

LOUISE SHERMAN SCHOON AND CORINNE HARDESTY
THE COMPLETE PORK COOKBOOK

Outdoor Pork Chops with Roasted Apples

To serve 8

8	pork loin or shoulder chops, 2.5 cm (1 inch) thick, trimmed of fat	8
12.5 cl	vegetable or olive oil	4 fl oz
2 tsp	salt	2 tsp
1 tsp	crushed sage leaves	1 tsp
1 tsp	crushed rosemary	1 tsp
1 tsp	ground ginger	1 tsp
1 tbsp	paprika	1 tbsp
1 tsp	pepper	1 tsp
8	large apples	8

Combine the oil, salt, sage, rosemary, ginger, paprika and pepper to make a marinade. Brush the chops generously with the marinade and leave them to stand for 1 hour. Grill them on a rack 12.5 cm (5 inches) above the coals for 35 minutes, or until cooked through. Brush the chops frequently with the marinade and turn once half way through the cooking time.

While the chops are cooking, roast the apples by skewering them on the tips of long skewers and holding them over the fire. Cook them, turning frequently, for 15 to 20 minutes. The apples should be golden-brown on the outside, hot and juicy and slightly soft inside.

THE OAKS II COLLECTION

Barbecued Spareribs from Canton

Chinese five-spice powder is a blend of equal parts of finely ground anise-pepper, star anise, cassia, cloves and fennel seeds. It can be bought from shops specializing in Chinese foods, as can hoisin sauce, rice wine and Chinese oyster sauce.

To serve 4

1.5 kg	lean pork spareribs, excess fat and membrane removed, cut in half crosswise, bony ends cracked	3 lb
4 tbsp	*hoisin* sauce	4 tbsp
60 g	sugar	2 oz
1 tbsp	rice wine or dry sherry	1 tbsp
1 tbsp	Chinese oyster sauce	1 tbsp
½ tsp	Chinese five-spice powder	½ tsp

Combine the *hoisin* sauce, sugar, rice wine or dry sherry, oyster sauce and five-spice powder. Rub the pieces of meat with this mixture and marinate for at least 4 hours. Set the spareribs over a drip pan on a rack placed 15 to 20 cm (6 to 8 inches) above medium-hot coals and grill them, turning occasionally, until they are browned, about 30 to 40 minutes.

MARGARET GIN AND ALFRED E. CASTLE
REGIONAL COOKING OF CHINA

Pork in Vermouth

Varkentje in Vermouth

To serve 4

8 to 12	pork spareribs, or 4 thick pork shoulder chops	8 to 12
12.5 cl	red vermouth	4 fl oz
12.5 cl	dry white vermouth	4 fl oz
½ tsp	lemon juice	½ tsp
½ litre	olive oil	16 fl oz
3	onions, finely chopped	3
4	garlic cloves, crushed	4
½ tsp	dried oregano	½ tsp
1	sweet red pepper, seeded and chopped	1
2 tsp	salt	2 tsp
	pepper	
1 tbsp	potato flour (optional)	1 tbsp

Place the pork in an earthenware bowl. Combine all the remaining ingredients, except the potato flour, and pour this marinade over the pork. Leave the meat to marinate for 4

hours, turning it occasionally.

Grill the spareribs or chops about 12.5 cm (5 inches) from a medium heat until they are nicely browned—about 7 minutes on each side. Baste occasionally with the marinade.

If you wish, heat the remaining marinade with the potato flour for 10 minutes or until thickened, and serve as a sauce.

HUGH JANS
VRIJ NEDERLAND

Pork Chops with Cold Green Chili Sauce

To serve 4

8	pork loin chops	8
3 tbsp	chili powder	3 tbsp
3 tbsp	tomato juice	3 tbsp
4	garlic cloves, crushed	4
1 tsp	salt	1 tsp
	dried oregano	
	Cold green chili sauce	
3	tomatoes, skinned, seeded and chopped	3
60 g	spring onions, chopped	2 oz
45 g	green chili peppers, seeded and chopped	1½ oz
2	pickled *jalapeño* chili peppers, seeded and finely chopped	2
1	garlic clove, crushed	1
2 tbsp	finely chopped parsley	2 tbsp
1 tsp	dried coriander leaves, soaked in 1 tbsp hot water, then drained	1 tsp
½ tsp	salt	½ tsp
	black pepper	
	sugar	

Combine the chili powder, tomato juice, garlic cloves, salt and a pinch of oregano to make a paste and spread the paste over both sides of each chop. Leave the chops to marinate overnight in the refrigerator.

To make the sauce, combine the chopped vegetables with the garlic and parsley, and add the soaked coriander, the salt and a pinch each of pepper and sugar. Chill the sauce for at least 1 hour before serving.

Grill the chops over hot coals, turning once, for about 20 minutes. Serve them with the cold chili sauce.

RONALD JOHNSON
THE AFICIONADO'S SOUTHWESTERN COOKING

Pork and Apple Skewers from Vierville

Brochettes de Vierville

To serve 6

1.5 kg	boneless pork shoulder, cut into 36 2 cm (¾ inch) cubes	3 lb
4	apples, each peeled, cored and cut into 8 pieces	4
1	onion, thinly sliced	1
½ tsp	dried thyme	½ tsp
1	bay leaf, crumbled	1
2 tbsp	calvados	2 tbsp
2 tbsp	oil	2 tbsp
	salt	
	crushed black peppercorns	
12.5 cl	double cream, warmed and lightly salted	4 fl oz

Combine the pork cubes, apple pieces, onion, thyme, crumbled bay leaf, calvados and oil, and leave to marinate for 30 minutes. Skewer the meat and apples and grill them over hot charcoal. First sear the meat very well on all sides by placing the skewers very, very close to the coals. Then raise the grill rack 12.5 cm (5 inches) above the coals and cook for another 15 to 20 minutes, turning the skewers at regular intervals.

As soon as they are cooked, place the skewers on a long platter. Season the meat and apples highly with salt and crushed black peppercorns, and dribble the warmed double cream over them.

MADELEINE KAMMAN
DINNER AGAINST THE CLOCK

Pork and Prune Skewers

To serve 2

350 g	boneless pork shoulder, cut into 12 2 cm (¾ inch) cubes	12 oz
10	prunes, soaked in warm water for 4 hours and stoned	10
2 tbsp	corn oil	2 tbsp
1 tsp	lemon juice	1 tsp
½ tsp	finely grated lemon rind	½ tsp

Mix the pork cubes and the prunes. Mix the corn oil, lemon juice and lemon rind. Roll the pork and prunes in the corn oil mixture and leave them to stand for 10 minutes or so. Without

drying them, thread the pork and prunes alternately on to two skewers. Sear the meat well on all sides, very close to the coals, then raise the grill rack 12.5 cm (5 inches) above the coals and cook for 15 minutes more, turning the skewers several times so that the meat browns evenly.

MADELEINE KAMMAN
DINNER AGAINST THE CLOCK

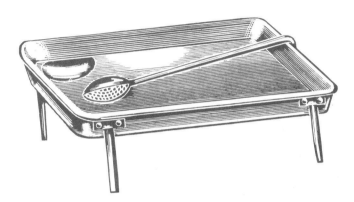

Skewered Asparagus with Pork

Yachae Sanjuk

As a variation on this recipe, the author suggests using beef instead of the pork.

To serve 4

125 g	lean boneless pork, cut into strips 1 cm (½ inch) wide and 7.5 cm (3 inches) long	4 oz
12	asparagus stalks, hard ends trimmed	12
1	garlic clove, crushed	1
1 tsp	sesame seed oil	1 tsp
1 tsp	sesame seeds	1 tsp
½ tsp	salt	½ tsp
	black pepper	

Parboil the asparagus stalks for about 5 minutes or until crunchy. Drain and set them aside. In a large bowl, combine the garlic with the sesame seed oil, sesame seeds, salt and a dash of black pepper. Add the asparagus and the pork strips and mix them well until the pork is coated on all sides with the sauce. Thread the pork and asparagus alternately on to four small skewers. Grill the skewers over medium-hot coals for 10 minutes or until the pork is well done.

JUDY HYUN
THE KOREAN COOKBOOK

Mixed Grill, Woodcutter's-Style

Il Piatto del Boscaiolo

To make polenta, sprinkle about 250 g (8 oz) of cornmeal into a pan containing about twice its volume of boiling salted water. Add the grain slowly, so that the water remains on the boil. As soon as you have added all the cornmeal, lower the heat and stir the polenta with a wooden spoon. Continue to cook the polenta, stirring continuously, for about 30 minutes. Each time it becomes too solid to stir, thin it by pouring in a ladleful of boiling water. When the polenta has acquired an elastic texture and comes away from the sides of the pan, turn it out on to a smooth work surface. Flatten it out to a thickness of about 1 cm ($\frac{1}{2}$ inch) and smooth the surface. Leave it to cool for at least 20 minutes, then cut it into squares with a sharp knife.

To serve 6

6	small pork cutlets, pounded until thin and halved	6
12	mushrooms, wiped with a damp cloth, stems separated from caps and trimmed	12
6	Italian pork sausages, halved	6
12	small squares of cooked polenta	12
	melted butter	
	salt and pepper	
4 tbsp	olive oil mixed with a little chopped rosemary	4 tbsp

Wrap each pork cutlet half round a mushroom stem, then thread them on to skewers with the mushroom caps and the sausages, alternating the ingredients.

Place the skewers on a very hot grill rack. Grill the skewers slowly about 15 cm (6 inches) from the heat for about 30 minutes, turning them frequently so that the meats cook evenly. While the skewers are cooking, sprinkle the polenta squares with a little melted butter and toast them on both sides until they are crisp.

Season the skewers with salt and pepper and serve them very hot, sprinkled with a little rosemary-flavoured oil and accompanied by the slices of toasted polenta.

FEAST OF ITALY

Country-Style Sausages

Botifarres o Salsitxes a la Pagesenca

Butifarras *(called* botifarres *in Catalan) are a speciality of Catalonia, in Spain. They are sausages made from pork, flavoured with white wine, garlic and spices. Black butifarras also include pig's blood. Each sausage is usually about*

12.5 cm (5 inches) long. They can be bought from shops that specialize in Spanish food.

Serve this dish accompanied by a good salad.

To serve 4

4	fresh *butifarras*, white or black, pricked with a fork	4
4	large potatoes, scrubbed but not peeled	4
8	field mushrooms	8
	salt	
4 tbsp	oil	4 tbsp
2	garlic cloves, chopped	2
4 tbsp	chopped parsley	4 tbsp
12.5 cl	*aïoli (page 163)*	4 fl oz

Bury the potatoes in the ashes of the fire and bake them for about 1$\frac{1}{2}$ hours. Place the *butifarras* close together on a rack over the hot coals or embers and cook them gently so that they remain whole. Turn them several times; they will take about 10 minutes to cook.

Sprinkle the mushrooms with salt, and with the oil, garlic and parsley, then grill them for about 7 minutes.

When the potatoes are cooked, cut them in half lengthwise and place them in a dish. Sprinkle them with salt. Put the *butifarras* in another dish, with a thin line of *aïoli* along each one, and arrange the field mushrooms by their side.

IGNASI DOMENECH
APATS

Sausages and Cheese in a Bag with Potatoes

Cervelas e Formaggio al Cartoccio con Patate

To serve 4

Four 100 g	*cervelas* or spiced pork sausages	Four 3$\frac{1}{2}$ oz
200 g	Gruyère cheese, rind removed	7 oz
1 tbsp	olive oil	1 tbsp
4	potatoes, scrubbed but not peeled	4

Slice the cheese about 5 mm ($\frac{1}{4}$ inch) thick, and cut it into 24 squares. Make six deep, crosswise cuts in each sausage, without slicing through completely. Place a square of cheese in each cut. Oil four sheets of foil and wrap a sausage in each sheet, closing up the ends tightly. Wrap the potatoes in foil.

Place the wrapped potatoes in the embers of the fire. After 20 minutes, place the wrapped sausages in the embers. Cook for 20 minutes and serve hot.

ANNA BASLINI ROSSELLI
100 RICETTE PER LA COLAZIONE SULL'ERBA

Roast Loin of Pork

Àrista di Maiale Arrosto

To serve 6 to 8

About 2 kg	loin of pork	About 4 lb
1	sprig fresh rosemary, leaves finely chopped, or 1 tsp finely chopped dried rosemary	1
2	garlic cloves, finely chopped	2
	salt and freshly ground pepper	

Combine the chopped rosemary and garlic with a teaspoon of salt and plenty of pepper.

With a small, sharp knife, make holes in the meat, going as close as possible to the bone. Insert some of the rosemary and garlic mixture into these holes, then sprinkle the outside of the meat with additional salt and pepper.

Skewer the meat on a spit and cook, turning, for about 2 hours or until the juices run clear when the meat is pierced. Serve hot or cold and carve carefully around the bones.

WILMA PEZZINI
THE TUSCAN COOKBOOK

Barbecued Pig

Lechón Asado

If Seville oranges are not available, use sweet oranges and sharpen the juice with 1 tablespoon of lemon juice. Annatto oil is made from annatto seeds, a pungent spice that imparts an orange colour to food; the seeds can be bought in shops specializing in Caribbean or South-East Asian foods. To make the oil, heat ½ litre (16 fl oz) of vegetable oil in a small saucepan; add 150 g (5 oz) of annatto seeds and cook them over a low heat for 5 minutes, stirring occasionally. Cool the liquid and strain it before use. The technique of fixing a whole pig to a spit is shown on pages 80-83.

In Puerto Rica, barbecued pig is the customary dish for picnics and other open-air parties. It is cooked over an open fire of charcoal built on layers of stone. Green plantains are peeled and roasted over the stones, to be eaten with the pig.

To serve 12 to 15

One 11.5 kg	suckling pig, cleaned	One 25 lb
24	garlic cloves	24
3 tbsp	dried oregano leaves	3 tbsp
1 tbsp	black peppercorns	1 tbsp
200 g	salt	7 oz
12.5 cl	Seville orange juice	4 fl oz
½ litre	annatto oil	16 fl oz

	Aji-li-mójili sauce	
8	large garlic cloves	8
8	black peppercorns	8
12	fresh chili peppers, seeded	12
12.5 cl	vinegar	4 fl oz
12.5 cl	lime juice	4 fl oz
4 tsp	salt	4 tsp
¼ litre	olive oil	8 fl oz

Crush and mix in a mortar the garlic cloves, oregano leaves, peppercorns and salt. Add the Seville orange juice and mix thoroughly. Make deep gashes on the pig's neck, under the lower jaw, on the loin, legs, shoulders and over the ribs. Rub the orange juice seasoning into the gashes and all over the inside and outside of the pig. Cover the pig with muslin and leave it overnight in a cool place.

Barbecue the pig in the traditional way, by passing a pole through its body. Tie the front legs very tightly round the pole. Do the same with the hind legs, stretching them as far as possible. Place the pig over an open fire of live charcoal placed over layers of stone, resting both ends of the pole on Y-posts. Rotate the pole constantly and slowly in order to roast the pig evenly. Baste it frequently with annatto oil. Cook the pig for about 7 hours or until the meat is well done, when all pink colour has disappeared and the meat becomes almost white.

To prepare the sauce, crush the garlic, peppercorns and chili peppers together in a mortar, then stir in the vinegar, lime juice, salt and olive oil. Mix thoroughly. Cut the roasted pig into serving pieces and serve it with the sauce.

CARMEN ABOY VALLDEJULI
PUERTO RICAN COOKERY

Serbian Meat Rolls

Serbischer Cevapcici

To serve 4

500 g	minced beef	1 lb
250 g	minced pork	8 oz
	salt and pepper	
	chopped onions	

Mix together the minced meats. Add plenty of salt and some pepper and work the mixture together well with your hands. Fashion small sausage-shaped rolls—5 cm (2 inches) long and the width of a finger—from the mixture. Grill the rolls quickly for about 6 minutes, turning them frequently so that they brown evenly. Serve the rolls with chopped onions.

MARIA HORVATH
BALKAN-KÜCHE

Cypriot Meat Rolls

Sheftalia

	To serve 4	
250 g	minced lamb	8 oz
250 g	minced pork	8 oz
1	large onion, finely chopped	1
1 tsp	finely chopped oregano	1 tsp
2 tbsp	finely chopped parsley	2 tbsp
	salt and pepper	
125 g	lamb's caul, rinsed, cut into 12 pieces	4 oz

Mix the meats, onion and herbs together in a bowl. Season with salt and pepper. Shape the mixture into 12 small rolls and wrap each roll separately in a piece of caul. Place the rolls on a wire rack over hot coals and grill them for 5 minutes, turning them frequently so that they brown evenly.

ANDREAS POUROUNAS
APHRODITE'S COOKBOOK

Grilled Hamburger

Yuk Sanjuk Kui

Bean curd is a soft white cake made from ground soy beans. It is available from health food and Oriental food shops. It should be stored in the refrigerator, covered in cold water; it will not keep for longer than a day or so. If it is unavailable, the author suggests substituting 60 g (2 oz) of breadcrumbs.

	To serve 2 to 4	
125 g	lean beef, minced	4 oz
125 g	lean pork, minced	4 oz
2	garlic cloves, crushed	2
1	spring onion, finely chopped	1
60 g	bean curd, diced	2 oz
1 tsp	sesame seeds	1 tsp
2 tsp	sesame seed oil	2 tsp
½ tsp	salt	½ tsp
1 tbsp	sugar	1 tbsp
	pepper	

In a bowl, combine the meat with the rest of the ingredients. Mix well. Shape the mixture into six flat hamburger patties. Grill the hamburgers over hot charcoal for 10 to 15 minutes, turning them once.

JUDY HYUN
THE KOREAN COOKBOOK

Belgrade Meat Dumplings with Onions

Belgrader Pljeskavica

The technique of skinning sweet peppers is shown on page 19.

	To serve 4	
350 g	boneless lean pork, minced	12 oz
350 g	boneless lean veal, minced	12 oz
4	onions, finely chopped	4
1	sweet red pepper, skinned, seeded and finely chopped	1
	salt and pepper	

Mix the pork and veal with 1 tablespoon of the chopped onion and the red pepper, and add salt and pepper. Mix well with your hands, then leave the mixture for 1 to 2 hours.

Form the mixture into small flat patties. Cook them quickly over a hot grill, for about 5 minutes on each side, or until they are evenly browned on both sides.

To serve, heap the remaining chopped onion in the middle of a flat dish and arrange the meat dumplings round the edge.

MARIA HORVATH
BALKAN-KÜCHE

Meat Cooked on a Tile

Carn a la Llosa

Butifarras, a Catalan speciality, are sausages made from pork flavoured with white wine, garlic and spices. They can be bought in shops specializing in Spanish food. Red pine mushrooms are found in the woods of Catalonia and Mallorca; large field mushrooms can be substituted. A large fireproof earthenware dish can be used instead of the tile.

	To serve 4	
4	lamb chops	4
4	*butifarras*	4
250 g	streaky bacon rashers	8 oz
3	garlic cloves, chopped	3
8	red pine mushrooms	8
30 cl	*aïoli (page 163)*	½ pint

Take a large earthenware tile and cover it liberally with bacon and garlic. Prepare a charcoal fire, place the tile on top and heat it until it becomes extremely hot—this will take about 30 minutes. When the tile is at the right temperature, place the chops, *butifarras* and mushrooms on it and grill them for 15 minutes, turning so that they cook evenly. Serve with the *aïoli*.

M. DEL CARME NICOLAU
CUINA CATALANA

Ukrainian Shashlik

To serve 6

250 g	lean salt pork or smoked bacon, cut into 2 to 2.5 cm (¾ to 1 inch) cubes	8 oz
250 g	fillet of beef, cut into 2 to 2.5 cm (¾ to 1 inch) cubes	8 oz
250 g	fillet of veal, cut into 2 to 2.5 cm (¾ to 1 inch) cubes	8 oz
250 g	fillet of pork, cut into 2 to 2.5 cm (¾ to 1 inch) cubes	8 oz
6	kidneys, fat and membranes removed, halved and cored	6
	freshly ground black pepper	
	paprika	
	salt	
12	spring onions, halved lengthwise	12
2 or 3	lemons, cut into wedges	2 or 3
3 or 4	tomatoes, cut into wedges	3 or 4

Thread the cubes of meat on skewers, alternating the different kinds of meat. Sprinkle with pepper and paprika and grill over hot coals for 15 minutes or until cooked through, turning often. Season the meats with salt before serving, and garnish with spring onions and wedges of lemon and tomato.

BARBARA NORMAN
THE RUSSIAN COOKBOOK

Mixed Skewered Meat

Raznjici

This is the Yugoslav version of the kebab or shish kebab. If it is served as a main course, allow two skewers per person.

To serve 8 to 10

500 g	lean boneless beef steak, cut into 2.5 cm (1 inch) cubes	1 lb
500 g	lean boneless lamb, cut into 2.5 cm (1 inch) cubes	1 lb
	salt and pepper	
5 tbsp	melted bacon fat	5 tbsp
2 tbsp	oil	2 tbsp
1 or 2	onions, chopped	1 or 2

Thread the cubes of meat, alternating beef and lamb, on to small skewers. Season them with salt and pepper. Heat the bacon fat and the oil in a small saucepan. When the mixture is warm, brush it over the meat and begin to grill the meat slowly over hot charcoal. Cook the meat for 15 to 20 minutes, brushing the cubes frequently with fat and turning the skewers so that the meat cooks evenly. Serve chopped onion separately on each plate.

MARIA KOZSLIK DONOVAN
THE BLUE DANUBE COOKBOOK

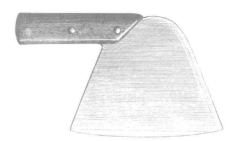

Mixed Roast-on-a-Spit

Il Girato Misto

The recipe below is not a definitive one. Many different meats can be used, and there are countless variations. Keep in mind that meats cooked on the same spit should need about the same cooking time. Serve the meats with a crisp, fresh salad.

To serve 4 to 6

500 g	pork tenderloin, cut into 8 large pieces	1 lb
1	guinea fowl, cleaned, washed and cut into 8 pieces	1
4	thick slices white bread, quartered	4
4	Italian pork sausages, halved	4
	salt and freshly ground black pepper	
8	fresh sage leaves	8
	olive oil	

About 1 hour before cooking time, build a strong fire with large pieces of fragrant wood. Sprinkle the pork, guinea fowl, bread and sausages generously with salt and pepper.

When most of the wood has burned to embers, start filling two spits. Skewer a piece of bread, then a piece of guinea fowl with a leaf of sage, a piece of bread, a piece of pork, a piece of sausage and so on until everything is used up. Brush everything generously with olive oil, put the spits into their slots near the fire and start turning them slowly. Baste repeatedly with olive oil.

After about 40 minutes, stop the spits and check if the guinea fowl, pork and sausages are cooked. If so, remove everything from the spits and serve at once.

WILMA PEZZINI
THE TUSCAN COOKBOOK

Mixed Meat and Poultry Roasted on a Spit

Arrosto Girato alla Fiorentina

Good, home-made white bread can be substituted for the Tuscan bread in this recipe. If a large spit is not available, the ingredients can be threaded on more than one spit.

A huge spit over a roaring fire of wood or charcoal is one of the trademarks of the Italian country villas. The spit has given its name, *girarrosto*, to a kind of restaurant in which specialities such as this dish are served. In Italy, a special pan called a *ghiotta* is placed under the spit itself. Potatoes are put in the *ghiotta* to cook so they can collect the delicious drippings from the meat cooking above on the spit. These *patate alla ghiotta* accompany the dish.

The bread commonly used for this dish is a Tuscan bread shaped in the form of a very long loaf, 3.5 cm (1½ inches) thick and baked for only 35 minutes. Because of its short baking time, the bread does not form a crust and retains a whitish colour, even if the dough is made with wholewheat flour.

To serve 12

850 g	loin of pork, cut into 12 pieces	1¾ lb
One 1.75kg	chicken, cut into 12 pieces	One 3½ lb
3	pigeons, quartered	3
12	spiced pork sausages, pricked with a fork	12
12	quail, drawn	12
12 to 14	bay leaves, halved	12 to 14
18 to 24	fresh sage leaves, halved	18 to 24
500 g	Tuscan bread, cut into pieces 2.5 cm (1 inch) wide and 1 cm (½ inch) thick	1 lb
	salt and freshly ground black pepper	
¼ litre	olive oil	8 fl oz
Fegatelli alla fiorentina (optional)		
150 g	caul	5 oz
45 g	fresh white breadcrumbs	1½ oz
2 tbsp	fennel seeds	2 tbsp
	salt and pepper	
500 g	pork liver, cut into 12 pieces	1 lb
6	bay leaves, halved	6

To make the *fegatelli*, if used, soak the caul in a small bowl of lukewarm water for 10 minutes. Meanwhile, combine the breadcrumbs, fennel seeds and a pinch each of salt and pepper in a large bowl and mix well. Carefully open the caul and spread it out on a board. Cut it into 12 pieces. Put the liver pieces into a large bowl and mix them well with the breadcrumb mixture. Place each piece of liver on top of a piece of caul. Add half a bay leaf to each piece and wrap the liver and bay leaf completely in caul. Secure with a toothpick until the *fegatelli* are safely threaded on to the spit.

Now thread the meats on to the spit in the following order: chicken piece, half a bay leaf, bread; pork loin piece, half a sage leaf, bread; pigeon quarter, half a bay leaf, bread; sausage, half a sage leaf, bread; quail, half a bay leaf, bread and, if using *fegatello*, half a sage leaf, bread. Continue until the spit is full. The bay leaves and sage leaves should alternate, but it does not matter which is next to which meat.

Season freely with salt and pepper and place the spit over a charcoal fire (the charcoal should be grey and there should be no flames). Cook the *arrosto* very slowly for about 1 hour, sprinkling the meat every so often with salt and brushing with the olive oil. When it is ready, remove the *arrosto* from the spit and serve immediately.

GIULIANO BUGIALLI
THE FINE ART OF ITALIAN COOKING

Tuscan Mixed Grill

The author suggests that you serve this dish with a rice pilaff (recipe, page 165) tossed with raisins which have first been plumped up by soaking in hot water.

To serve 6

6	small slices loin of pork	6
6	small pieces boned chicken	6
6	slices pig's liver	6
6	small lamb cutlets	6
12	rashers lean bacon, halved	12
24	fresh sage leaves	24
2	sprigs rosemary, ground in a mortar	2
	salt and freshly ground pepper	
6 to 8 tbsp	olive oil	6 to 8 tbsp
3 or 4	juniper berries, crushed, or ½ tsp fennel seeds, bruised	3 or 4

Thread a slice of pork, a piece of chicken, a slice of liver and a lamb cutlet on to each of six skewers, interspersing each piece of meat with a bacon strip and a sage leaf. Sprinkle the skewers with the rosemary and pepper.

Place the skewers side by side in a shallow baking dish and pour the olive oil over them. Add the juniper berries (or fennel seeds) and marinate for 3 to 4 hours.

Grill the skewers over charcoal, turning frequently, for about 15 minutes or until the meats are cooked but still juicy. Sprinkle with salt before serving.

JANA ALLEN AND MARGARET GIN
"OFFAL" GOURMET COOKERY FROM HEAD TO TAIL

Giant Mixed Grill on Skewers

Mixed Grill en Brochettes "Gargantua"

	To serve 4	
600 g	boneless lean loin of veal, cut across the grain into slices 1 cm (½ inch) thick	1¼ lb
500 g	beef fillet, cut across the grain into slices 1 cm (½ inch) thick	1 lb
350 g	boneless lean loin of lamb, cut across the grain into slices 1 cm (½ inch) thick	12 oz
6	thick rashers bacon	6
2	sweet green peppers, seeded, blanched in boiling water for 1 minute	2
2	onions, thinly sliced	2
8	bay leaves, halved	8
	salt and freshly ground black pepper	
	dried thyme and oregano	
	Herb marinade	
35 cl	olive oil	12 fl oz
2	sprigs thyme or ½ tsp dried thyme	2
2	bay leaves	2
1	sprig rosemary or ¼ tsp dried rosemary	1
¼ tsp	crushed black peppercorns	¼ tsp

Cut the meats, bacon and sweet green peppers into 2.5 cm (1 inch) squares. Thread the meat, vegetables and bay leaves on to four very long skewers as follows: one slice of sweet green pepper; one slice of beef; one slice of onion; one slice of veal; one slice of sweet green pepper; one slice of bacon; half a bay leaf; one slice of lamb; one slice of bacon; one slice of onion. Repeat the sequence three or four times for each skewer, pushing the meat close together.

Make the marinade by mixing the oil with the herbs and the peppercorns. Using a brush, coat the skewered meat and vegetables carefully with marinade. Leave the skewers on a rack for 15 to 20 minutes to allow the excess oil to drain off.

Sprinkle the skewers with a few pinches of dried thyme and oregano and grill them over a medium heat, turning them once only, until the meats have browned nicely—about 10 minutes on each side.

LOUISETTE BERTHOLLE (EDITOR)
SECRETS OF THE GREAT FRENCH RESTAURANTS

Poultry and Game

Grilled Poussins

Pollos a la Parrilla

Serve the poussins in a large dish with a good lettuce or endive salad and accompany it with a highly seasoned sauce served in a sauceboat.

	To serve 6	
3	poussins or very small chickens	3
	salt	
	oil	
15 g	butter	½ oz
1 tsp	mustard	1 tsp
	dry white breadcrumbs	

Clean the poussins and split them in half, lengthwise, crushing them gently with a long, heavy knife to break the bones so that they lie flat on the rack whilst cooking. Season the pieces with salt and brush them well with oil. Place them on a very hot grill and cook them for about 10 minutes on each side, or until cooked through. Mix together the butter and mustard to form a paste. Spread the paste all over the cooked poussins and dust them with the breadcrumbs. Return them to the grill to cook for another 2 minutes, or until browned.

MAGDALENA ALPERI
TRATADO COMPLETO DE COMIDAS Y BEBIDAS

Tex-Mex Chicken Galveston-Style

	To serve 4	
One 1.75 to 2 kg	chicken, backbone removed, split in half lengthwise	One 3½ to 4 lb
1	lemon, halved	1
6	garlic cloves, finely chopped	6
1 tbsp	cayenne pepper	1 tbsp
2 tbsp	paprika	2 tbsp

Rub each piece of chicken well on both sides with half a lemon. Rub each piece with garlic, then with cayenne pepper and paprika. Place the pieces, breast side up, in a shallow baking dish and leave to stand, uncovered, in a cool place (but do not refrigerate) for 24 hours.

Place the chicken halves, skin side down, on a rack high above the coals of a covered grill. Cover and grill, turning the chicken several times, until tender—about 1½ hours.

BERT GREENE
HONEST AMERICAN FARE

Devilled Grilled Chicken

Pollo alla Diavola

Serve the chicken hot with salad and baked or fried potatoes.

	To serve 2 to 4	
1	small chicken, halved, each piece pounded flat	1
3 tbsp	olive oil	3 tbsp
1	lemon, juice strained	1
1	garlic clove, crushed	1
1	bay leaf, crumbled	1
1	sprig fresh rosemary, leaves finely chopped, or 1 tsp finely chopped dried rosemary	1
	salt and pepper	

Make a marinade with all the ingredients except the chicken, whisking well to incorporate the oil. Put the chicken into the marinade for 2 hours and turn it over after 1 hour.

Take the chicken out of the marinade and put it on the grill rack. Allow it to cook, basting with the marinade, for about 20 minutes on each side, or until the juices from the thigh run clear when the chicken is pierced.

WILMA PEZZINI
THE TUSCAN COOKBOOK

Grilled Chicken Kyushu-Style

Toriniku No Nanbanyaki

If mirin *is unobtainable, sherry can be substituted.*

	To serve 4	
1	chicken, jointed	1
3 tbsp	sake	3 tbsp
1½ tbsp	mirin	1½ tbsp
4 tbsp	soy sauce	4 tbsp
3	spring onions, finely chopped	3
2	sweet red peppers, finely chopped or ¼ tsp cayenne pepper	2
1	egg yolk	1
1 tbsp	flour	1 tbsp

Mix together the *sake, mirin* and soy sauce and marinate the chicken pieces in this mixture for 15 minutes. Remove the chicken pieces from the marinade and add the spring onions and sweet peppers or cayenne pepper to the marinade with the egg yolk and flour. Beat the mixture until very smooth.

Grill the chicken pieces over medium-hot coals for about 10 minutes on each side. Remove them from the grill and brush them with the sauce, then return them to the grill. Continue cooking the chicken joints until they are done, about 30 minutes in all, brushing them three or four times on each side with the sauce. The addition of the egg yolk in the sauce will produce a very high glaze, but care must be taken not to cook the chicken over too hot a grill since the sauce burns easily.

PETER AND JOAN MARTIN
JAPANESE COOKING

Barbecued Chicken with Polynesian Barbecue Sauce

Kumquats resemble very tiny oranges and are eaten whole, including the rind. If they are unavailable, substitute one tangerine or one small orange, and include the rind.

	To serve 4	
Two 1 kg	chickens, cut into quarters	Two 2 to 2½ lb
4 tbsp	honey	4 tbsp
½	lemon, juice strained	½
6	kumquats, finely chopped	6
½ tsp	ground ginger	½ tsp
2 tbsp	grated orange rind	2 tbsp
4 tbsp	orange juice	4 tbsp
4 tbsp	soy sauce	4 tbsp
¼ tsp	freshly ground pepper	¼ tsp

Blend together the honey, lemon juice, kumquats, ginger, orange rind, orange juice, soy sauce and pepper. Pour this sauce over the chicken pieces and marinate them for 4 to 5 hours in the refrigerator, turning them once every hour.

Place your barbecue rack 15 to 20 cm (6 to 8 inches) above hot glowing coals. Grill the chicken, turning the pieces from time to time, until the juices flow clear when a thigh is pricked—about 45 minutes to 1 hour. Baste the pieces with the marinade during the las 15 minutes of cooking.

ANN CHANDONNET
THE COMPLETE FRUIT COOKBOOK

Chicken in East-West Sauce

This sauce was invented at the Yildizlar restaurant in Beirut. It freezes well. Serve the chicken with a green salad.

To serve 6

One 1.5 to 2 kg	chicken, jointed	One 3 to 4 lb
500 g	sweet red peppers, sliced and seeded	1 lb
125 g	fresh red chili peppers, sliced and seeded	4 oz
8 to 12.5 cl	olive oil	3 to 4 fl oz
1	large lemon, juice strained	1
	salt	

Cook the sweet red peppers and chili peppers in boiling salted water until tender, about 10 minutes, and then put them through the medium disc of a food mill, or purée them in a blender. Mix the olive oil and lemon juice into this hot purée and add extra salt if necessary. Leave to cool.

Rub the sauce over the chicken joints and leave to marinate overnight. Then grill the chicken with the sauce still on it, over hot charcoal, for about 40 minutes, turning once.

JANE GRIGSON
JANE GRIGSON'S VEGETABLE BOOK

Indian Barbecued Chicken

Tandoori Murghi

To serve 6

Three 1 kg	very young, tender chickens	Three 2 to 2¼ lb
1½	lemons, juice strained	1½
2	large garlic cloves	2
1 tbsp	chopped fresh ginger root	1 tbsp
1 tsp	ground roasted cumin seeds	1 tsp
½ tsp	ground cardamom	½ tsp
½ tsp	cayenne pepper	½ tsp
1 tbsp	paprika	1 tbsp
8 cl	yogurt	3 fl oz
	ghee or vegetable oil	

Cut the wings off the chickens. Remove the neck-bones carefully. Place the chickens on a cutting board and quarter them neatly. Then pull away the skin, using kitchen paper for a better grip if necessary. (Reserve the wings, neck and skin for the stock-pot.) Prick the chicken all over with a fork or a thin skewer. Make diagonal slashes, 1 cm (½ inch) deep and 2.5 cm (1 inch) apart, on the meat. Put the chicken in a large bowl.

Add the lemon juice to the chicken, and rub it into the slashes and all over for 2 minutes. Cover the bowl and

marinate the chicken for 30 minutes.

Put all the remaining ingredients except the *ghee* into a blender or food processor and blend until reduced to a smooth sauce. (Alternatively, the garlic and ginger may be crushed to a paste and blended with the remaining ingredients.)

Pour this marinade over the chicken pieces and mix, turning and tossing, to coat all the pieces well. Cover and marinate for 4 hours, or refrigerate for two days, turning several times. Take the chicken from the refrigerator at least 1 hour before cooking to bring it to room temperature. The chicken is now ready to be grilled.

Fire the charcoal well in advance (about 1½ hours before you are ready to begin cooking), so that a white ash forms over the surface of the charcoal. This is when the charcoal is at its hottest. Place the rack at least 12.5 cm (5 inches) away from the heat and rub it generously with oil. Place the chicken pieces, slashed side up, on the rack and brush them with *ghee* or vegetable oil. Let the chicken cook, without turning, for 10 minutes. Turn, baste the other side, and cook for 10 minutes. Continue to cook, turning and basting the chicken every 10 minutes, until it is done, 30 to 40 minutes.

JULIE SAHNI
CLASSIC INDIAN COOKING

Chicken Breasts in Red Sauce

Dak Kui

Red bean paste (kochu chang) is a sweet paste made from soy beans; it is sold in tins in Oriental food shops and will keep for months refrigerated in a covered jar.

To serve 2 to 4

2	chicken breasts, skinned, boned and halved	2
2	spring onions, finely chopped	2
3	garlic cloves, crushed	3
4 tsp	red bean paste	4 tsp
1 tbsp	sesame seed oil	1 tbsp
1 tbsp	sesame seeds	1 tbsp
1 tbsp	sugar	1 tbsp
1 tbsp	soy sauce	1 tbsp
	black pepper	

Flatten the chicken breasts by pounding them with the flat side of a heavy knife. Score the flesh diagonally across the grain. For the marinade, combine the remaining ingredients in a bowl; add the chicken breasts and mix well until the breasts are coated on all sides with the marinade. Grill the breasts over medium-hot coals for 5 minutes on each side. To serve, cut the breasts into 5 cm (2 inch) pieces.

JUDY HYUN
THE KOREAN COOKBOOK

Grilled Chicken Breast Rolls

Filets de Volaille en Crottes d'Ane

To serve 4

4	chicken breasts, boned	4
1½ tbsp	*fines herbes* (chopped parsley, chervil, chives and tarragon)	1½ tbsp
1 tbsp	finely chopped shallot	1 tbsp
	dried oregano	
90 to 125 g	mushrooms, finely chopped	3 to 4 oz
½	lemon, juice strained	½
About 3 tbsp olive oil		About 3 tbsp
	salt and coarsely ground pepper	

Remove the skin from the chicken breasts and trim them neatly, making certain that no fragments of bone remain. Each is composed of two muscles known as the fillet and the *filet-mignon*. They are connected only by a fragile membrane except at one edge. Open them out so that the opened breast is vaguely heart shaped, and flatten each one with the side of a large knife. Mix the *fines herbes*, shallot, a pinch of oregano, the mushrooms, lemon juice, 3 tablespoons of olive oil and pepper to aste on a platter. Spread the chicken breasts out on the platter. Marinate them for 1 hour, gently turning them round and over two or three times.

Salt the inside surface of each fillet lightly, spread it well with the chopped vegetables from the marinade and roll it up, holding it together with toothpicks. Salt the outside of each roll lightly, and grill the breasts on a preheated grill for 10 to 12 minutes, turning them every 2 to 3 minutes. They should be golden-brown. Baste the coloured surfaces regularly, adding more olive oil to the marinade if necessary.

RICHARD OLNEY
HOUSE AND GARDEN MAGAZINE

Chicken on a Spit

To serve 4

One 2 kg	chicken	One 4 lb
2 tsp	salt	2 tsp
2	medium-sized apples, peeled, cored and quartered	2
60 g	celery leaves	2 oz

Lemon basting sauce		
2 tsp	paprika	2 tsp
1 tsp	sugar	1 tsp
1 tsp	salt	1 tsp
½ tsp	black pepper	½ tsp
¼ tsp	dry mustard	¼ tsp
	cayenne pepper	
175 g	butter, melted	6 oz
12.5 cl	lemon juice	4 fl oz
12.5 cl	hot water	4 fl oz
	Tabasco sauce	
2 tbsp	grated onion (optional)	2 tbsp

Rub the cavity of the chicken with the salt and place the apple quarters and celery leaves in the cavity. To close the body cavity, sew it up or skewer it and lace it with string. Fasten the neck skin to the back with a skewer. Tie the wings to the body. Insert a spit through the chicken. Tie the drumsticks to the spit by looping string over the tip ends and round the spit. Be sure the chicken is well balanced.

To make the basting sauce, stir the paprika, sugar, salt, pepper, mustard and a small pinch of cayenne pepper into the melted butter. Blend in the lemon juice, hot water and a few drops of Tabasco, and the grated onion, if used.

Place the chicken over hot coals, with a drip pan underneath it. Cook the chicken for about 1½ hours or until the skin is well browned and beginning to split. Baste often to keep the skin moist and to add flavour. When the chicken is done, carve it and serve it with the remaining sauce, heated.

STAFF HOME ECONOMISTS, CULINARY ARTS INSTITUTE (EDITORS)
THE OUTDOOR GRILL BOOK

Egyptian Chicken Kebabs

To serve 6 to 8

4	large chicken breasts, skinned, boned and cut into 16 squares each	4
1 tbsp	yogurt	1 tbsp
¼ tsp	salt	¼ tsp
¼ tsp	ground turmeric	¼ tsp
½ tsp	curry powder	½ tsp
⅛ tsp	ground cardamom	⅛ tsp
1 tsp	lemon juice	1 tsp
1 tsp	vinegar	1 tsp
16	thin slices onion	16
8	small tomatoes, halved	8

Combine the yogurt, salt, turmeric, curry powder, cardamom, lemon juice and vinegar and marinate the squares of chicken in this mixture for at least 30 minutes. Thread the chicken, slices of onion and tomatoes on to skewers in the following order: two squares of chicken, one slice of onion, two squares of chicken, half a tomato. Repeat until all the ingredients have been used up. Grill the skewers over hot coals, 15 cm (6 inches) from the heat source, for 5 to 10 minutes, or until the chicken pieces are evenly browned.

JANE NOVAK
TREASURY OF CHICKEN COOKERY

Chicken on Skewers

Yakitori

If mirin *is unobtainable, sherry can be substituted.*

These delicious little titbits are hardly substantial enough for a full meal, but are an excellent accompaniment to drinks.

To serve 6

500 g	boned chicken, cut into bite-sized pieces	1 lb
6	chicken livers, halved or quartered	6
4	leeks, white part only, cut into 2.5 cm (1 inch) lengths	4
1	onion, cut into bite-sized pieces	1
2	sweet green peppers, seeded, cut into bite-sized pieces	2
1	garlic clove, finely chopped	1
2.5 cm	fresh ginger root, finely chopped	1 inch
12.5 cl	soy sauce	4 fl oz
4 tbsp	*mirin*	4 tbsp
4 tbsp	*sake*	4 tbsp
2 tsp	sugar	2 tsp
$\frac{1}{4}$ tsp	cayenne pepper	$\frac{1}{4}$ tsp

Arrange two of the chicken pieces and one each of the pieces of liver, leek, onion and sweet pepper on oiled metal or bamboo skewers, starting and ending with the chicken.

Put the chopped garlic and ginger into a small saucepan with the soy sauce, *mirin, sake,* sugar and cayenne pepper. Bring to the boil and pour over the skewered chicken; allow the skewers to marinate for 30 minutes. Heat the grill and, when it is hot, place the skewers over it, cooking them for 2 to 3 minutes on each side. Take them from the grill, dip them into the marinade again and grill them again until the chicken is done—about another 5 minutes.

PETER AND JOAN MARTIN
JAPANESE COOKING

Chicken Breasts and Livers on a Skewer

To serve 6

500 g	boned chicken breasts, cut into 3.5 cm (1½ inch) squares	1 lb
500 g	chicken livers, trimmed and halved	1 lb
6 tbsp	olive oil	6 tbsp
1	garlic clove, crushed	1
1 tbsp	chopped thyme, tarragon or rosemary	1 tbsp
	cherry tomatoes	

Mix together the oil, garlic and chopped herbs. Put the meat into a bowl, pour the flavoured oil over it and mix thoroughly. Drain the meat and reserve the oil. Alternate pieces of chicken and pieces of liver on skewers, adding cherry tomatoes as often as you like. Place a piece of perforated foil on the grill, over a very hot charcoal fire, as close to the coals as possible. Put the skewers on the foil and cook the meat rapidly, turning the skewers several times and basting them with the reserved flavoured oil. If the fire is hot enough, 10 to 15 minutes should be enough time to cook the meat. Serve at once.

MOLLY FINN
SUMMER FEASTS

Chicken Liver Kebabs

Spiedini di Fegatini di Pollo

To serve 6

1.2 kg	chicken livers, cleaned and halved or quartered	2¾ lb
50 g	butter, melted	2 oz
600 g	mushrooms, sliced	1¼ lb
50 g	dry breadcrumbs	2 oz

Heat half the butter in a frying pan, add the chicken livers and cook just until they have changed colour but are not cooked through—approximately 2 minutes. Toss the sliced mushrooms in the remaining butter. Thread the livers and mushrooms alternately on to skewers, roll them in the dry breadcrumbs, and grill over a moderate heat for 6 to 8 minutes, turning the skewers several times.

VINCENZO BUONASSISI
CUCINA ALL'ARIA APERTA

Goose Liver Shashlik

Szaszłykz Watróbek Gesich

To serve 4

500 g	goose livers	1 lb
100 g	pork fat or smoked bacon	3½ oz
100 g	onions, sliced	3½ oz
30 g	lard or butter, melted	1 oz
	salt and pepper	

Cut the livers into 24 slices about 4 cm (1½ inches) long. Slice the pork fat or bacon into 20 pieces of the same size.

Thread the livers on to four skewers, alternating them with the slices of onion and pork fat or bacon. Brush the skewers with the melted lard or butter. Grill the skewers over hot coals, turning frequently, for about 6 minutes, or until the livers are browned on the outside but still pink in the middle. Season the skewers with salt and pepper after 4 minutes. Serve them with boiled rice.

HELENA HAWLICZKOWA
KUCHNIA POLSKA

Roast Guinea Fowl

Perlhuhn vom Grill

Serve this dish with grilled tomatoes or grilled bananas. The guinea fowl can also be halved and cooked on the grill.

To serve 2

1	young guinea fowl, trussed	1
	salt	
	paprika	
4	sprigs parsley	4
60 g	butter, melted, or 4 tbsp oil	2 oz

Lightly salt the inside of the guinea fowl and rub paprika over the outside. Place the parsley sprigs in the cavity.

Thread the guinea fowl on to the spit. Baste it with melted butter or oil and cook it for 40 to 50 minutes, continuing to baste it often during the cooking time. It should be evenly browned and cooked through.

ILSE FROIDL
DAS GEFLÜGEL-KOCHBUCH

Guinea Fowl Roasted in Clay

Faraone à la Kreis

Modelling clay can be used to wrap the guinea fowl. It can be bought at shops selling artists' materials, and should be kneaded vigorously before use.

To serve 2

One 900 g	guinea fowl	One 1¾ lb
250 g	streaky bacon rashers	8 oz
5 to 7	juniper berries	5 to 7
	chopped thyme	
2 or 3	sage leaves, chopped	2 or 3
60 g	butter	2 oz
	salt and pepper	

Take a sheet of greaseproof paper or strong foil large enough to wrap the guinea fowl, butter it, and dampen it lightly all over with water. Lay the bacon on it. In a mortar, make a paste from the juniper berries, a large pinch of chopped thyme, the sage and the butter, and season with salt and pepper. Rub this vigorously over the guinea fowl, inside and out, and place the bird on the bacon. Wrap the bird up well in the bacon and the paper and secure it tightly with string. Wrap another layer of paper round, then surround this parcel with a layer about 3 cm (1¼ inches) thick of wet clay.

Bury the wrapped guinea fowl in hot ashes for about 2½ hours. Break open the clay mould, remove both sheets of paper and serve the guinea fowl immediately.

KATINKA MOSTAR
FEINE WILDBRET-REZEPTE

Burmese-Style Guinea Fowl

Parelhoen à la Birmanienne

Serve this dish with rice, mango chutney and melted butter.

To serve 6

3	guinea fowl	3
¼ tsp each	ground coriander, pepper, turmeric, cumin and cinnamon	¼ tsp each
10 cl	olive oil	3½ fl oz
1	lemon, juice strained	1
120 g	clarified butter	4 oz
6	small bananas, halved	6
	flour	
6	sprigs watercress	6

Using scissors, split the guinea fowl by cutting to one side of the backbone from the tail to the neck. Lay the birds, breast up, on a flat surface. Place the palm of your hand over the breast and press down firmly to break the breastbone. With a small sharp knife, make a slit in the loose skin between the legs. Gently bend the legs inwards and insert them through the slit in the skin.

Mix the spices together well and rub them thoroughly into the guinea fowl. Leave the birds to marinate for at least 2 hours in the oil and lemon juice.

Roast the guinea fowl slowly on the grill for about 25 minutes, brushing them from time to time with clarified butter. Dip the bananas in flour and grill them for 4 minutes, brushing them with butter several times.

Serve the guinea fowl garnished with the bananas and sprigs of watercress.

WALTER BICKEL AND RENÉ KRAMER
WILD EN GEVOGELTE IN DE INTERNATIONALE KEUKEN

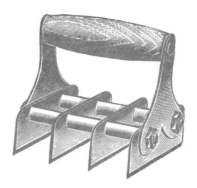

Barbecued Lemon Duck

The author suggests that the duck should be served with boiled rice seasoned with spicy nuoc mam *sauce—made by mixing together ¼ litre (8 fl oz) of Oriental fish sauce or light soy sauce, 45 g (1½ oz) of finely chopped fresh ginger root, two crushed cloves of garlic, 1 teaspoon of chili powder, 3 tablespoons of lemon juice, 2 tablespoons of sugar and 4 tablespoons of water. Lemon wedges and a salad of lettuce, chives, cucumber and bean sprouts should also accompany the duck.*

To serve 4

One 2 to 2.5 kg	duck, quartered	One 4 to 5 lb
4	spring onions, finely chopped	4
1 tsp	freshly grated ginger root	1 tsp
2 tsp	ground turmeric	2 tsp
2 tbsp	dark soy sauce	2 tbsp
1 tsp	sugar	1 tsp
½ tsp	grated lemon rind	½ tsp
	salt and black pepper	

Mix together the spring onions, ginger, turmeric, soy sauce, sugar, lemon rind, salt and pepper. Spread this mixture over the duck pieces and leave them to marinate for 4 hours. Grill the duck pieces, 7.5 to 10 cm (3 to 4 inches) from the coals, for about 25 minutes on each side, or until the meat is well done and the skin is crisp. Serve hot.

MAY WONG TRENT
ORIENTAL BARBECUES

Marinated Duck

Marinierte Ente

To serve 6

One 2 kg	fat young duck, rinsed inside and out and patted dry	One 4 lb
1 tsp	paprika	1 tsp
	ground ginger	
	ground cinnamon	
	grated nutmeg	
	onion salt	
30 g	parsley, finely chopped	1 oz
	freshly ground black pepper	
2 tbsp	sugar	2 tbsp
3 tbsp	full-bodied dry red wine	3 tbsp
	soy sauce	
5 tbsp	oil	5 tbsp
2 tbsp	salt	2 tbsp
500 g	grapes, skinned and seeded	1 lb

Mix together the paprika, a pinch each of ginger, cinnamon, nutmeg and onion salt, the parsley, pepper, sugar, red wine and a dash of soy sauce. Blend to a paste with 3 tablespoons of the oil. Spread this mixture over the inside and outside of the duck, then wrap the duck securely in foil and allow it to marinate in a cold place for at least 24 hours.

Pat the duck inside and out again, and reserve the marinade left in the foil. Brush the duck with the rest of the oil and grill it on a spit for about 70 minutes, brushing it now and then with the reserved marinade. Fifteen minutes before the end of the cooking time, dissolve the salt in 4 tablespoons of hot water and baste the duck with this several times, so that the skin becomes crisp. Carve the duck and serve it immediately, garnished with the grapes.

MECHTHILD PIEPENBROCK
GRILL VERGNÜGEN

Angolan Duck with Grilled Papaya

To serve 4

One 2.5 kg	duck, halved or quartered	One 5 to 5½ lb
4 tbsp	corn oil	4 tbsp
12	cloves	12
1	fresh chili pepper, seeded and chopped	1
12.5 cl	orange juice	4 fl oz
2 tbsp	lime juice	2 tbsp
75 g	sweet green pepper, seeded, finely chopped	2½ oz
¼ tsp	salt	¼ tsp
	Grilled papaya	
2	firm papayas, peeled, halved and stoned	2
60 g	butter, melted	2 oz
⅛ tsp	freshly grated nutmeg	⅛ tsp
½ tsp	salt	½ tsp

Place the duck pieces in a shallow glass dish. Mix together the oil, cloves, chili pepper, orange juice, lime juice, sweet pepper and salt, and pour this mixture over the duck. Marinate the duck for 2 hours at room temperature, turning the pieces occasionally. Grill the duck over hot charcoal until it is nicely brown and the juices run clear when the flesh is pierced with a skewer, 10 to 20 minutes on each side.

Just before the duck is cooked, place the papayas in a bowl with the melted butter, nutmeg and salt. Turn them to coat them. Grill the papaya halves over the coals until they are just heated through, about 1 minute on each side.

MAGGIE WALDRON
FIRE AND SMOKE

Roasted Quail

Cailles Rôties

To serve 2

4	quail, drawn and trussed	4
1	thin sheet pork back fat, cut into 4 pieces	1
4	large vine leaves	4

Cover each quail with a vine leaf, then wrap it in a piece of pork fat. Thread the quails on a spit, passing the spit crosswise through their bodies, and cook them over a hot fire, turning constantly, for about 30 minutes.

TANTE MARIE
LA VÉRITABLE CUISINE DE FAMILLE

Quail Grilled over Charcoal

Putpudutsi Pecheni

To serve 2

4	quail, drawn	4
	salt and freshly ground black pepper	

Place each quail on its back on a chopping board, and slice it lengthwise along the breastbone, leaving the two sides joined at the back. Spread the bird open and pound gently with a meat pounder to flatten it, at the same time working in some salt and freshly ground black pepper. Arrange the prepared birds on a greased, hot rack over glowing charcoal and grill them, turning once, until they are cooked through and nicely browned—about 10 minutes. Serve at once.

SEMEYNO SUKROVISHTE

Marinated Grilled Quail

To serve 4

12	quail, drawn and split lengthwise	12
¾ litre	dry white wine	1¼ pints
1 tbsp	wine vinegar	1 tbsp
1	bay leaf	1
2	sprigs fresh thyme or 1 tsp dried thyme	2
	salt and pepper	
125 g	celery, chopped	4 oz
2	garlic cloves, crushed	2
125 g	butter, melted	4 oz

Combine the wine, vinegar, bay leaf, thyme, salt and pepper, celery and garlic, and marinate the quail in this mixture in the refrigerator for 8 hours. Remove the birds from the marinade, rinse them and pat them dry. (Discard the marinade or keep it in the freezer for a second use.)

Place the quail, cut side down, on an oiled barbecue rack and cook for about 20 minutes, or until browned, turning them from time to time and basting with melted butter.

DOMINIQUE D'ERMO
DOMINIQUE'S FAMOUS FISH, GAME AND MEAT RECIPES

Barbecued Quail

Guatlles a la Brasa

To serve 4

4	quail, drawn, innards chopped	4
16 to 20	garlic cloves, finely chopped	16 to 20
4 tbsp	finely chopped parsley	4 tbsp
60 g	butter	2 oz
4	fresh vine leaves	4
4	rashers bacon	4

Add the garlic, parsley and butter to the chopped innards. Stuff the quail with this mixture. Encase each quail in a vine leaf and wrap a rasher of bacon round each leaf. Cook the quail on a preheated rack over a fire of vine shoots until the bacon is golden-brown on all sides, about 20 minutes. Serve the quail at once.

ELIANA THIBAUT COMELADE
CUINA ROSSELLONESA I DE LA COSTA BRAVA

Small Birds Spit-Roasted

Paulákia stin Soúvla

The technique of threading small birds on a spit is demonstrated on page 58.

Small birds, grilled on spits over coals, are served at many Greek village cafés with cheese or fried eggs on the side, a delicacy since ancient times.

To serve 4

12	quail or other small game birds, drawn and trussed	12
	salt and pepper	
About 4 tbsp	olive oil	About 4 tbsp
$\frac{1}{2}$ tsp	dried thyme	$\frac{1}{2}$ tsp
About $\frac{1}{2}$	lemon, juice strained	About $\frac{1}{2}$

Rub the birds with salt and pepper and thread them on a metal spit. Combine the olive oil, thyme and lemon juice in a bowl and beat lightly with a fork until well mixed. Brush the birds with this mixture. Grill them over a charcoal fire for 7 to 10 minutes, turning them often to cook all sides and basting frequently with the oil and lemon mixture; make up more of the mixture if necessary.

THEONIE MARK
GREEK ISLANDS COOKING

Spit-Roasted Woodcocks

Bekasa Pechena

The technique of threading small birds on a spit is demonstrated on page 58.

In this recipe, the birds may be served with their innards, or the innards can be removed after grilling, then chopped, seasoned to taste, and spread on the bread.

To serve 4

4	woodcocks	4
	salt	
20 cl	dry red wine	7 fl oz
10 cl	tomato juice	$3\frac{1}{2}$ fl oz
1	small loaf white crusty bread, halved lengthwise, each half cut across into 2 pieces	1
	lemon juice	
	olive oil	

Pluck each bird and singe the skin over an open flame. Peel the skin off the head and remove the eyes. Take out the gizzard but otherwise leave the woodcocks undrawn. Season the birds with salt, then draw the head forwards and run the beak through the lower part of the neck. Secure the wings and legs with string if you wish.

Thread the birds on a spit. In a small bowl, mix the wine with the tomato juice. Roast the woodcocks close to and at the side of the hot embers of a wood fire, placing a pan containing the pieces of bread—crust side down—under the birds to catch their cooking juices. Grill the birds for 30 minutes, turning the spit slowly the whole time and brushing the birds often with the wine and tomato mixture.

When the birds are cooked, remove them from the spit and place each bird on a warmed serving plate, on top of a slice of the bread. Sprinkle the birds with a little lemon juice and olive oil and serve immediately.

SEMEYNO SUKROVISHTE

Roast Woodcocks

Bécasses Rôties

The technique of preparing woodcocks for spit-roasting is described in the previous recipe on page 133.

	To serve 4	
2	woodcocks	2
	salt and pepper	
1	sheet pork back fat, cut in half	1
4	slices white bread, toasted	4

Season the woodcocks with salt and pepper; truss each bird, then bard it with a piece of pork fat and tie it securely. Thread the birds on a spit. Place the slices of toasted bread in a drip pan and position the pan under the spit so that the roasting juices drop on to the toast. Roast the woodcocks, turning frequently, for about 30 minutes. Cut the woodcocks in half and serve each half on a slice of the toast.

TANTE MARIE
LA VÉRITABLE CUISINE DE FAMILLE

Spit-Roasted Partridges

Kuropatwy i Przepiórki Pieczone

The same recipe may be used for quail, which require about 18 minutes' roasting time.

	To serve 2	
2	partridges, drawn	2
	salt	
150 g	pork back fat, thinly sliced	5 oz
4 or 6	sage leaves (optional)	4 or 6
60 g	butter, melted	2 oz
2	slices white bread	2
2 tbsp	stock (*page 167*)	2 tbsp

Salt the birds moderately inside and outside, then wrap each bird in thin slices of pork back fat and tie with scalded cotton thread. Two or three sage leaves may be placed inside each bird to enhance the flavour of the meat.

Roast the partridges on a spit for about 25 minutes, basting them from time to time with a tablespoonful of melted butter.

Fry the bread in the remaining butter. Remove the threads from the birds, leaving on the covering of attractively browned pork fat, and place each bird on a slice of fried bread. Stir the stock into the juices in the drip pan and pour this sauce over the birds.

MARIA LEMNIS AND HENRYK VITRY
OLD POLISH TRADITIONS IN THE KITCHEN AND AT THE TABLE

Pigeon Grilled over Charcoal

Pigeonneau Grillé sur Charbon de Bois

Instead of using skewers, you can place the birds directly on the grill rack. Turn them several times during cooking.

	To serve 6	
6	pigeons, drawn and trussed	6
75 g	butter	2½ oz
4 tsp	paprika	4 tsp
1 tsp	cumin	1 tsp
1	garlic clove, crushed	1
	salt	
30 cl	water	½ pint

Place the pigeons in a saucepan. Add the butter, half the paprika, half the cumin and the garlic. Salt lightly. Add the water, cover the pan and put it on a gentle heat. Allow the pigeons to simmer for about 1 hour or until they are cooked through. Then remove them from the saucepan and boil down their cooking liquid until about $\frac{1}{4}$ litre (8 fl oz) remains. Allow this sauce to cool, then stir in the remaining paprika and cumin. Brush the pigeons with this mixture.

Thread each pigeon on to a skewer and grill them, turning constantly, over charcoal for 20 minutes. Serve very hot.

AHMED LAASRI
240 RECETTES DE CUISINE MAROCAINE

Young Rabbit Spit-Roasted with Mustard

	To serve 4	
1	young wild rabbit, gutted	1
	salt and pepper	
1 tbsp	chopped thyme	1 tbsp
1	bay leaf	1
90 g	butter	3 oz
4 tbsp	Dijon mustard	4 tbsp

Place the rabbit on the spit and season it with salt and pepper. Put into your drip pan the thyme, bay leaf and butter. Baste the rabbit with this mixture while it is roasting. When it is three-quarters cooked, after about 30 minutes, coat it with the mustard and continue cooking it for about 10 minutes more, or until it is browned and cooked through.

SYLVAIN CLUSELLS
COOKING ON TURNING SPIT AND GRILL

Roast Rabbit

Conejo Asado

To serve 4

1	medium-sized rabbit, gutted	1
½ tsp	salt	½ tsp
45 g	lard	1½ oz
4 tbsp	chopped parsley	4 tbsp
2	garlic cloves, chopped	2
8 cl	dry white wine	3 fl oz

Sprinkle the rabbit with salt and thread it on a spit. Place it on a grill above glowing coals. When it is half-cooked, after about 20 minutes, remove it from the fire, rub it with lard and sprinkle it with the parsley and garlic. Then return it to the fire for another 20 minutes. Sprinkle a little wine over the rabbit before finally removing it from the grill.

ANTONIO ARAGONES SUBERO
GASTRONOMIA DE GUADALAJARA

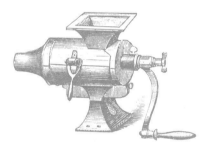

Grilled Young Rabbit

If you use wild rabbits for this recipe, they should be hung for several days before they are eaten. Hutch rabbits, however, do not need hanging.

To serve 6 to 8

2	plump young rabbits, split in half lengthwise and pounded flat	2
	oil	
	Basting sauce	
1 tsp	salt	1 tsp
1 tsp	pepper	1 tsp
3 tbsp	oil	3 tbsp
2 tbsp	lemon juice	2 tbsp
	dried sage	
½	garlic clove, crushed	½

To make the basting sauce, mix together the salt, pepper, oil, lemon juice, a pinch of dried sage and the garlic.

Brush the rabbit halves with oil and place them on a grill rack. Sear them over hot coals until both sides are brown. Raise the rack and grill them slowly for about 25 minutes, basting them frequently with the sauce and turning them often. Test the rabbit pieces by piercing one with a skewer. If the juices run clear, the rabbit is cooked.

JOHN AND MARIE ROBERSON
THE COMPLETE BARBECUE BOOK

Country Rabbit

The technique of jointing a rabbit is shown on page 56.

This is an old Romany recipe which was ideally suited to their open-air life. The gypsies would kill, skin and joint a rabbit, gather the ingredients growing wild in the fields and cook it on the camp fire. It is best suited to a young, fresh rabbit, but if this is unavailable, make sure that you marinate the rabbit for at least double the stated time.

To serve 4

1	young rabbit, cut into joints	1
125 g	mushrooms, chopped	4 oz
1	garlic clove, crushed	1
1 tsp	chopped parsley	1 tsp
1 tsp	chopped chives	1 tsp
4	juniper berries, crushed	4
2 tbsp	oil	2 tbsp
1 tbsp	gin	1 tbsp
	salt and freshly ground black pepper	

Wipe the portions of rabbit with a kitchen towel. With a sharp knife, make one or two incisions in each portion to enable the marinade to permeate the meat more thoroughly. Arrange the joints in a shallow dish suitable for marinating, and sprinkle the mushrooms over them. Mix the remaining ingredients together and pour this marinade over the rabbit pieces. Leave them in a cool place to marinate for about 2 hours, basting the meat occasionally.

Drain the rabbit joints carefully, so as not to shake off any bits of the marinade which may be sticking to them. Cook the joints over an open wood or charcoal fire until tender—10 to 15 minutes. Turn the pieces while they are cooking so that they brown evenly, and paint them with the marinade to prevent the meat from becoming too dry. Serve the rabbit immediately with baked potatoes.

HENRIETTA GREEN
THE MARINADE COOKBOOK

Burgundian Roast Hare

Le Lièvre Rôti à la Bourguignonne

The technique of larding a joint of meat is shown on page 56.

To serve 2

1	hare, gutted, liver and blood reserved, forequarters and hindquarters removed	1
60 g	pork fat, cut into strips	2 oz
60 g	butter, melted	2 oz
	salt	
12.5 cl	stock (*page 167*)	4 fl oz
4 tbsp	dry white wine	4 tbsp
4 tbsp	*glace de viande (page 167)*	4 tbsp
½	lemon, juice strained	½
1	shallot, chopped	1
2 or 3	small gherkins, chopped	2 or 3

Lard the saddle of hare with the pork fat and fix it on to the spit. After 5 minutes of cooking, baste it with the melted butter and season with salt. Fifteen minutes later, season again with salt. In the drip pan, place half the stock, the wine, the *glace de viande* and the lemon juice. Baste with this mixture and continue to cook for a total of about 1 hour.

Pour the sauce from the drip pan into a small saucepan. Add the hare's liver pounded with the blood and the remaining stock. Heat the sauce gently, without boiling, to thicken it slightly. Sieve the sauce into a sauceboat containing the shallot and gherkins. Serve with the hare.

PAUL MÉGNIN
300 MANIÈRES DE CUIRE ET ACCOMMODER LE GIBIER

Grilled Venison

To serve 2

2	tender venison steaks or chops	2
	olive oil	
	salt and pepper	
75 g	butter, melted	2½ oz
1	lemon, juice strained	1

Brush the steaks or chops with olive oil, then sprinkle them with salt and pepper. Place them on a rack over a very hot fire and sear them for 10 seconds on each side. Brush each side again with olive oil and grill for 2 more minutes on each side.

Mix together the melted butter, 1 teaspoon of salt, ¼ teaspoon of pepper and the lemon juice and serve this sauce with the steaks or chops.

FRANK G. ASHBROOK AND EDNA N. SATER
COOKING WILD GAME

Saddle or Loin of Venison

Comber Jeleni ze Śmietana

The technique of larding a joint of meat is shown on page 56.

Serve with salad and a tart fruit compote or jelly.

To serve 6 to 8

One 2 kg	saddle or loin of venison	One 4 lb
	salt and pepper	
175 g	salt pork, cut into thin strips	6 oz
60 g	butter, melted	2 oz
¼ litre	soured cream	8 fl oz
1 tbsp	flour	1 tbsp
	Marinade	
1	large onion, sliced	1
1	bay leaf	1
1	large carrot, sliced	1
½	celery root	½
½	Hamburg parsley root	½
20	black peppercorns	20
10	whole allspice berries	10
1	sprig thyme	1
¾ litre	red wine vinegar	1¼ pints
1.5 litres	water	2½ pints

Boil all the marinade ingredients together for 30 minutes, then allow the marinade to cool completely. Place the meat in a deep dish just large enough to hold it and pour the marinade over it. There should be enough marinade to cover the meat. Leave the meat to marinate for at least 24 hours, and preferably for two to four days.

Rub the meat with salt and sprinkle it sparingly with pepper. Lard the meat generously with the salt pork. Thread the meat on a spit and place a pan beneath the spit to catch the drippings. Roast the meat over hot coals, basting frequently with the melted butter. After the butter has been used up, baste the meat with the soured cream. After the first 20 minutes, reduce the heat and continue to cook the venison for about 40 minutes more.

Stir the flour into the juices in the drip pan, blending it in to avoid lumps, and cook it gently for 3 minutes to make a sauce. Slice the venison fairly thin and serve it with the sauce.

MARJA OCHOROWICZ-MONATOWA
POLISH COOKERY

Fish and Shellfish

Fresh Grilled Anchovies

To serve 4

16	fresh anchovies	16
1	lemon, juice strained	1
3 tbsp	olive oil	3 tbsp
½ tsp	paprika	½ tsp
2	garlic cloves, finely chopped	2
	salt and freshly ground black pepper	
	parsley sprigs	
	lemon wedges	

Add half the lemon juice to the oil, paprika and garlic, and season with salt and pepper. Marinate the anchovies for 15 minutes in this mixture. Then place the anchovies on a very hot grill and cook for 4 minutes on each side, while basting the fish with the excess marinade. Pour the remaining lemon juice over the grilled anchovies and serve them hot, garnished with parsley sprigs and lemon wedges.

GRANT BLACKMAN
AUSTRALIAN FISH COOKING

Grilled Sardines

Sardinas Asadas

To serve 4

24	large fresh sardines, wiped with a cloth but not gutted	24
	salt	
10 cl	olive oil	3½ fl oz
4 tbsp	finely chopped parsley	4 tbsp
100 g	butter	3½ oz

Season the sardines with salt and the oil and place them on a rack over a fire of wood or oak charcoal. Cook for about 5 minutes on each side. Place in a serving dish, sprinkle with the chopped parsley and dot with the butter.

NESTOR LUJAN AND JUAN PERUCHO
EL LIBRO DE LA COCINA ESPAÑOLA

Sardines on a Tile

Sardinas a la Teja

These sardines are traditionally cooked on large Spanish roof tiles. A large fireproof earthenware dish or an unglazed quarry tile could be substituted.

This is a typical dish from the Basque provinces of Spain.

To serve 4

24	very fresh sardines	24
	salt	
	lettuce leaves	

Salt the sardines. Lay the lettuce leaves on an earthenware tile which has been preheated over hot charcoal for about 30 minutes. Place the sardines on top of the lettuce, head to tail. Cook them for about 3 minutes on one side and then on the other, making sure that the tile is heated evenly. Serve the fish on the same tile.

MAGDALENA ALPERI
TRATADO COMPLETO DE COMIDAS Y BEBIDAS

Charcoal Grilled Sardines

To serve 2

16	small fresh sardines, cleaned, rinsed and dried	16
	coarse salt	
	olive oil	
2	fresh bread rolls	2

Bury the sardines in coarse salt and let them cure for 1 hour. Dig them out and brush off most of the salt, but not all of it. Rub the sardines with olive oil. Place them on a rack about 7.5 cm (3 inches) above hot coals and cook them until brown on both sides—about 5 minutes on each side.

To eat the sardines, lay a grilled fish on the bottom half of a roll. Tap the fish gently with the other half of the roll to break the skin, then peel it off. Pick the layer of fish off the bones with your fingers and eat it, then turn the fish over and do likewise to the other side. Use the same half of roll to hold each new fish and by the time you have eaten eight fish, the roll will be saturated with sardine oil; then eat the roll too.

HOWARD MITCHAM
THE PROVINCETOWN SEAFOOD COOKBOOK

Sardines Grilled over Hot Coals

Sardinas a la Brasa

To serve 4

12	fresh sardines, cleaned, heads removed, opened out flat	12
8 cl	oil	3 fl oz
	salt and white pepper	
1	sprig oregano	1
2	garlic cloves, chopped	2
2 tbsp	chopped parsley	2 tbsp

Oil the sardines and grill them, skin side down, over a vigorous fire. When they are cooked, after 5 minutes, season them with salt and place them in a serving dish.

Fry the oregano, garlic, parsley and a pinch of white pepper in the remaining oil. Strain the oil and sprinkle it over the sardines before serving them.

M. DEL CARME NICOLAU
CUINA CATALANA

Salted Sardines with Peppers

Sardinas Salpimentonadas

Salting the sardines for 12 to 24 hours, as recommended by the author, impregnates them with a strong taste of salt. For a less salty flavour, leave them in salt for 1 to 2 hours only.

To serve 4

24	fresh sardines, cleaned	24
125 g	salt	4 oz
1	sweet green pepper, seeded and cut into strips	1
6	hot chili peppers, seeded and cut into strips	6

Cover the sardines with the salt and allow them to stand for 12 to 24 hours. Then place them on a rack over hot coals. Immediately, slit each sardine along the back and place pieces of green pepper and chili pepper in the openings. When the sardines are cooked on one side, turn them and cook on the other side—about 7 minutes' cooking in all. Serve the sardines as soon as they are removed from the rack.

MANUEL M. PUGA Y PARGA (PICADILLO)
LA COCINA PRACTICA

Devilled Herrings

Arenques a la Diabla

To serve 4

8	small herrings, cleaned	8
	salt and pepper	
	oil	
100 g	dry breadcrumbs	3½ oz
	cayenne pepper	
	vinaigrette (*page 163*)	

Season the herrings with salt and pepper, oil them and roll them in the breadcrumbs. Dust them with cayenne pepper and grill them for 3 to 4 minutes on each side, or until they are browned and cooked through. Place them on a serving dish and serve with vinaigrette sauce.

IGNACIO DOMENECH
PESCADOS Y MARISCOS

Whole Fish on the Spit or Grilled

Machchi Seekhi

A whole cod or six small whiting could be used for this recipe.

To serve 6

One 1.5 kg	fish or 6 small fish, cleaned, heads and tails removed	One 3 lb
½ tsp	paprika	½ tsp
4 tbsp	coriander seeds	4 tbsp
½ tsp	salt	½ tsp
¼ tsp	freshly ground black pepper	¼ tsp
6	cardamom pods	6
1 tbsp	aniseeds or dill	1 tbsp
2	onions	2
2	garlic cloves	2
1	sweet green pepper	1
2 tbsp	chopped mint	2 tbsp
4 tbsp	chopped parsley	4 tbsp
15 cl	yogurt, whipped	¼ pint
1	lemon or lime, juice strained	1
60 g	*ghee*	2 oz

Lightly roast the paprika and coriander in a frying pan, then grind them with the other spices, the onions, the garlic, the sweet pepper and the herbs. Use them to make a paste with the yogurt and lemon or lime juice. Prick the fish all over and rub the paste over the fish and in the cavity. Leave to stand for 30 minutes to 1 hour.

Preheat the grill. Place the fish on a spit or on the rack over a drip pan. Cook for about 15 minutes, or until the paste is dry but not burning. Baste with the drippings and cook over a slightly reduced heat until tender—about 25 minutes for the large fish, 10 to 15 minutes for the small fish. If you are using the rack, turn the fish over once. Test for doneness by piercing the fish right through with a thin, sharp skewer; if the flesh flakes easily, the fish is done. When the surface begins to scorch, baste with the *ghee*. Increase the heat again and let the skin crisp for a minute or two. Serve immediately.

DHARAMJIT SINGH
INDIAN COOKERY

Fish Parcels

To serve 8

8	fillets of white fish	8
	salt and pepper	
125 g	mushrooms, sliced	4 oz
125 g	onions, chopped	4 oz
30 g	capers	1 oz
60 g	butter	2 oz
30 cl	single cream	½ pint
	chopped parsley	

Put each fish fillet on a double thickness of buttered foil and sprinkle with salt and pepper. Arrange the mushrooms, onions and capers over the fish and dot the fillets with butter. Pour over the cream. Wrap the foil loosely over the fish to make neat parcels. Cook on the grill rack over hot coals for 25 to 30 minutes. Serve the fish on a dish with the cooking juices and sprinkle with chopped parsley.

BARBARA LOGAN
BARBECUE AND OUTDOOR COOKERY

Grilled Cod Fillets

Filety z Dorsza z Rusztu

To serve 4

600 g	cod fillets (or other sea fish), skinned and cut into pieces 1 cm (½ inch) thick	1¼ lb
	salt and pepper	
3 tbsp	olive oil	3 tbsp
1 tbsp	white wine vinegar or lemon juice	1 tbsp

Dust the fish fillets with salt and pepper. Mix together 1 tablespoon of the oil and the vinegar or lemon juice and sprinkle this over the fish. Leave the fillets for 30 minutes to 1 hour, turning them over a few times. Drain them and grill them on a hot oiled rack for 5 minutes on each side, brushing them from time to time with the remaining oil.

HELENA HAWLICZKOWA
KUCHNIA POLSKA

Tandoori Fish

Use a firm, white fish such as cod or haddock.

To serve 2 or 3

One 1 kg	fish, cleaned	One 2 lb
1	medium-sized onion, finely chopped	1
6	garlic cloves, crushed	6
2.5 cm	fresh ginger root, finely chopped	1 inch
1	hot green chili pepper, seeded and chopped, or cayenne pepper	1
1	lemon, juice strained	1
1 tbsp	coriander seeds, ground	1 tbsp
1 tsp	cumin seeds, ground	1 tsp
2 tsp	fennel seeds or aniseeds, ground	2 tsp
5	cardamom pods, seeds removed and ground	5
1 tsp	ground cinnamon	1 tsp
	salt and black pepper	
1 tsp	paprika	1 tsp
15 cl	yogurt or oil	¼ pint
	clarified butter or oil for basting	
	Garnish	
1	onion, thinly sliced into rings	1
1	lemon, cut into wedges	1
	chopped fresh coriander, mint leaves or flat-leafed parsley	

Put the onion, garlic, ginger, chili pepper or a generous pinch of cayenne pepper, lemon juice, spices, salt and pepper and paprika in a food processor and blend them to a paste. Blend in the yogurt or oil.

Make a few diagonal incisions in the skin of the fish. Rub the paste inside and out with your hands and leave the fish for at least 2 hours. Roast the fish on a spit or cook it on a grill over moderate coals, basting it with clarified butter or oil, until the flesh begins to flake and the skin is crisp—about 15 minutes.

Serve the fish with onion rings and lemon wedges and sprinkle it with coriander, mint leaves or flat-leafed parsley.

CLAUDIA RODEN
PICNIC

Fish Ball Satay

Sesatée Ikan

Galingale is a root similar to ginger. Galingale (laos) *and lemon grass* (sereh) *can be bought in Oriental food shops.*

To serve 4

750 g	cod, haddock or other white, firm-fleshed fish, cleaned, boned and finely chopped	1½ lb
½	coconut, flesh grated and toasted until golden-brown	½
1	onion, finely sliced	1
1 tsp	ground coriander	1 tsp
½ tsp	ground cumin	½ tsp
1 tbsp	finely sliced lemon grass	1 tbsp
¼ tsp	pepper	¼ tsp
5	slices galingale	5
3	garlic cloves, finely sliced	3
1 tsp	sugar	1 tsp
1	leek, finely sliced	1
1 tbsp	chopped parsley	1 tbsp
2	eggs, yolks separated from whites, yolks lightly beaten, whites lightly whisked	2
	flour or dry breadcrumbs	
½ litre	coconut milk (*page 167*)	16 fl oz

Mix together and pound the coconut, onion, coriander, cumin, lemon grass, pepper, galingale, garlic and sugar. Place three-quarters of this mixture in a bowl and stir in the leek, parsley, egg yolks and, finally, the fish. Form this mixture into small balls and roll them first in the egg white and then in flour or dry breadcrumbs. Thread the balls on to skewers and barbecue them over a gentle fire for 10 minutes, or until the balls are golden-brown, turning them often. The remaining spice mixture should be added to the coconut milk and used to baste the fish balls from time to time during cooking.

J. CATENIUS VAN DER MEIJDEN
GROOT NIEUW VOLLEDIG INDISCH KOOKBOEK

Grilled Mackerel

Grillierte Makrelen

To serve 4

4	mackerel, cleaned	4
1	lemon, juice strained	1
	salt	
4 tbsp	mixed chopped fresh fennel leaves, parsley, thyme and chervil	4 tbsp
1 or 2	garlic cloves, finely chopped	1 or 2
8 cl	oil	3 fl oz
4	lemon slices	4

Cut several deep slashes on each side of each mackerel, then sprinkle the mackerel with a little lemon juice and salt, inside and outside. Stuff each fish with chopped herbs and a little of the garlic. Mix together the remaining garlic, lemon juice and the oil. Grill the fish over hot embers for 5 minutes on each side, or until cooked through, brushing them from time to time with the oil and lemon mixture. Serve the mackerel garnished with lemon slices.

FRISCH VOM GRILL

Grilled Mackerel Cadiz-Style

Caballa Asada a la Gaditana

To serve 1

One 250 g	mackerel, cleaned	One 8 oz
	salt	
4 tbsp	olive oil	4 tbsp
2	tomatoes, 1½ chopped, ½ thinly sliced	2
1	small onion, finely chopped	1
1	small sweet green pepper, finely chopped	1
2 tbsp	vinegar	2 tbsp

Season the fish with salt and coat it liberally with half the olive oil. Grill the fish on a barbecue of glowing wood charcoal, with no ashes, for about 5 minutes on each side.

Mix together the chopped tomato, onion and green pepper and the tomato slices. Place this salad on a serving dish. When the mackerel is cooked, place it on the dish with the salad. Stir together the remaining oil, the vinegar and a little salt and pour this dressing over the fish and the salad.

LUIS BETTONICA
COCINA REGIONAL ESPAÑOLA

Mackerel Grilled over Embers

Pechena Pryasna Riba

In this recipe the fish is grilled in a hinged wire basket. After grilling, do not wash the basket; just place it over the hot embers to allow the heat to burn up any particles that have stuck to the wire. Then rub the basket with clean wrapping paper—not newspaper. This method of cleaning helps to prevent the food sticking to the wire during grilling.

To serve 5

1 kg	mackerel fillets	2 to 2½ lb
2 tsp	salt	2 tsp
1 tsp	freshly ground black pepper	1 tsp
5 tbsp	vegetable oil	5 tbsp
1 or 2	lemons, juice strained	1 or 2
2 tbsp	finely chopped parsley	2 tbsp

Prepare a wood or charcoal fire. When it is glowing red, throw some of the ash over it. This will prevent the dripping oil from the fish flaming on the embers.

Season the mackerel fillets with the salt and arrange them in a large, hinged basket. Grill the fish, skin side down, until the skin is browned and blistered—about 4 minutes. Then turn the wire basket over to let the fillets take colour on the other side—about 4 minutes more.

Remove the fish carefully from the basket on to heated serving plates. Sprinkle the fillets with the pepper, the vegetable oil, and lemon juice to taste, and garnish them with the chopped parsley.

DR. GEORGI SHISHKOV AND STOIL VOUCHKOV
BULGARSKI NATSIONALNI YASTIYA

Mackerel with Lemon Leaves

Caballas con Hojas de Limonero

Lemon verbena or lemon balm leaves can be used instead of lemon tree leaves in this recipe.

To serve 4

4	small mackerel, cleaned and boned	4
125 g	lemon tree leaves	4 oz
8 cl	oil	3 fl oz

Cover the rack with some of the lemon leaves. Place the fish on the rack over a low heat and sprinkle them with drops of oil from time to time. When the lemon leaves are burnt, the mackerel is cooked on one side. Place a new layer of leaves on the rack and turn the fish over to cook them completely. Serve the mackerel on a bed of fresh lemon leaves.

MANUEL VAZQUEZ MONTALBAN
LA COCINA CATALANA

Stuffed Mackerel

Caballas Rellenas

To cook mussels, scrub their shells clean and put them in a large heavy pan with a chopped onion, a crushed garlic clove, a bay leaf, some thyme and a splash of white wine. Cover the pan, place it over a high heat and cook the mussels for 3 to 5 minutes, or until all the shells have opened. The flesh can then be pulled free of the shell.

As an alternative, make a stuffing for the mackerel from streaky bacon, garlic and parsley.

To serve 4

4	small mackerel, cleaned, opened out flat and boned	4
3	eggs, hard boiled	3
1	garlic clove, crushed	1
2 tbsp	chopped parsley	2 tbsp
12	live mussels, cooked, shelled and chopped	12
1 tbsp	oil	1 tbsp
	salt	

Make a paste from the hard-boiled eggs, garlic, parsley, mussels and oil. Add salt to taste. Fill the mackerel with this stuffing. Tie the fish with fine string and grill them over a low fire, turning once, for 12 minutes, or until cooked through.

MANUEL VAZQUEZ MONTALBAN
LA COCINA CATALANA

Mackerel on Skewers

Makrelen am Spiess

To serve 1

2	small mackerel, cleaned	2
	salt	
2	bay leaves	2
	olive oil	
	lemon juice	
	parsley sprigs	

Salt the insides of the fish and stick each one, lengthwise, on a skewer with a bay leaf. Cook the mackerel on the grill, turning them often and basting them with oil and sprinkling them with lemon juice. When they are ready, after about 10 minutes, pull the fish off their skewers, place them in a dish, decorate round the edge with parsley sprigs and serve.

MARIA HORVATH
BALKAN-KÜCHE

Barbecued Tuna Fish

Atún a la Brasa

The author recommends serving this dish accompanied by mayonnaise that has been flavoured with a dash of mustard, or by tartare sauce (recipe, page 163).

	To serve 4	
750 g	fresh tuna, cut into 4 steaks	1½ lb
About 8 cl	oil	About 3 fl oz
2 tbsp	white wine vinegar	2 tbsp
	salt	
4	sprigs thyme (optional)	4
500 g	tomatoes, skinned and seeded	1 lb
4	garlic cloves, roasted in the ashes of the fire for about 20 minutes, then peeled	4
4 tbsp	chopped parsley	4 tbsp

Leave the tuna to marinate in the oil, vinegar and a pinch of salt for 1 hour. Grill the fish, basting it continually with the marinade, supplemented by more oil if necessary, and turning it once, until it is cooked through but still firm—about 12 minutes. A sprig of thyme can be placed beside each steak to give extra flavour.

Press the tomatoes and garlic through a sieve and mix them with the parsley. Heat this sauce gently and serve a large spoonful of it on each tuna steak.

MANUEL VAZQUEZ MONTALBAN
LA COCINA CATALANA

Grilled Tuna Fish

Atun Emparrillado

Salmon steaks may be prepared in the same way.

	To serve 4	
4	tuna steaks, 1 cm (½ inch) thick, cut from the middle of the fish	4
8 cl	olive oil	3 fl oz
	salt and pepper	
1 tsp	paprika	1 tsp
1	lemon, juice strained	1

Brush the fish steaks lightly with oil and place them on the rack over hot charcoal. Grill for 15 minutes, turning them several times, until they are golden-brown on both sides. Season with oil, salt and pepper, paprika and lemon juice.

JOSÉ GUARDIOLA Y ORTIZ
CONDUCHOS DE NAVIDAD Y GASTRONOMIA ALICANTINA

Grilled Swordfish

Pesce Spada alla Griglia

Cod, halibut or turbot may be used instead of swordfish.

	To serve 6	
Six 200 g	swordfish steaks	Six 7 oz
3	garlic cloves, slivered	3
	rosemary sprigs	
	olive oil	
	salt and pepper	

Stick garlic slivers and tiny sprigs of rosemary into the fish. Smear the steaks with oil and sprinkle with salt and pepper. Grill over medium-hot coals for about 15 minutes.

VINCENZO BUONASSISI
CUCINA ALL'ARIA APERTA

Anchovied Swordfish Steaks

Cod, halibut or turbot may be used instead of swordfish.

	To serve 2	
Two 250 g	swordfish steaks, cut 2.5 cm (1 inch) thick	Two 8 oz
15 g	butter	½ oz
1	anchovy fillet, soaked and drained	1
	cayenne pepper	

Wipe the steaks well. Combine the butter and the anchovy fillet, crushing the fillet as it is blended, and adding a scanty pinch of cayenne pepper. Coat the steaks with the anchovied butter and grill them over bright coals for 3 minutes on one side, then 5 minutes on the other side, until cooked through.

MEL MARSHALL
COOKING OVER COALS

Swordfish en Brochette

Kiliç Şişte

If swordfish is unobtainable, substitute another firm-fleshed fish such as halibut, cod or turbot.

	To serve 6	
1 kg	swordfish	2 to 2½ lb
2	lemons, thinly sliced	2
4	tomatoes, sliced	4

	Marinade	
½	lemon, juice strained	½
2 tbsp	olive oil	2 tbsp
1	small onion, grated, juice strained, pulp discarded (optional)	1
1½ tsp	paprika	1½ tsp
12	bay leaves	12
2 tsp	salt	2 tsp

	Lemon and oil dressing	
1	lemon, juice strained	1
2 to 3 tsp	olive oil	2 to 3 tsp
1 or 2	sprigs parsley, chopped	1 or 2

Dice the swordfish into pieces about 2.5 by 4 by 5 cm (1 by 1½ by 2 inches). (Do not worry about the exact size. The important thing is to make the pieces of more or less uniform size.) Mix together the ingredients for the marinade and leave the pieces of swordfish in it for 4 to 6 hours.

Remove the pieces of fish and thread them on skewers, with the long side of each piece parallel to the skewer. Insert slices of lemon and tomato between the pieces of fish. Grill the skewers on both sides over a charcoal fire, brushing them frequently with the leftover marinade. This should take about 10 minutes or a little longer.

Mix together the ingredients for the dressing. Serve the swordfish skewers hot, accompanied by the dressing.

ALAN DAVIDSON
MEDITERRANEAN SEAFOOD

Swordfish or Shark Steaks Grilled in Lettuce Leaves

For an even more aromatic flavour, toss a handful of fennel seeds or some dried fennel branches over the coals just before putting on the fish.

To serve 4

Four 250 g	swordfish or shark steaks	Four 8 oz
1	lettuce, leaves separated	1
1	lemon, juice strained	1
4 tbsp	olive oil	4 tbsp
2 tbsp	fennel seeds	2 tbsp
½ tsp	salt	½ tsp
2	garlic cloves, finely chopped	2
2 tbsp	finely chopped parsley	2 tbsp

Mix together the lemon juice, oil, fennel seeds, salt, garlic and parsley. Marinate the fish in this mixture for several hours at least; all day or overnight is even better.

Spread some of the lettuce leaves flat and lift the fish steaks on to them, keeping a fair amount of marinade on each piece. Dribble some more marinade on top. Cover each steak with more lettuce leaves and tie it with kitchen string. If you like, place the fish packets in a hinged grilling basket that will hold them snugly.

Grill the fish over white-hot coals for about 10 minutes on each side, depending on the thickness of the steaks.

THR GREAT COOKS' GUIDE TO FISH COOKERY

Shark Brochettes

To serve 4

750 g	shark, boned and cut into chunks about 3 cm (1¼ inches) square	1½ lb
1 tbsp	lemon juice	1 tbsp
4 tbsp	olive oil	4 tbsp
½	onion, finely chopped	½
1 tbsp	chopped basil	1 tbsp
¼ tsp	salt	¼ tsp
¼ tsp	black pepper	¼ tsp
2	firm tomatoes	2
2	rashers bacon	2

Marinate the pieces of shark for 30 minutes in the lemon juice, olive oil, onion, basil, salt and pepper. Cut the tomatoes and bacon into similar-sized pieces. Thread a piece of fish, bacon, fish, tomato, until one skewer is filled. Repeat the process on the other three skewers. Place them on a preheated grill, baste them with the marinade, turn them every minute and grill for 12 minutes.

GRANT BLACKMAN
AUSTRALIAN FISH COOKING

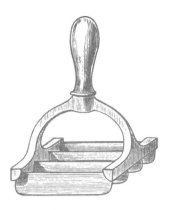

Tope en Brochette

Tope is a member of the shark family. A firm-fleshed fish such as porbeagle, swordfish or fresh tuna can be substituted.

Leftover sauce can be kept in a tightly corked bottle in the refrigerator for several weeks. It can be used for meat too.

To serve 6

5	tope steaks, 12.5 to 15 cm (5 to 6 inches) in diameter, skinned, each cut into 6 chunks and boned	5
125 g	green streaky bacon, cut into 2.5 cm (1 inch) squares	4 oz
125 g	smoked streaky bacon, cut into 2.5 cm (1 inch) squares	4 oz
250 g	mushrooms, halved	8 oz
6	large bay leaves, each cut into 4 pieces	6
	salt and pepper	
	melted butter for basting (optional)	

Barbecue sauce (optional)

15 g	bacon fat, or a small piece of fatty salt pork	½ oz
1	medium-sized onion, chopped	1
2 or 3	sticks celery, leaves chopped	2 or 3
1½ tbsp	wine vinegar	1½ tbsp
1	lemon, juice strained	1
1 tbsp	Worcestershire sauce	1 tbsp
1½ tbsp	brown sugar	1½ tbsp
¼ litre	tomato ketchup (*page 165*)	8 fl oz
1 tbsp	French mustard	1 tbsp
	salt and pepper	

Arrange the tope chunks in six lines and fit the bacon, mushrooms and bay leaves equitably in between. Now it's an easy matter to thread the skewers. Season them and brush

them with melted butter and grill them on a moderate heat for 10 to 15 minutes, turning two or three times, until the fish is opaque to the centre. Serve with buttered rice.

Instead of the melted butter, the fish can be basted with barbecue sauce made in the following way. Melt the bacon fat or render down the fatty salt pork, and fry the onions and celery leaves gently until they begin to turn yellow. Add the remaining ingredients and simmer for 10 minutes. Taste and adjust the seasoning. Serve some of the sauce with the brochettes and rice.

JANE GRIGSON
FISH COOKERY

Sea Fish Skewers

Brochettes de Poissons de Mer

These skewers may be made with one kind of fish only, or with a mixture of fish. If you wish, you can throw twigs of aromatic dried fennel on to the coals a few moments before the end of the cooking time; the smoke will accent the aroma of the fish.

To serve 4

1 kg	conger eel, monkfish or other firm-fleshed sea fish, cleaned, skinned, boned, and cut into 3 cm (1¼ inch) cubes	2 to 2½ lb
2	small shallots	2
4	garlic cloves	4
½ tsp	dried fennel	½ tsp
½ tsp	dried thyme	½ tsp
4 tbsp	olive oil	4 tbsp
2 tbsp	lemon juice	2 tbsp
16	large prawns, peeled and halved, or 32 live mussels, scrubbed	16

Combine in a blender the shallots, garlic cloves, dried fennel and thyme, olive oil and lemon juice. Process until thoroughly blended. Pour this mixture over the cubes of fish and leave to marinate for 2 hours.

Meanwhile, if using mussels, cook them with a little court-bouillon or water in a tightly covered saucepan over a high heat for 5 minutes or until they have all opened. Allow the mussels to cool, then remove them from their shells.

Thread the fish cubes on to skewers, alternating them with prawn halves or with mussels. Grill over medium-hot coals for 10 to 12 minutes.

MARIO V. BONDANINI (EDITOR)
GASTRONOMIE DE PLEIN AIR

Charcoal-Grilled Fish
Psári tis Sháras

To serve 4 to 6

Two 750 g to 1 kg	sea bream, red snapper, grouper or bass, cleaned	Two 1½ to 2 lb
	salt and pepper	
1 tbsp	chopped fresh oregano leaves or ¼ tsp dried oregano	1 tbsp
	Lemon-oil dressing	
12.5 cl	olive oil	4 fl oz
3 tbsp	lemon juice	3 tbsp
1	garlic clove, lightly crushed	1
¼ tsp	white pepper	¼ tsp

Combine all the ingredients for the dressing in a bowl and beat them vigorously with a fork or whisk until well mixed. Let the dressing stand at room temperature for at least 1 hour.

Season the inside cavities of the fish with salt and pepper, rubbing it in with your fingers. Using a brush, baste the entire outside of the fish with some of the lemon-oil dressing and coat a hinged wire rack with it. When the burning charcoal is hot, place the fish in the basket and hold it about 5 to 7.5 cm (2 to 3 inches) from the coals. Turn the basket over and over and baste the fish continuously with dressing until they are cooked—approximately 30 minutes, depending on the thickness of the fish. Remove the fish to a platter, sprinkle them with the remaining lemon-oil dressing and garnish them with the oregano.

THEONIE MARK
GREEK ISLANDS COOKING

Whole Grilled Fish

To serve 8

One 3 to 3.5 kg	fish (salmon, sea bass, etc.), cleaned, head and tail removed	One 6 to 8 lb
12	rashers bacon	12
10	sprigs parsley	10
	salt and white pepper	
35 to 50 cl	dry white wine	12 to 16 fl oz

Lay eight of the bacon rashers and all the parsley sprigs inside the fish. Season it inside and out with salt and pepper. Lay four bacon rashers on top of the fish. Place the fish on a double layer of aluminium foil large enough to enclose it completely. Fold the edges of the foil up round the fish and pour the wine over the fish. Secure the package tightly and place it 10 to 12.5 cm (4 to 5 inches) from medium-hot coals. Cook the fish for 45 minutes to 1 hour, or until the flesh is opaque when pierced behind the gills. To serve, unwrap the fish and remove the bacon rashers and parsley.

MARIAN BURROS
PURE AND SIMPLE

Egyptian Fish Kebab
Samak Kebab

This dish is traditionally accompanied by *babaghanoush* "salad", which is made as follows. Bake in a preheated 180°C (350°F or Mark 4) oven, just as they are, three medium-sized aubergines and one smallish onion for 1 hour or until they are soft. Cut them in half, cool them, scoop out the flesh and mash it up with four finely chopped garlic cloves. Combine this mixture with 200 g (7 oz) of *tahini* (sesame paste), a tablespoonful of vinegar and the juice of three lemons, adding seasoning and a pinch of ground cumin and blending the whole well. Garnish with parsley and a few black olives.

To serve 4

750 g	filleted sea bass or other firm-fleshed fish, cut into 1.5 cm (½ inch) cubes	1½ lb
3	lemons, juice strained	3
3	onions, grated, juice strained, pulp discarded	3
4	bay leaves	4
2 tsp	ground cumin	2 tsp
	salt and pepper	
400 g	small tomatoes, quartered	14 oz
	olive oil	
60 g	parsley, finely chopped	2 oz
	lemon wedges	

Combine the lemon juice, onion juice, bay leaves, ground cumin and salt and pepper. Leave the cubes of fish in this marinade for 30 minutes.

Impale the cubes of fish alternately with the tomato quarters on thin, stainless steel skewers. Brush with olive oil and grill the skewers over charcoal for 5 to 6 minutes, turning several times. Serve the skewers on a bed of chopped parsley, garnished with lemon wedges.

ALAN DAVIDSON
MEDITERRANEAN SEAFOOD

Sea Bass or Red Mullet Grilled with Fennel

Grillade au Fenouil

It is advisable to have a second hot dish in readiness to receive the fish and its strained juices, for when it comes to serving the fish, nobody wants burnt fennel on his or her plate.

	To serve 4	
1	large sea bass, cleaned, or red mullet, cleaned but with liver left intact	1
	dried fennel stalks	
	olive oil	
About 4 tbsp	Armagnac or brandy	About 4 tbsp

Make two deep crosswise incisions on each side of the fish. Stick two or three short pieces of fennel in the incision through which the intestines of the fish were removed. Paint the fish all over with oil, and grill it on each side for about 7 minutes or until cooked through, turning it over once only. On a long, fireproof serving dish, arrange a bed of dried fennel stalks. Remove the rack with the fish on it from the grill and place it over the fennel. In a soup ladle or small saucepan, warm the Armagnac or brandy; set light to it and pour it flaming into the dish. The fennel catches alight and burns, giving out a strong scent which flavours the dish.

ELIZABETH DAVID
FRENCH PROVINCIAL COOKING

Bass Grilled with Fennel

Le Loup Grillé au Fenouil

The Mediterranean bass is identical to the sea bass; the two fish are cooked in exactly the same way.

	To serve 4	
One 1 kg	bass, scaled, cleaned and deeply slashed on each side	One 2 to 2½ lb
	olive oil	
	dried fennel stalks	
	pastis or other anise-flavoured liqueur	
	butter	
	lemon quarters	

Brush the fish all over with olive oil. Grill it over wood coals, allowing 10 to 15 minutes for each side.

When the cooking is almost done, throw a few fennel stalks on to the coals and turn the fish in the aromatic smoke. At the last minute, remove the fish to a serving platter, pour on a little pastis and set it alight.

Serve the fish with butter and lemon quarters.

MARIO V. BONDANINI (EDITOR)
GASTRONOMIE DE PLEIN AIR

Grilled Red Mullet

Triglie alla Griglia

Salsa verde *is a piquant vinaigrette flavoured with parsley, capers, anchovy fillets, garlic and mustard.*

If the fish is absolutely fresh, it has such a marvellous flavour of the sea that it is absurd to serve any sauce with it. Town fish can do with a little melted butter and parsley, or a *salsa verde.*

	To serve 1	
1	medium-sized red mullet, cleaned but with the liver left intact	1
	olive oil	

Make a couple of incisions crosswise on each side of the fish. Brush it with oil. Cook it over hot charcoal for about 7 minutes on each side—it will be golden and crackling.

ELIZABETH DAVID
ITALIAN FOOD

Charcoal-Grilled Red Mullet

When you clean red mullet, leave the liver intact, as it has an excellent flavour and is considered a great delicacy.

	To serve 4	
4	red mullet, cleaned	4
2 tbsp	olive oil	2 tbsp
15 g	butter, melted	½ oz
2	garlic cloves, finely chopped	2
1 tbsp	chopped fennel leaves	1 tbsp
1 tbsp	orange juice	1 tbsp

Mix together the olive oil, melted butter, garlic, fennel and orange juice, and marinate the fish in this mixture for 1 hour. Grill the fish on a preheated rack for 8 minutes on each side, basting with the marinade.

GRANT BLACKMAN
AUSTRALIAN FISH COOKING

Barbecued Red Mullet Mariner-Style

Molls a la Brasa de Mariners

The author recommends that this dish should be cooked on the beach over a fire of broom, rosemary and other aromatic herbs found along the coast of Mallorca. The fish can be wrapped in vine leaves, as shown in the demonstration on page 74.

	To serve 4	
4	red mullet, cleaned but with the liver left intact	4
	salt	
1	onion, chopped	1
500 g	tomatoes, skinned, seeded and sliced	1 lb
1 tbsp	chopped capers	1 tbsp
	pepper	
1 tbsp	chopped oregano	1 tbsp
4 tbsp	olive oil	4 tbsp
1 tbsp	water	1 tbsp

Season the mullet lightly with salt and place them over the fire. Cook them for about 7 minutes on each side. When the fish are cooked, skin them and carefully extract the liver.

Whilst the fish are cooking, prepare a salad with the onion and tomatoes. Mix together the capers, a little pepper, the oregano, oil and a little water. Pound the livers with this dressing, pour it over the salad and serve with the grilled fish.

IGNASI DOMENECH
APATS

Grilled Red Mullet with Olives

Rouget Grillé aux Olives

	To serve 2	
One 500 to 600 g	red mullet, cleaned but with the liver left intact	One 1 to 1¼ lb
4 tbsp	olive oil	4 tbsp
2 to 3 tbsp	red or white wine	2 to 3 tbsp
	salt	
2 tbsp	chopped wild thyme	2 tbsp
2 tbsp	chopped fennel leaves (optional)	2 tbsp
About 12	black olives, stoned	About 12
	orange or lemon slices	

Score the mullet across twice on both sides, and marinate it for an hour or so in a little olive oil and the wine (either red or white, for mullet is one of the few fish which can be success-

fully cooked in red wine). Sprinkle the fish with salt, wild thyme and some chopped fennel leaves if you have them.

The fish will take about 10 to 15 minutes to grill, being started off close to the heat, over a drip pan. Turn it over once and, when the second side is crackling and crisp, move the grilling rack further away from the heat.

When the fish is cooked, remove it carefully to the serving dish. Put the drip pan with the juices and the black olives over a high heat for a few seconds; then pour the contents of the pan over the fish and garnish with slices of orange or lemon.

This dish is also good cold.

ELIZABETH DAVID
FRENCH PROVINCIAL COOKING

Mullet Grilled with Anchovy Sauce

	To serve 4	
4	large or 8 small red mullet	4
30 g	clarified butter	1 oz
	salt and pepper	
	Anchovy sauce	
5	salt anchovies, soaked, filleted, rinsed and drained	5
4	garlic cloves	4
2 tbsp	tomato purée (*page 164*)	2 tbsp
1 tbsp	chopped parsley	1 tbsp
4 tbsp	oil	4 tbsp
¼ litre	white wine	8 fl oz
12.5 cl	fish fumet (*page 167*) or water	4 fl oz
15 g	butter, mashed with 1 tbsp flour	½ oz

Score the mullet on each side, rub with clarified butter, season with salt and pepper, and grill on a preheated grill for 5 to 8 minutes on each side, depending on the size of the fish.

To make the sauce, pound the anchovies, garlic, tomato purée, parsley and oil into a smooth paste. Heat the wine to simmering point, add the fumet or water and the anchovy paste and simmer for 15 minutes. Add the butter and flour mixture and cook, stirring, for a few more minutes until the sauce has thickened. Serve the sauce poured over the fish.

GRANT BLACKMAN
AUSTRALIAN FISH COOKING

Red Mullet in Fennel

To serve 4

Four 125 g	red mullet, cleaned	Four 4 oz
	salt and pepper	
$\frac{1}{2}$	lemon, juice strained	$\frac{1}{2}$
1 tbsp	olive oil	1 tbsp
2 tbsp	chopped fennel	2 tbsp
60 g	fat bacon, coarsely chopped	2 oz
30 g	parsley, chopped	1 oz

Make regular incisions in the fish. Season them and marinate for 3 hours in the lemon juice, oil and fennel.

Add the bacon and parsley to the marinade. Wrap each red mullet in a sheet of greaseproof paper, adding to each parcel a little of the marinade mixture. Secure the ends of the paper and grill the four parcels very gently for about 15 minutes. Serve the fish in their paper. Use scissors to cut open the greaseproof paper wrapper round the red mullet on the plate of each guest; the aroma which rises is simply superb.

SYLVAIN CLUSELLS
COOKING ON TURNING SPIT AND GRILL

Red Mullet in Parcels

Salmonetes Envueltos

To serve 6

12	small red mullet, cleaned	12
	salt and pepper	
12	thin rashers lean bacon	12
6	bay leaves, halved	6

Season the fish with salt and pepper, wrap a bacon rasher round each fish and secure it with a cocktail stick. Insert half a bay leaf between the bacon and the fish.

Grill the fish parcels over medium-hot charcoal, turning them over several times so that they cook evenly. When the fish are ready, in about 10 minutes, remove the bay leaves and the sticks. Serve hot.

MAGDALENA ALPERI
TRATADO COMPLETO DE COMIDAS Y BEBIDAS

Barbecued Grey Mullet

Llisses a la Brasa

To serve 4

Four 350 g	grey mullet, cleaned	Four 12 oz
17.5 cl	oil	6 fl oz
	salt and pepper	

Make several incisions along each side of each fish. Season the oil with salt and pepper and marinate the mullet in it for 30 minutes. Then cook them on a grill for about 20 minutes, turning them once and basting them occasionally with the oil.

LUIS RIPOLL
NUESTRA COCINA

Grey Mullet with Pomegranate Juice

Muggine al Sugo di Melagrana

To obtain the juice from a pomegranate, press it all over with your hands to crush the structure of membranes inside. Then cut a small slit in the skin to allow the juice to drain out. Strain the juice before using it.

This is a recipe from the vicinity of Comacchio, on the Adriatic coast of Italy, where the grey mullet are especially good in the autumn and winter. Do not gut the fish, since, like the red mullet (to which the grey mullet is not related), they gain added flavour by being cooked with gut in place.

To serve 2

2	grey mullet, cleaned	2
1	lemon, juice strained	1
About 8 cl	olive oil	About 3 fl oz
	salt and pepper	
1 or 2	pomegranates, juice strained	1 or 2

Mix together the lemon juice and 4 tablespoons of the olive oil, and marinate the fish in this mixture for about 15 minutes. Then grill them on both sides, for about 10 minutes each side, taking care to salt and pepper them and to baste them sufficiently with olive oil. When they are cooked, put them between two soup plates at the side of the fire and leave them for 5 minutes so that they will soak up instead of losing the juices which will continue to be exuded. Finally, and this is the distinctive feature of the dish, sprinkle them generously with pomegranate juice instead of the usual lemon juice.

ALAN DAVIDSON
MEDITERRANEAN SEAFOOD

Grilled Lamprey

Llampuga Torrada

Instead of the garnish given here, this dish may be served with sweet red peppers, roasted and then dressed with oil, chopped garlic and salt.

To serve 4

1 kg	lamprey, cleaned and cut into thick slices	2 to 2½ lb
¼ tsp	salt	¼ tsp
2	lemons, juice strained	2
30 g	parsley, chopped	1 oz
4	garlic cloves, chopped	4
¼ tsp	cayenne pepper	¼ tsp
8 cl	oil	3 fl oz

Sprinkle the lamprey with salt and half of the lemon juice, and leave for 1 hour or so. Rinse the fish in clean water and let it drain. Cook the slices of fish on a preheated grill for about 3 minutes on each side; do not overcook the slices or they will dry out. Transfer the cooked fish to a serving dish and cover it with the parsley and garlic. Sprinkle over the cayenne pepper and oil, and the remaining lemon juice.

JUAN CASTELLO GUASCH
¡BON PROFIT! (EL LIBRO DE LA COCINA IBICENCA)

Grilled Perch

Sandacz z Rustztu

Serve the grilled fish with potatoes and lettuce or salad.

To serve 4

One 800 g to 1 kg	perch, cleaned and filleted, each fillet cut into 2 or 3 square pieces	One 1¾ to 2 lb
	salt	
45 g	butter, 20 g (¾ oz) melted, the rest cut into small pieces	1½ oz
1 tsp	chopped parsley	1 tsp

Season the fish with salt and leave for 1 hour. Dry the pieces and brush them with the melted butter. Brush the rack with oil and grill the fish on it for about 10 minutes, depending on the thickness of the pieces, turning them over after 5 minutes.

When the pieces are browned, prick one with a fork to see if the juices start to run. If they do, the fish is ready to serve. Arrange the pieces on a serving dish, put a piece of butter on each piece and sprinkle the parsley over.

HELENA HAWLICZKOWA
KUCHNIA POLSKA

Fisherman's Trout

La Truite du Pêcheur

Perfect accompaniments to this dish are thinly sliced cucumber with lemon juice, and a new potato cooked in its skin. The trout can be replaced with mackerel, using fennel tips or dill.

To serve 1

1	trout, sliced down the belly and cleaned, head and tail left intact	1
	salt and pepper	
15 g	butter, kneaded with 1 tsp chopped fresh sorrel	½ oz

Place the trout on the rack 15 cm (6 inches) from ash-covered coals. When the skin becomes loose, in about 5 minutes, turn the trout over and repeat the procedure. When it is done on both sides, season the trout with salt and pepper and add the sorrel butter to the inside.

JULIETTE ELKON
A BELGIAN COOKBOOK

Trout from the Bierzo Valley, León

Truchas al Estilo del Bierzo

This is the typical way of preparing freshly caught trout on the banks of the Bierzo.

To serve 4

4	trout, cleaned	4
60 g	pork fat, cut into 4 long pieces	2 oz

Stuff each trout with a piece of pork fat and grill the trout over a hot wood fire for about 12 minutes, turning once. When they are done, eat them without further seasoning or dressing.

COCINA REGIONAL ESPAÑOLA

Grilled Trout

Trota alla Griglia

To serve 6

6	trout, cleaned	6
12.5 cl	olive oil	4 fl oz
	salt and pepper	
3	garlic cloves, chopped	3
4 tbsp	chopped parsley	4 tbsp

Brush the insides of the trout with oil and sprinkle the cavities with salt and pepper. Mix the garlic and parsley and use this mixture to stuff the trout. Brush the outsides with oil. Grill the fish for 8 to 10 minutes, turning once.

VINCENZO BUONASSISI
CUCINA ALL'ARIA APERTA

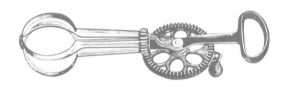

Trout Baked in Paper

Truchas Asadas

To flavour olive oil, heat it gently with a clove of garlic and a sprig of a herb such as rosemary or thyme, just until it sizzles. Then strain the oil and use it as required.

To serve 1

1	trout, cleaned	1
	salt	
1 tbsp	chopped parsley	1 tbsp
30 g	fresh white breadcrumbs	1 oz
About 1 tbsp	lemon juice	About 1 tbsp
	flavoured olive oil	
10 cl	dry white wine	3½ fl oz

Salt the inside of the trout and stuff it with the parsley and breadcrumbs, and a few drops each of lemon juice and flavoured oil. Wrap the fish in brown paper that has been soaked in the wine for 30 minutes. Bury the wrapped fish in the hot ashes and embers of the fire and remove it after 15 minutes. Serve it sprinkled with a few more drops of lemon juice.

ANTONIO ARAGONES SUBERO
GASTRONOMIA DE GUADALAJARA

Citrus-Barbecued Trout

For an extra garnish you may wish to add sliced mushrooms or almonds prior to barbecuing. If so, turn the trout packages once while they are on the grill so that the mushrooms or nuts do not stick to the foil.

To serve 4

4	trout, cleaned	4
60 g	butter, softened	2 oz
	salt and pepper	
2½	lemons, juice of 2 strained, the half lemon cut lengthwise into 4 pieces	2½
½	small onion, cut lengthwise into 4 pieces	½
2	limes, juice strained	2

Rub the trout all over with the butter and sprinkle them with salt and pepper. Insert a piece of lemon and a piece of onion into the the cavity of each trout. Place each trout on a separate piece of heavy-duty aluminium foil and sprinkle lemon and lime juice equally over all four fish. Wrap the foil tightly round the trout and place the packages on the grill rack over fairly hot coals. Barbecue the fish for 20 minutes. There is no need to turn the fish.

KAREN GREEN AND BETTY BLACK
HOW TO COOK HIS GOOSE (AND OTHER WILD GAMES)

Greek Grilled Eel

Cheli tis Skaras

The technique of preparing an eel is shown on page 72.

This is delicious with a salad of tomatoes and *feta* cheese.

To serve 4

1 to 1.5 kg	eel, skinned, cleaned and cut into 5 cm (2 inch) thick slices	2 to 3 lb
	salt and pepper	
4 tbsp	olive oil	4 tbsp
2	lemons, juice of one strained, the other cut into wedges	2
4 tbsp	chopped parsley	4 tbsp

Sprinkle the eel slices with salt and pepper, brush them with some olive oil and grill them for about 10 minutes on each side. Serve at once on a platter, garnished with the lemon wedges, sprinkling the eel with the remaining olive oil, the lemon juice and the chopped parsley.

EVA ZANE
GREEK COOKING FOR THE GODS

Japanese Grilled Eel

Kabayaki

The technique of preparing an eel is shown on page 72. If mirin is unobtainable, sherry can be substituted.

Eel-eating is such a popular pastime in Japan during August when it is thought that eel's health-giving properties are particularly effective against the debility caused by summer heat, that eel restaurants have a difficult time keeping up with the demand. Records of this particular recipe have been found as early as the 13th century.

To serve 4

1	eel, cleaned, head and backbone removed, flesh cut lengthwise into 4 fillets	1
5 tbsp	dark soy sauce	5 tbsp
12.5 cl	*mirin*	4 fl oz
	oil	

Combine in a small saucepan the soy sauce and the *mirin*. Bring the mixture to the boil and cook it until it has reduced to about two-thirds of its original volume.

Heat the grill. When it is hot, lightly oil the eel fillets and the rack to prevent sticking, and place the eel pieces on the rack over the grill. Grill them for about 5 minutes on each side. Remove them from the rack and brush them with the soy sauce and *mirin* mixture, then return them to the rack. Baste the fillets with the mixture two or three times on each side and cook them for a total of about 10 minutes longer, or until the eel is done and the sauce has formed a shiny glaze on the surface. Serve the eel immediately, with a tablespoon or two of the leftover sauce poured over the top of each fillet.

PETER AND JOAN MARTIN
JAPANESE COOKING

Grilled Eel with Bercy Butter

Gegrilde Paling met Bercy Boter

The technique of preparing eels for grilling is shown on page 72. To prepare poached beef marrow, first ask your butcher to saw beef marrow bones into 10 cm (4 inch) sections. Place the bones in a saucepan with enough water to cover them. Bring the water to the boil, reduce the heat and simmer for a few minutes. Drain, then shake each bone gently over a plate to slip the marrow out in one piece. It can then be cut into cubes.

Serve this dish with potatoes and a fresh salad.

To serve 4 to 6

1 kg	fat eels	2 to 2½ lb
	salt and freshly ground black pepper	
	olive oil	

Bercy butter

2 tbsp	finely chopped shallots	2 tbsp
¼ litre	dry white wine	8 fl oz
1 tbsp	finely chopped parsley	1 tbsp
1 tbsp	cubed, poached beef marrow	1 tbsp
1 tsp	mustard	1 tsp
30 g	chopped hazelnuts	1 oz
	salt and pepper	
	lemon juice	
200 g	butter, softened	7 oz

Cut the eels with diagonal cuts into portions 7.5 cm (3 inches) wide. Score the skin at 1 cm (½ inch) intervals, and sprinkle the pieces with salt and plenty of black pepper. Brush them with olive oil and grill them gently for 10 minutes, turning them several times so that they cook evenly.

Simmer the shallots in the wine until the liquid is reduced by half. Stir in the parsley, marrow, mustard and hazelnuts. Season, and add lemon juice. Stir in the softened butter. Cover the bottom of a serving dish with the Bercy butter and arrange the grilled eel portions on top.

HUGH JANS
VRIJ NEDERLAND

Spit-Roasted Eel

Anguilla Arrosto

The technique of preparing an eel is shown on page 72.

The flesh of eel is rich and spit-roasting is a good way of cooking it. The skin is left on, since it forms a protective crust which prevents the flesh itself from hardening during the cooking—and it can easily be peeled off afterwards.

The dish is often accompanied in northern Italy by *mostarda di Cremona*, which can be bought in Italian food shops. It is made of whole fruits—tiny pears and oranges, apricots and cherries—and slices of melon, preserved in sugar syrup and flavoured with mustard oil and garlic.

To serve 4

1	large eel, cut across into sections 8 to 10 cm (3 to 4 inches) thick	1
	sage leaves, bay leaves or rosemary sprigs	
	salt	

Impale the sections of eel on the spit, with sage leaves, bay leaves or sprigs of rosemary in between. Place a drip pan under the spit and roast the eel for 8 minutes, basting it frequently with its own fat drippings and plenty of salt. Towards the end of cooking, the fire should be very hot.

ALAN DAVIDSON
MEDITERRANEAN SEAFOOD

Grilled Eel

The technique of preparing eels is shown on page 72. To give the eels a particularly delicious flavour, the author suggests grilling them over the embers of a fire of vine prunings, as is done by the eel fishermen of the river Loir in France.

	To serve 6	
2 or 3	eels, skinned and cut into 4 to 5 cm (1½ to 2 inch) pieces	2 or 3
	salt and black pepper	
2 tbsp	wine vinegar	2 tbsp
1	lemon, juice strained	1
About 8 cl	olive oil	About 3 fl oz
	bay leaves	
60 g	dry white breadcrumbs	2 oz
	lemon quarters	

Put the eel pieces in a flat dish, season well and sprinkle over the wine vinegar, the lemon juice and enough olive oil to ensure that the pieces are coated lightly. Leave for 2 hours.

Thread the eel pieces on to skewers, alternating them with bay leaves. Grill over a moderate heat until the flesh separates from the bone without too much trouble (test a thin piece), about 8 minutes. As they cook, brush them from time to time with such marinade as remains in the dish. When they are done, brush them over again, this time with fresh olive oil, and sprinkle them liberally with the breadcrumbs. Return them to the grill for a few minutes, until the breadcrumbs are appetizingly browned. Serve with lemon quarters.

JANE GRIGSON
FISH COOKERY

Eel Kebabs from Travemünde

Aalspiesse Travemünde

The technique of preparing an eel is shown on page 72.

	To serve 4	
One 750 g	eel, gutted, skinned and cut diagonally into 12 pieces	One 1½ lb
2	lemons, juice of 1 strained, the other cut in quarters	2
8 cl	dry white wine	3 fl oz
	salt and freshly ground white pepper	
1	small dried chili pepper, seeded and chopped	1
1	bay leaf	1
13	small sprigs dill	13
8 cl	oil	3 fl oz
12	large mushroom caps, cleaned	12
½	cucumber, unpeeled, cut into 1.5 cm (⅔ inch) slices	½
100 g	piece fatty bacon, cut into 2 cm (¾ inch) cubes	3½ oz
1	sweet red pepper, seeded and cut into squares	1
½ tsp	paprika	½ tsp

Mix the lemon juice with the white wine, some salt and pepper, the chili pepper, bay leaf and a sprig of dill. Stir in 2 tablespoons of oil and marinate the pieces of eel in this mixture for 50 minutes to 1 hour. Place the mushroom caps in the wine marinade too, so that they do not discolour.

Remove the pieces of eel from the marinade, dry them lightly and push a sprig of dill into the centre of each piece. Dry the mushroom caps and thread an eel piece, a mushroom, a cucumber slice, a bacon cube and a piece of red pepper on to each of four metal skewers. Continue threading the ingredients in sequence until they are all used up. Then brush the kebabs with oil and sprinkle them lightly with the paprika. Brush the grill rack with oil and grill the kebabs on it for 5 to 8 minutes, turning them frequently. Serve the kebabs with lemon quarters.

MECHTHILD PIEPENBROCK
GRILL VERGNÜGEN

Eels Cooked on a Spit

Anguilles à la Broche

Instead of using skewers, you can tie the eels to the spit with a length of string.

This recipe requires some preparation the day before, as the eels must be given a preliminary poaching. However, the spit-roasting is a spectacular sight, and the dish is very good to eat. It is best if you can poach the eels in a fish kettle as this allows them to remain straightened out rather than coiled up.

To serve 8 to 10

Two 700 to 900 g	eels	Two 1½ to 1¾ lb
2	carrots, finely chopped	2
2	turnips, finely chopped	2
1	small stick celery, finely chopped	1
2 litres	water	3½ pints
1	bay leaf	1
1	sprig parsley	1
	salt and pepper	
½ litre	dry white wine	16 fl oz
2	eggs, lightly beaten	2
125 g	dry breadcrumbs, seasoned	4 oz

Place the carrots, turnips and celery in a saucepan with the water. Add the bay leaf and parsley, season with salt and pepper and bring to the boil. Cook for 1 hour, then strain and discard the vegetables and herbs. Pour the cooking liquid into a fish kettle and add the white wine. Boil for 10 minutes, then leave to cool completely.

Tie a piece of string round the head of each eel and suspend each one from a nail. With a small sharp knife, make a slit in the skin right round the body, just below the gills. Roll back the skin for about 1 cm (½ inch), then grasp the loose skin firmly in a cloth and pull it towards the tail to skin the eels. Cut off their heads and tails, open their stomachs and remove the entrails, then wash the stomach cavities.

Place the eels in the cold cooking liquid in the fish kettle over a gentle heat. Bring the contents to a gentle simmer and cook for 20 minutes. Leave the eels to cool in the cooking liquid until the next day.

When you are ready to barbecue the eels, take them from their poaching liquid. Using a brush, paint beaten egg over each eel, then sprinkle on breadcrumbs; brush on more egg and sprinkle on more breadcrumbs until all the egg and breadcrumbs have been used up.

Arrange the eels on either side of a spit, and keep them in place by fixing small skewers through the eels and at right angles to the spit. Wrap the whole thing up in a piece of oiled greaseproof paper and grill, turning frequently, for about 20 minutes.

Remove the greaseproof paper and place the spit directly on the grilling rack, very close to the coals, for a few seconds on each side, to brown the breadcrumb coating.

CÉLINE VENCE
LE BARBECUE EN 10 LEÇONS

Barbecued Prawns
Gambes a la Brasa

The technique of preparing large prawns for grilling is demonstrated on page 70.

To serve 4

12 or more	Mediterranean or Pacific prawns in their shells	12 or more
12.5 cl	aïoli (page 163)	4 fl oz

Prepare a fire of burning vine shoots or brushwood and place a metal baking sheet or slate on top to heat for about 30 minutes. Place the prawns on the baking sheet or slate and cook them for 5 to 6 minutes on each side. Transfer them to a hot serving dish and serve them at once, with *aïoli*.

ELIANA THIBAUT COMELADE
CUINA ROSSELLONESA I DE LA COSTA BRAVA

M. C. Charcoaled Prawns

The technique of de-veining prawns is shown on page 70.

To serve 4

1 kg	large raw prawns, rinsed in cold water, shells snipped open along the back, de-veined	2 lb
3	garlic cloves, chopped	3
1	medium-sized onion, chopped	1
1 tsp	dry mustard	1 tsp
1 tsp	salt	1 tsp
12.5 cl	olive or peanut oil	4 fl oz
3 tbsp	lemon juice	3 tbsp
30 g	parsley, finely chopped	1 oz

Place the prawns in a bowl. Combine the remaining ingredients and pour them over the prawns. Marinate the prawns in the refrigerator for at least 5 hours. Drain the prawns and arrange them on a grill rack over hot coals. Cook them for 5 to 8 minutes, turning once. Serve the prawns in their shells.

THE JEKYLL ISLAND GARDEN CLUB (EDITORS)
GOLDEN ISLES CUISINE

Charcoal-Grilled Prawns

To serve 4

24	raw Dublin Bay or Pacific prawns, shelled	24
24	anchovy fillets	24
12	slices lean bacon, cut in half lengthwise	12

Split the prawns deeply down the back, remove the intestinal thread and insert an anchovy fillet in each split. Wrap half a slice of bacon round each prawn, securing it with a toothpick. Grill the prawns in a hinged wire rack over coals, turning several times, until the bacon is crisp, about 5 minutes or less. Do not overcook the prawns or they will dry out.

NANCY FAIR MCINTYRE
IT'S A PICNIC!

Garlic-Grilled Prawns

The technique of de-veining prawns is shown on page 70.

To serve 6

12	raw Pacific or Dublin Bay prawns, shells snipped open along the back, de-veined and rinsed in cold water	12
$\frac{1}{4}$ litre	olive oil	8 fl oz
1	lemon, juice strained	1
3	garlic cloves, crushed	3
2 tbsp	finely chopped parsley	2 tbsp
$\frac{1}{4}$ tsp	ground cloves	$\frac{1}{4}$ tsp

Make a marinade from the olive oil, lemon juice, garlic, parsley and ground cloves. Marinate the prawns in this mixture for 2 to 3 hours, then drain them and place them in a hinged wire basket. Grill the prawns for 4 to 5 minutes on each side, or until the flesh has turned white and opaque. Serve the prawns in their shells, with a little marinade poured over them, if desired.

THE EDITORS OF LADIES' HOME JOURNAL
ADVENTURES IN COOKING

Prawn Kebabs

The technique of de-veining prawns is shown on page 70.

To serve 4

500 g	raw Pacific prawns, shelled and de-veined	1 lb
6 to 8	rashers bacon, rind removed, each cut into halves or thirds	6 to 8
60 g	butter, melted	2 oz
4 tbsp	lemon juice	4 tbsp

Wrap each prawn in a piece of bacon and thread them on to four bamboo skewers. Combine the melted butter and the lemon juice and brush this mixture over the kebabs.

Grill the kebabs over hot coals for 10 to 15 minutes, or until the prawns are cooked and the bacon is lightly brown and crisp. Turn the kebabs frequently while cooking and, before serving, brush them again with the melted butter and lemon juice. Pour any remaining butter into a small bowl or jug and serve it with the kebabs.

ELIZABETH SEWELL
BARBECUE COOKBOOK

Prawn Satay

The author recommends using Japanese soy sauce (also known as tamari *or* shoyu *sauce), which can be bought in Oriental and health food shops.*

To serve 4

500 g	raw prawns, shelled	1 lb
	Satay sauce	
$\frac{1}{4}$ litre	coconut milk (*page 167*)	8 fl oz
1 tsp	salt	1 tsp
$\frac{1}{8}$ tsp	ground ginger	$\frac{1}{8}$ tsp
1 tbsp	brown sugar	1 tbsp
$\frac{1}{2}$ tsp	chili powder	$\frac{1}{2}$ tsp
1 tbsp	soy sauce	1 tbsp
1 tbsp	lime juice	1 tbsp

In a shallow bowl, combine all the ingredients for the sauce. Marinate the prawns in the satay sauce at room temperature for 30 minutes, turning them frequently. Remove the prawns from the marinade with a slotted spoon and thread them, head to tail, on to bamboo or metal skewers, three or four to each skewer. Grill the prawns over charcoal for about 2 minutes on each side, or until done to your taste, but do not overcook them. When grilling the prawns, baste them liberally with the remaining satay sauce.

ALEX D. HAWKES (EDITOR)
THE SHRIMP COOKBOOK

Skewered Crayfish

Brochetas de Cigalas

To serve 4

12	crayfish tails	12
1	sweet green pepper, cut into 8 pieces	1
12	small onions	12
1	sweet red pepper, cut into 8 pieces	1
8 cl	oil	3 fl oz
1	lemon, juice strained	1
	salt	

Thread each of four skewers in the following order: green pepper, onion, crayfish, red pepper, onion, crayfish, green pepper, onion, crayfish, red pepper.

Grill the skewers over hot charcoal for 5 minutes, turning them frequently and basting them with a mixture of the oil and lemon juice, seasoned with a little salt.

IGNACIO DOMENECH
PESCADOS Y MARISCOS

Barbecued Spiny Lobsters

Llagostes a la Brasa

The technique of preparing lobsters is shown on page 70. The author recommends serving the barbecued lobsters with mayonnaise (recipe, page 163) or tomato purée (recipe, page 164) and a good salad.

To serve 4

Two 400 to 500 g	spiny lobsters, split in half lengthwise	Two 14 oz to 1 lb
8 cl	vinaigrette (*page 163*)	3 fl oz
	white pepper	
	dried thyme, powdered	
	dried bay leaves, powdered	

Prepare a fire of vine shoots or charcoal. Brush the lobster flesh with the vinaigrette and dust it lightly with the pepper, thyme and bay. Place the lobster halves on an oiled, preheated rack. Cook the lobsters for 10 to 15 minutes on each side (depending on their size), sprinkling them from time to time with more vinaigrette.

ELIANA THIBAUT COMELADE
CUINA ROSSELLONESA I DE LA COSTA BRAVA

Grilled Crawfish with Basil Butter

Langouste Grillée au Beurre de Basilic

To serve 2

Two 500 g or one 1 kg	crawfish or spiny lobsters, split lengthwise	Two 1 lb or one 2 to 2½ lb
	salt and pepper	
2 tbsp	olive oil	2 tbsp
100 g	butter	3½ oz
20	basil leaves, roughly chopped	20

Season the crawfish or lobsters with salt and pepper and sprinkle with olive oil. Grill them, shell side downwards, for 5 minutes, and then flesh side downwards for 5 minutes.

Meanwhile, put the butter with the basil in a small saucepan and let the butter melt over a low heat.

Turn the crawfish flesh side up and sprinkle liberally with the basil butter. Without turning them, continue to cook the crawfish for 10 minutes for two small ones, or 20 minutes for one large one, basting frequently with the basil butter.

Serve with no further embellishment.

ROGER VERGÉ
CUISINE OF THE SUN

California Grilled Lobster

The technique of preparing a lobster is shown on page 70.

To serve 2

One 1 kg	live lobster	One 2 to 2½ lb
150 g	butter	5 oz
	salt and black pepper	
1 tsp	paprika	1 tsp
1	lemon, cut into wedges	1
	watercress	

Plunge the lobster into vigorously boiling salted water and cook it for 4 minutes. Remove it from the water, allow it to cool sufficiently to handle, then split it down the middle and rinse out the gravel sac and the black intestinal vein.

Mix together 30 g (1 oz) of the butter, a pinch each of salt and pepper and the paprika. Spread half this mixture on the meat side of the lobster pieces and grill them over charcoal, meat side down, for 6 minutes. Turn the lobster pieces, spread on the remaining butter mixture and continue to cook for approximately 10 minutes more.

Garnish the lobster pieces with lemon wedges and watercress, and serve at once with the remaining butter, melted.

THE BROWN DERBY COOKBOOK

Special Barbecued Lobsters

The technique of preparing lobsters is shown on page 70.

To serve 8

4	cooked lobsters, split in half lengthwise, intestinal vein and gravel sac removed	4
125 g	butter, melted	4 oz
2	garlic cloves, crushed	2
1	lemon, juice strained	1
	salt and pepper	
	watercress	
8	lemon wedges	8

Crack the lobster claws, remove the flesh from them and add it to the flesh in the shells. Mix together the melted butter, garlic, lemon juice, salt and pepper and brush the lobsters with this sauce. Cook the lobsters, shell-side down, on a rack over medium coals for 12 to 15 minutes, basting them several times with the sauce. Place the lobsters on a serving dish and garnish them with watercress and the lemon wedges.

BARBARA LOGAN
BARBECUE AND OUTDOOR COOKERY

Lobster Kebabs

Hummerfleisch am Spiess

To cook a lobster, plunge it into a large pan of boiling salted water. Hold it under the surface with tongs for 2 minutes. Turn down the heat, cover the pan and simmer the lobster for about 10 to 12 minutes. Sauce Colbert is a variation of béarnaise sauce (recipe, page 164) which is flavoured by the addition of a little melted glace de viande *(recipe, page 167).*

To serve 2

One 750 g	lobster, cooked, tail meat removed and sliced	One 1½ lb
250 g	large mushrooms, sliced	8 oz
125 g	goose, turkey or calf's liver, sliced	4 oz
	melted butter mixed with salt and pepper	
	herb butter (*page 162*)	
	Sauce Colbert	

Thread slices of lobster, mushroom and liver, one after another, on to skewers. Brush with seasoned, melted butter. Grill the skewers for 12 to 15 minutes. Cover the skewers with herb butter and serve them with Sauce Colbert.

THEODOR BOTTIGER
SCHALEN UND KRUSTENTIERE

Skewered Scallops and Cucumbers with Dill

Brochettes de Saint-Jacques et Concombres à l'Aneth

Aromatics such as sliced carrot and onion and chopped parsley may be added to the court-bouillon.

Normally a coral butter would accompany the skewered scallops. Poach 90 g (3 oz) of the scallop corals (the remainder left attached to the scallops and skewered) in a court-bouillon made from 8 cl (3 fl oz) each of water and white wine, flavoured with a little dill. After 3 minutes, sieve the corals and reduce the court-bouillon by boiling it over a medium heat until only a tablespoonful remains. Whisk the sieved corals and the reduced court-bouillon into about 125 g (4 oz) of softened butter. Whip 8 cl (3 fl oz) of double cream and whisk it into the mixture. Season to taste.

If you use dried dill weed, soak it for 10 minutes or so in the lemon juice before assembling the marinade.

To serve 4

500 g	shelled scallops, halved across the grain if very large, rinsed and sponged dry	1 lb
300 to 350 g	cucumbers	10 to 12 oz
	salt	
	Marinade	
1 tbsp	finely chopped fresh dill leaves and tender flower buds, or 1 tsp dried dill weed	1 tbsp
1	lemon, juice strained	1
4 tbsp	olive oil	4 tbsp
	salt and pepper	

Peel the cucumbers and, if they are small and firm and the seeds are still unformed, cut them into 1 cm (½ inch) sections. Split larger ones into halves or quarters, seed them and cut them into sections approximating the dimensions of the scallops. Parboil the cucumber pieces for about 1 minute in strongly salted water and drain.

Mix together the ingredients for the marinade and marinate the cucumbers and scallops for about 1 hour. Skewer alternating cucumber sections and scallops, and grill them in a hinged grilling basket over a fairly intense bed of coals for 8 to 10 minutes, basting regularly with the marinade.

RICHARD OLNEY
SIMPLE FRENCH FOOD

Scallops on Skewers

Coquilles Saint-Jacques en Brochettes

To serve 4

8 to 16	scallops, shells removed, cleaned	8 to 16
200 g	fat bacon, cut into 3 cm (1¼ inch) squares, blanched for 3 to 4 minutes in boiling water	7 oz
	salt and pepper	
About 10 cl	olive oil, or 60 g (2 oz) butter, melted	About 3½ fl oz
4	shallots, finely chopped	4
4 tbsp	finely chopped parsley	4 tbsp

Thread the scallops and the bacon pieces alternately on to four skewers. Sprinkle salt and pepper over the skewers and brush them generously with some of the olive oil or melted butter. Grill the skewers over hot coals for about 5 minutes, turning several times.

Meanwhile, fry the shallots and parsley in a little more oil or butter for about 1 minute. When the scallops are cooked, serve them very hot, covered in the shallots and parsley.

TANTE MARIE
LA VÉRITABLE CUISINE DE FAMILLE

Charcoal-Grilled Scallops

The authors suggest that the scallops can also be cooked on skewers with slices of aubergine, tomatoes and mushrooms.

To serve 6

1 kg	scallops, shells removed	2 lb
12.5 cl	oil	4 fl oz
4 tbsp	lemon juice	4 tbsp
2 tsp	salt	2 tsp
¼ tsp	white pepper	¼ tsp
250 g	thinly sliced bacon, each slice cut in half lengthwise and then crosswise	8 oz
	paprika	

Place the scallops in a bowl. Combine the oil, lemon juice, salt and pepper. Pour this over the scallops and leave them to marinate for 30 minutes, stirring occasionally. Remove the scallops, reserving the sauce for basting. Wrap each scallop in a piece of bacon and fasten the bacon with a toothpick. Baste the scallops with a little of the reserved sauce and place them in a well-oiled, hinged wire basket. Cook them about 10 cm (4 inches) from moderately hot coals for 5 minutes. Baste them

with the reserved sauce and sprinkle them with paprika. Turn the scallops and cook them for 5 to 7 minutes longer, or until the bacon is crisp.

JANE CHEKENIAN AND MONICA MEYER
SHELLFISH COOKERY

Mussels on the Spit

To serve 4

40	mussels, scrubbed	40
4 tbsp	white wine	4 tbsp
2	small shallots, chopped	2
	salt and white pepper	
12	button mushrooms, cut into 40 thin slices	12
30 g	butter	1 oz
40	thin rashers green streaky bacon	40
1½ tbsp	flour, sifted	1½ tbsp
2	eggs, well beaten	2
45 g	fine white breadcrumbs	1½ oz
3 tbsp	olive oil	3 tbsp
	dried fennel	
	parsley sprigs	

Place the mussels, wine, shallots and a little pepper in a saucepan. Cover tightly and cook over a high heat for 3 to 5 minutes, until the mussels have opened. Shell the mussels.

Sweat the mushrooms quickly in the butter and season with salt. Wrap a mussel and mushroom slice in each rasher of bacon, and assemble 10 mussels on each skewer.

Next, prepare three plates for your coating. Put the flour on a dinner plate, the eggs in a shallow dish, and the breadcrumbs on to another dinner plate. Very gently dip each skewerful of mussels first into the flour, then into the beaten egg and finally into the breadcrumbs, making sure that the latter adhere well all round.

Flavour the olive oil with a pinch each of fennel, salt and pepper. Brush the breadcrumbed mussels on their skewers gently with the oil and then either roast them on a vertical spit or grill them well over a gentle heat for about 5 minutes, basting from time to time with the oil.

Serve on a long dish, garnished with parsley sprigs.

SYLVAIN CLUSELLS
COOKING ON TURNING SPIT AND GRILL

Grilled Oysters au Gratin

To serve 6 to 8

48	oysters, shelled	48
1 tsp	salt	1 tsp
100 g	fine dry breadcrumbs	3½ oz
250 g	butter, melted	8 oz

Mix the salt and the breadcrumbs together in a shallow dish. Pour the melted butter into a shallow bowl. Drain the oysters, rolling them well in a clean napkin to make them as dry as possible. Take each oyster upon a fork (thrust through the tough muscle), dip it into crumbs, then into butter, then into crumbs again. Arrange the oysters in a hinged wire rack and grill them over a bright coal fire for about 3 minutes, turning the wire rack every 5 to 10 seconds. When the oysters are plump and their juices run, they are done. Serve them at once.

U.S. DEPARTMENT OF COMMERCE, BUREAU OF FISHERIES
ECONOMIC CIRCULAR NO. 18

Oysters en Brochette

To serve 1

4	oysters, shelled	4
2 tsp	lemon juice	2 tsp
	salt and freshly ground black pepper	
4	mushroom caps	4
1	long, thin rasher bacon	1
	melted butter	
1 tbsp	finely chopped parsley	1 tbsp
1	lemon wedge	1

Sprinkle the oysters with the lemon juice, salt and pepper. At the end of the skewer, place a mushroom cap. Next, put the end of the bacon strip, then an oyster, then loop the bacon round the oyster on to the skewer again, add another mushroom, another oyster, and continue until you have used all four oysters, weaving the bacon between each item.

Brush the skewered oysters with melted butter and grill them over hot charcoal, turning them several times, for about 3 minutes. Sprinkle with the chopped parsley and serve with a lemon wedge.

JAMES BEARD
JAMES BEARD'S NEW FISH COOKERY

Barbecued Squid

To serve 4 to 6

1.5 kg	squid, cleaned, skinned and cut into rings	3 lb
1 to 6	garlic cloves, finely chopped	1 to 6
60 g	butter	2 oz
2	lemons, juice strained	2

Fry the garlic in 15 g (½ oz) of the butter until it is lightly browned. Add the rest of the butter and the lemon juice. Allow the butter to melt, then set the sauce aside.

Thread the rings of squid on to skewers. Grill the rings over red-hot coals for 2 to 3 minutes on each side, or until brown. Serve the squid pieces hot with the lemon-garlic butter.

ISAAC CRONIN
THE INTERNATIONAL SQUID COOKBOOK

Grilled Cuttlefish

Tintenfisch vom Rost

To prepare a cuttlefish, wash it in cold water; then, with a sharp knife, slit the back from head to tail, pressing until the blade strikes the cuttlebone. Ease apart the sides of the cut to expose the oval cuttlebone, and, with your fingers, gently ease the bone out. Peel away and discard the membrane covering the viscera, then scoop out and discard the viscera. If the cuttlefish is small, it can be cooked whole in this recipe. If it is large, cut off the tentacles and cut the body pouch into rings.

To serve 4

4	small whole cuttlefish, or 8 rings cut from 1 large cuttlefish body	4
	salt	
1	lemon, juice strained	1
4 tbsp	olive oil	4 tbsp
	coarsely chopped flat-leafed parsley	
1	lemon, cut into quarters	1

Sprinkle the cuttlefish with salt and trickle a little lemon juice and olive oil over them. Place them on a grill over hot charcoal and cook them for about 10 minutes, brushing them several times with a mixture of the remaining lemon juice and olive oil, and turning the pieces so that they cook evenly on both sides. Sprinkle the cuttlefish with chopped parsley and garnish them with lemon quarters.

FRISCH VOM GRILL

Miscellaneous Delicacies

Cheese in Vine Leaves

The technique of wrapping cheese in vine leaves is shown on page 78; depending on the size of the slices of cheese, you may only need to use two vine leaves for each slice. The author recommends using a good melting cheese such as Gruyère, Emmenthal, Bel Paese, Cheddar or fontina for this recipe.

To serve 4		
4	thick slices cheese	4
16 to 20	vine leaves	16 to 20
4	slices bread	4

Wrap up each slice of cheese in four or five vine leaves. Put the packages over a gentle fire until the cheese has melted and absorbed the distinct tang of the vine leaves—about 10 minutes. Serve on slices of bread.

CLAUDIA RODEN
PICNIC

Grilled Goat's Cheese

Fromages de Chèvre au Gril

The author recommends using Chabichou du Poitou, a French goat's milk cheese, for this recipe. Chabichou is formed into small cylinders or flat-topped cones, then rolled in powdered charcoal which forms a matt, blue-black coating on its outer surface. The cheese hardens and dries as it matures; the author suggests using mature Chabichou because the drier the cheese, the better it will taste after it has been grilled.

To serve 4		
4	small mature goat's cheeses	4
2 tbsp	oil	2 tbsp
4	slices freshly toasted bread	4
	freshly ground black pepper	

Lightly scrape the surface of the cheeses with a knife, but do not remove all the skin. Brush the cheeses with the oil, then place them on a rack over a fairly high heat for 2 minutes before turning them over. Cook them for 3 minutes more. Serve immediately, each cheese accompanied by a slice of toast and seasoned with pepper.

CÉLINE VENCE
LE BARBECUE EN 10 LEÇONS

Bread and Cheese Skewers

Crostini alla Provatura

This recipe is traditionally made with Roman *provatura*, a fresh, soft cheese which is the size and shape of an egg. Cut from the home-made bread as many pieces as there are slices of cheese, plus six more.

To serve 6		
500 g	*provatura* or *mozzarella* cheese, cut into medium-thick slices	1 lb
	salt and pepper	
	home-made white bread, cut into pieces the same size and thickness as the cheese	
135 g	butter, 15 g (½ oz) melted	4½ oz
4	large anchovy fillets, chopped	4

Season the cheese with salt and pepper. Thread the bread and cheese alternately on to six skewers, beginning and ending each one with a slice of bread. Cook the skewers over the embers of a wood fire, turning and basting them from time to time with the melted butter. The bread and cheese should become brown and slightly smoked.

While the *crostini* are cooking, mix the chopped anchovy fillets and the remaining butter. Cook them gently in a small frying pan until the anchovies have dissolved into the butter to make a sauce.

Arrange the *crostini* in a heated serving dish and pour the hot anchovy butter over the top.

ADA BONI
ITALIAN REGIONAL COOKING

Mixed Grill with Cheese

"Mixed Grill" de Fromage

For this recipe, select a combination of two or more firm cheeses. Cheddar, Cheshire, Gruyère, Emmenthal, Jarlsberg, fontina, provolone, Gouda and Edam are all suitable cheeses.

To serve 4 to 6		
500 to 750 g	firm cheese, cut into 1 cm (½ inch) slices	1 to 1½ lb
	finely chopped parsley or basil leaves, or grated nutmeg, or ground cinnamon or fennel seeds, or freshly ground black pepper	

Grill the slices of cheese about 15 to 20 cm (6 to 8 inches) from the coals, turning them once with a metal spatula, until the cheese is cooked but not melted—about 3 minutes in all. Place the cheese slices on heated plates and season them to taste with parsley or basil, or nutmeg, cinnamon or fennel seeds, or simply with pepper.

LE BARBECUE

Melted Cheese Valais-Style

La Raclette Valaisanne

This method of melting half a raclette cheese in front of an open fire and then scraping out the pale sizzling mass originates in the canton of Valais in Switzerland and derives its name from the French verb racler, to scrape. The cheeses used are semi-hard ones such as Gomser, Bagnes and Orsières, which are produced in Valais; they weigh about 5 kg (11 lb)

when whole and are about 10 cm (4 inches) thick. Raclette cheeses can be bought in shops specializing in Swiss food and in many good delicatessens.

To serve 8		
½	semi-hard Swiss cheese, weighing about 2.5 kg (5 lb)	½
	black pepper	
8	potatoes, boiled in their jackets	8
16	gherkins	16
16	pickled onions	16

Have ready eight warmed, heat-resistant plates. Position a small trestle table or a flat rock in front of the flickering heat of a fierce fire, preferably made with logs or wood charcoal. Place the cheese on the trestle table or rock, with the cut side facing the heat. After about 30 seconds, when the cheese begins to melt and bubble, turn it away from the fire and, holding it with one hand, use the back of a knife to scrape out the creamy melted cheese on to one of the warmed plates. Season the bubbling cheese with pepper, add a potato, some gherkins and pickled onions, and serve it.

Replace the cheese in front of the fire, positioning it so that the whole of the cut surface is exposed and the cheese will melt evenly and easily. After another 30 seconds, scrape off the melted cheese and serve the second portion, and so on. As the cheese melts, fold the bubbling edges of the two flat surfaces inwards; this will produce the crusty titbit known as the *religieuse*, which is highly prized by lovers of *raclette*.

MARIO V. BONDANINI (EDITOR)
GASTRONOMIE DE PLEIN AIR

Grilled Frogs' Legs

To serve 6		
12	pairs frogs' legs	12
6	slices bread, toasted and buttered	6
	Marinade	
17.5 cl	oil	6 fl oz
5 tbsp	lemon juice	5 tbsp
	salt and freshly ground pepper	
1	garlic clove, crushed	1

Mix together the ingredients for the marinade and marinate the frogs' legs in the mixture for 30 to 45 minutes. Turn them in the marinade three or four times.

Place the frogs' legs in a hinged wire rack and grill them over moderate coals, basting them with the marinade every few minutes. Cook for 5 to 6 minutes on each side, or until done. Serve on the slices of crisp buttered toast.

JOHN AND MARIE ROBERSON
THE COMPLETE BARBECUE BOOK

Standard Preparations

Dry Salt Marinade

This marinade is particularly good with pork. The meat can be left in the salting mixture for up to 48 hours.

To make about 350 g (12 oz)

300 g	coarse salt	10 oz
2 tbsp	juniper berries	2 tbsp
1 tsp	black peppercorns	1 tsp
5	allspice berries	5
1 tbsp	dried thyme	1 tbsp
3	bay leaves, crumbled	3

In a large mortar, grind the juniper berries, peppercorns, allspice berries and thyme to a coarse powder. Then add the crumbled bay leaves and salt, and grind until the ingredients are thoroughly blended.

Paste Marinade

To make about 12.5 cl (4 fl oz)

5	allspice berries	5
3	blades mace	3
15	cardamom pods, seeds removed and reserved, husks discarded	15
2	bay leaves, crumbled	2
10	dried chili peppers, stemmed and seeded	10
1 to 2 tbsp	olive oil	1 to 2 tbsp

In a mortar, pound the allspice and mace with a pestle. Add the cardamom seeds, crumbled bay leaves and chili peppers. Grind them to a fine powder, then dribble in enough olive oil to form a thick paste.

Cardamom and pepper paste: Grind together ¼ teaspoon of cardamom seeds, ¼ teaspoon of black peppercorns and a pinch of crushed red chili peppers in a mortar. Add about 2 tablespoons of olive oil—just enough to make a paste.

Thyme and chervil paste: Mix together 2 tablespoons of finely chopped fresh thyme, 15 g (½ oz) of finely chopped fresh chervil, ½ teaspoon of salt and ¼ teaspoon of freshly ground black pepper. Add just enough olive oil to form a moist paste.

Oil Marinade

To make about 15 cl (¼ pint)

4 tbsp	olive oil	4 tbsp
2	garlic cloves, finely chopped	2
2 tsp	finely chopped fresh thyme or 1 tsp mixed dried herbs	2 tsp
2 tbsp	finely chopped parsley	2 tbsp
3	shallots, finely chopped (optional)	3
2 tbsp	grated orange rind (optional)	2 tbsp
	salt and freshly ground black pepper	

Combine the oil with the garlic, herbs, parsley and shallots and orange rind, if used. Season with salt and pepper.

Oil and ginger marinade: Combine 4 tablespoons of olive oil with 2 tablespoons of chopped fresh ginger root and 4 tablespoons each of grated orange rind and chopped garlic.

Oil, parsley and lemon marinade: In a mortar, pound 2 garlic cloves and half a tablespoon of coarse salt together to make a smooth paste. Add half a tablespoon of lemon juice, then gradually stir in 12.5 cl (4 fl oz) of olive oil and 1 tablespoon of finely chopped parsley.

Lime, Orange and Garlic Marinade

To prepare enough of this marinade for a whole small pig, as demonstrated on pages 80-83, you will need to double the quantities given here.

To make about ¾ litre (1¼ pints)

35 cl	lime juice	12 fl oz
¼ litre	orange juice	8 fl oz
12.5 cl	olive oil	4 fl oz
2 to 3	garlic heads, cloves coarsely chopped	2 to 3
75 g	coarse salt	2½ oz
2 tsp	freshly ground black pepper	2 tsp
3	bay leaves	3

Thoroughly combine all the ingredients together in a bowl.

Yogurt Marinade

This marinade is particularly suitable for lamb or chicken.

To make about 55 cl (18 fl oz)

½ litre	yogurt	16 fl oz
4 tbsp	olive oil	4 tbsp
2	garlic cloves, finely chopped	2
2 tsp	chopped mint leaves	2 tsp
	freshly ground black pepper	

Whisk the yogurt to a smooth consistency, then stir into it the oil, garlic and mint. Season to taste with pepper.

Wine and Oil Marinade

If this marinade is used for fish, a few sprigs of dill can be added to the mixture.

To make about ¾ litre (1¼ pints)

½ litre	dry white or red wine	16 fl oz
12.5 cl	olive oil	4 fl oz
1	onion, thinly sliced	1
2	carrots, thinly sliced	2
4	sprigs parsley	4
12	blades chives	12
	freshly ground black pepper	

Combine the wine and oil with the onion, carrot, parsley and chives. Season with pepper.

Flavoured Butter

To make about 300 g (10 oz)

250 g	butter	8 oz

Soften the butter at room temperature, or beat it to make it pliable. Using a wooden spoon or a pestle, work in the prepared flavouring of your choice. Using a flexible scraper, press the butter through a fine-meshed drum sieve. Use the butter immediately, or cover and refrigerate.

Sweet red pepper butter: Roast one or two sweet red peppers in a 220°C (425°F or Mark 7) oven, or grill them, for 20 to 30 minutes, turning them frequently so that their skins blister evenly. Leave them to cool, covered with a damp cloth, then pull away the stems and seeds and strip off the skins. Press the pepper flesh through a sieve and place the resulting purée in another sieve lined with damp muslin to allow excess liquid to drain off. Mix the purée into the butter and sieve again.

Herb butter: Remove the stems from 60 g (2 oz) of mixed parsley, chives, tarragon and chervil. Blanch the leaves in boiling water for 1 minute, then drain and press them in a towel to dry. Blanch two finely chopped shallots for 1 minute, then drain and dry in the same way. Place the herbs and the shallots in a mortar and pound them with a little coarse salt to a fine purée. Pound the purée into the butter and sieve.

Lemon butter: Work the grated peel and strained juice of three lemons into the softened butter.

Olive and anchovy butter: Grate the rind of half an orange and squeeze and strain its juice. Remove the stones from six black olives. Soak, fillet, rinse and dry two salt anchovies. Blanch eight to 10 sage leaves. Finely chop the olives, anchovies and sage leaves together and combine them with the orange rind and juice. Pound into the butter.

Mustard butter: Work 2 tablespoons of Dijon mustard, or more to taste, into the softened butter.

Chili Relish

Salsa Cruda

To make ¾ litre (1¼ pints)

2	fresh hot chili peppers, stemmed, seeded and finely chopped	2
2	medium-sized onions, chopped	2
6	garlic cloves, finely chopped	6
6	tomatoes, skinned, seeded and coarsely chopped	6
45 g	fresh coriander leaves, coarsely chopped	1½ oz
	coarse salt	
6 tbsp	fresh lime juice or 4 tbsp vinegar	6 tbsp
4 tbsp	olive oil	4 tbsp

Combine the chili peppers, onions, garlic, tomatoes and coriander leaves in a large bowl. Add a large pinch of salt and stir in the lime juice or vinegar. Stir in the olive oil, taste the sauce and add more salt if necessary. Cover the bowl and leave the sauce to stand for 30 minutes to allow the flavours to mingle.

Avocado Sauce

To make about 35 cl (12 fl oz)

2	avocados	2
12.5 cl	lime juice	4 fl oz
1 tbsp	olive oil	1 tbsp
	coarse salt	
	freshly ground black pepper	

Cut each avocado in half. Remove the stones and scoop out the flesh with a large spoon. Place the flesh in a large bowl and mash it with a fork. Use a whisk to incorporate the lime juice and olive oil, beating until the sauce is light. Add coarse salt and pepper to taste.

Vinaigrette

The proportion of vinegar to oil may be varied according to the strength of the vinegar or the tartness of the food to be sauced, but one part vinegar to four or five parts oil is a good ratio. If desired, lemon juice may be substituted for the vinegar.

To make about 15 cl (¼ pint)

1 tsp	salt	1 tsp
¼ tsp	freshly ground pepper	¼ tsp
2 tbsp	wine vinegar	2 tbsp
12.5 cl	olive oil	4 fl oz

Put the salt and pepper into a small bowl. Add the vinegar and stir until the salt has dissolved. Then stir in the olive oil.

Mayonnaise

To prevent curdling, the egg yolks and oil should be at room temperature and the oil should be added very gradually at first. Mayonnaise will keep for several days in a covered container in a larder or refrigerator. Stir it well before use. One to 2 teaspoons of Dijon mustard may be mixed in with the vinegar or lemon juice.

To make about ½ litre (16 fl oz)

3	egg yolks	3
1 tbsp	wine vinegar or lemon juice	1 tbsp
½ litre	olive oil	16 fl oz
	salt and pepper	

Put the egg yolks in a bowl and whisk until smooth. Add the vinegar or lemon juice and mix thoroughly. Whisking constantly, add the oil, drop by drop to begin with. When the sauce starts to thicken, pour the remaining oil in a thin, steady stream, whisking rhythmically. If the mayonnaise becomes too thick, thin it with a little more vinegar or lemon juice or warm water. Season with salt and pepper.

Basil mayonnaise: Blanch 45 g (1½ oz) of fresh basil leaves in boiling water for 3 seconds, then drain them and plunge them immediately into cold water. Pat the leaves dry and chop them finely. Combine them with the egg yolks and whisk them vigorously for 1 minute. Then proceed as for plain mayonnaise, using lemon juice rather than wine vinegar to sharpen the sauce.

Tomato and basil mayonnaise: Stir 4 tablespoons of tomato purée (*recipe, page 164*) into the basil mayonnaise.

Tartare sauce: Add chopped sour gherkins, capers and chopped *fines herbes* to taste to the finished mayonnaise.

Aïoli

The ratio of olive oil to egg yolk can be varied according to taste: one yolk will take between 17.5 cl (6 fl oz) and ½ litre (16 fl oz) of oil. The amount of garlic used is also a matter of individual preference; you can include as much as one clove per person. To prevent curdling, both oil and egg yolks should be at room temperature before use.

To make about ¾ litre (1¼ pints)

3	large garlic cloves	3
1 tsp	sea salt	1 tsp
2	egg yolks	2
60 cl	olive oil	1 pint
1 to 2 tsp	lemon juice	1 to 2 tsp
1 to 2 tsp	warm water	1 to 2 tsp

In a marble mortar, pound the garlic and salt to a purée with a wooden pestle. Add the egg yolks and stir with the pestle until they turn pale in colour. Add the olive oil, drop by drop, to the side of the mortar, stirring constantly and always in the same direction. When the sauce starts to thicken, pour in the oil in a thin, steady stream, still stirring constantly. When the sauce is quite stiff, add the lemon juice and the water. Stir in the remaining oil until the sauce is thick.

Béarnaise Sauce

To make about 30 cl (½ pint)

20 g each	chopped tarragon and chervil	⅔ oz each
15 cl	dry white wine	¼ pint
4 tbsp	white wine vinegar	4 tbsp
2	shallots, finely chopped	2
3	egg yolks	3
¼ litre	olive oil or 250 g (8 oz) butter, cut into small cubes	8 fl oz
	water or lemon juice (optional)	

Reserve a teaspoonful each of chopped tarragon and chervil. Put the remaining herbs, the wine, vinegar and chopped shallots into an enamelled or stainless-steel saucepan. Boil until only about 2 tablespoons of syrupy liquid remain. Strain the reduction into a clean pan and add the egg yolks to the liquid Place the pan in a bain-marie and whisk until the mixture thickens slightly. Little by little, add the oil or the butter cubes, whisking all the time and adding more as each addition is absorbed. When all the oil or butter is used up, beat until the sauce is thick and creamy. Thin it, if desired, with a little water or lemon juice. Stir in the reserved herbs.

Tomato Purée

When fresh, ripe tomatoes are not available, use canned Italian plum tomatoes. The sauce can be flavoured with herbs other than those given below; parsley, basil, oregano and marjoram are all suitable substitutes. If summer-ripened garden tomatoes are used, no sugar is necessary.

To make about 30 cl (½ pint)

750 g	very ripe tomatoes, chopped	1½ lb
1	onion, finely chopped	1
2	garlic cloves, chopped (optional)	2
1 tbsp	olive oil	1 tbsp
3 or 4	sprigs fresh thyme or 1 tsp dried thyme	3 or 4
1	bay leaf	1
1 to 2 tsp	sugar (optional)	1 to 2 tsp
	salt and freshly ground pepper	

In a large enamelled or tin-lined pan, gently fry the onion and the garlic, if used, in the oil until they are soft but not brown. Add the other ingredients and simmer gently, uncovered, for about 30 minutes, stirring occasionally with a wooden spoon. When the tomatoes have been reduced to a thick pulp, press the mixture through a sieve, using a wooden pestle.

Return the purée to the pan and cook it, stirring frequently, over a low heat, for about 30 minutes. Season the purée to taste just before serving.

Barbecue Sauce

To make about 20 cl (7 fl oz)

2	garlic cloves	2
½ tsp	salt	½ tsp
½ tsp	paprika	½ tsp
4 tbsp	clear honey	4 tbsp
3 tbsp	tomato purée (*left, below*)	3 tbsp
4 tbsp	orange juice	4 tbsp
4 tbsp	white or red wine vinegar	4 tbsp
6 tbsp	soy sauce	6 tbsp

Crush the garlic and salt together in a mortar, then add the paprika and grind it in. Stir in the honey, then the remaining ingredients, one at a time, stirring well after each addition to ensure that they are well blended. The sauce is then ready to be used as a marinade, if desired.

To thicken the sauce for use as a basting liquid, transfer the mixture to a pan, bring it to the boil over medium heat, then simmer it gently, stirring often, until it reduces to the consistency you require.

Tomato Barbecue Sauce

To make about 10 cl (3½ fl oz)

12.5 cl	tomato purée (*left*)	4 fl oz
½ tsp	chili powder	½ tsp
½ tsp	dry mustard	½ tsp
1 tbsp	Worcestershire sauce	1 tbsp
45 g	brown sugar	1½ oz
4 tbsp	vinegar	4 tbsp
1	slice lemon	1
¼ tsp	Tabasco sauce	¼ tsp
	salt and pepper	

Combine all the ingredients together in a saucepan over a medium heat. Bring to the boil, stirring constantly, then simmer, stirring occasionally, for about 15 minutes, or until the liquid has the consistency of a thick basting sauce.

Tomato Ketchup

To make about 1.5 litres (2½ pints)

3 kg	firm ripe tomatoes, skinned, seeded and coarsely chopped	6 lb
175 g	onions, chopped	6 oz
75 g	sweet red pepper, seeded and chopped	2½ oz
1½ tsp	celery seeds	1½ tsp
1 tsp	allspice berries	1 tsp
1 tsp	mustard seeds	1 tsp
1	stick cinnamon	1
250 g	sugar	8 oz
1 tbsp	salt	1 tbsp
35 cl	vinegar	12 fl oz

In a heavy enamelled or stainless-steel pan, combine the tomatoes, onions and sweet pepper. Bring to the boil, stirring constantly, then reduce the heat to low and simmer for 20 to 30 minutes, or until the vegetables are soft. Purée the vegetables, a small batch at a time, through a food mill or a sieve into a clean pan. Cook over a medium heat, stirring frequently, until the mixture thickens and is reduced to about half its original volume—about 1 hour. Tie the celery seeds, allspice berries, mustard seeds and cinnamon stick in a piece of muslin and add them to the tomato mixture together with the sugar and salt. Stirring frequently, simmer the mixture gently, uncovered, for about 30 minutes. Then stir in the vinegar and continue to simmer until the ketchup reaches the desired consistency—about 10 minutes. Remove the bag of spices; taste the ketchup and adjust the seasoning.

Pour the hot ketchup into hot, sterilized jars, leaving 2.5 cm (1 inch) of space at the top of the jar. Cover each jar quickly and tightly with its lid. Set the jars on a rack in a deep cooking pot, pour in enough hot (not boiling) water to cover them by 2.5 cm (1 inch), cover the pot tightly and bring the water to the boil over a medium heat. Boil for 10 minutes. Remove the jars from the pot with tongs and leave them to cool at room temperature. The ketchup will keep for up to one year.

Pilaff

Other grains, such as pearl barley or cracked wheat (*burghul*) can be used to make a pilaff instead of rice. To make a saffron and tomato pilaff, add a pinch of saffron to the rice just before pouring on the boiling liquid; at the end of the cooking time, stir in one or two skinned, seeded and chopped tomatoes which have been heated through in butter for a minute or two. To make a herb pilaff, stir in 4 to 6 tablespoons of finely chopped mixed herbs at the end of the cooking time.

To serve 4

350 g	long-grain rice	12 oz
1	onion, finely chopped	1
75 g	butter	2½ oz
1 litre	boiling water or stock	1¾ pints
	salt	

Melt 30 g (1 oz) of the butter in a heavy pan over a low heat. Add the onion and sauté it briefly in the butter. Pour in the rice and stir it gently with a wooden spoon for 2 to 3 minutes or until each grain is coated in butter and has turned opaque. Pour in the boiling water or stock and add salt. Stir the rice once to ensure that no grains have stuck to the bottom, then turn down the heat to very low, so that the water just simmers, and cover the pan. Simmer the rice, undisturbed, for 18 to 20 minutes. When all the liquid has been absorbed, take the pan off the heat. Add the remaining butter, cut into small pieces; use two forks to gently incorporate the butter into the rice.

Stuffed Mushrooms

To make 24

24	large mushroom caps	24
12.5 cl	olive oil	4 fl oz
3 tbsp	lemon juice	3 tbsp
1	sweet red pepper, seeded and finely chopped	1
5	garlic cloves, finely chopped	5
6	shallots, finely chopped	6
20 g	parsley, finely chopped	⅔ oz
90 g	fresh white breadcrumbs	3 oz
	salt and freshly ground black pepper	

To make the marinade, combine all but 2 tablespoons of the olive oil with the lemon juice. Marinate the mushroom caps in this mixture for up to 2 hours. Drain the mushroom caps and reserve the marinade.

Heat the remaining oil in a frying pan and sauté the sweet red pepper, garlic and shallots in it for about 5 minutes, or until they are soft but not brown. Remove the pan from the heat, add the parsley and 4 tablespoons of the reserved marinade and stir in the breadcrumbs. Season the stuffing with salt and pepper to taste, then pack it into the mushroom caps.

Grill the stuffed mushrooms on an oiled rack 10 to 15 cm (4 to 6 inches) above medium-hot coals for 8 to 10 minutes, or until they are heated through.

Pork Sausages

The technique of making pork sausages is demonstrated on page 36. Finely chopped fennel, parsley, thyme or savory may be substituted for the sage. For a very smooth sausage-meat, pass the meats through the grinder twice.

To make 2.5 kg (5 lb)

2 kg	boneless, fatty neck end of pork, cut into pieces, connective tissue trimmed off	4 lb
500 g	loin of pork, cut into pieces	1 lb
5 tbsp	coarse salt	5 tbsp
	freshly ground black pepper	
2 tbsp	finely chopped fresh sage	2 tbsp
6	large garlic cloves, finely chopped	6
About 4 metres	sausage casing, soaked in tepid, acidulated water for 30 minutes and rinsed	About 4 yards

Pass the meats through a grinder using the medium disc. Mix the minced meats with the salt, pepper, sage and garlic. Fry a spoonful of the mixture in a frying pan for 2 to 3 minutes, or until the juices run clear; taste the fried meat and adjust the seasoning of the remaining sausage mixture if necessary.

Fit a sausage-making attachment to the meat grinder. Ease the entire sausage casing over its nozzle, leaving a finger's length hanging loose. Make a knot in the end. Fill the grinder's bowl with the sausage mixture and turn the handle to fill the casing. Slip the casing evenly away as it fills. When the casing is about 75 cm (30 inches) long, pull 15 cm (6 inches) of empty casing from the tube, cut it in the middle and knot it. Tie off the remaining casing and continue to make sausages until the mixture is used up.

Prick each sausage several times. Cook the sausages 10 to 15 cm (4 to 6 inches) above medium-hot coals for 8 to 10 minutes on each side or until golden-brown.

Mushroom and Bacon Stuffing

To make about 1 kg (2 to 2½ lb)

1 kg	mushrooms, finely chopped	2 to 2½ lb
250 g	lean bacon, coarsely diced	8 oz
30 g	butter	1 oz
2 tbsp	lemon juice	2 tbsp
1½ tbsp	chopped thyme and winter savory	1½ tbsp

Melt the butter in a large pan set over a medium heat. Add the mushrooms and, stirring occasionally, sauté them until the mushroom liquid has evaporated—about 15 minutes. Place the mushrooms in a mixing bowl and add the lemon juice.

In a frying pan, sauté the bacon over medium heat until it is crisp—about 5 minutes. Drain the bacon and add it to the mushrooms together with the herbs.

Duxelles Stuffing

The technique of filling a salmon with this stuffing is demonstrated on page 68.

To make about 350 g (12 oz)

15 g	butter	½ oz
½	large onion, finely chopped	½
1	small garlic clove, finely chopped (optional)	1
250 g	mushrooms, finely chopped	8 oz
2 tbsp	chopped parsley	2 tbsp
1	egg	1
½	lemon, juice strained	½
About 125 g	fresh breadcrumbs	About 4 oz
	salt and pepper	
	grated nutmeg	

In a sauté pan, melt the butter and sweat the onion and garlic, if used, until they are soft but not brown. Increase the heat, add the mushrooms and sauté them briefly until they soften slightly. Remove the pan from the heat and transfer the mixture to a large mixing bowl. Add the chopped parsley, egg, lemon juice and most of the breadcrumbs. With your hands, mix the ingredients together thoroughly. Add salt, pepper and grated nutmeg to taste. If the mixture feels wet, bind it further by mixing in the rest of the breadcrumbs.

Fish Fumet

To make about 2 litres (3½ pints)

1 kg	fish heads, bones and trimmings, rinsed and broken into convenient pieces	2 to 2½ lb
1 each	onion, carrot and leek, sliced	1 each
1	stick celery, cut into pieces	1
	bay leaf	1
2	sprigs thyme	2
2	sprigs parsley	2
½ litre	red or white wine	16 fl oz
About 2 litres	water	About 3½ pints
	salt	

Place the fish, vegetables and herbs in a large pan. Add the wine and enough water to cover the fish and season lightly with salt. Place the pan over a low heat. With a large shallow spoon, skim off the scum that rises to the surface as the liquid reaches a simmer. Keep skimming until no more scum rises, then cover and simmer for about 30 minutes. Strain the fumet through a colander lined with dampened muslin.

Veal Stock

To make about 3 litres (5 pints)

1 kg	knuckle of veal, including meaty veal	2 to 2½ lb
1 kg	shin or leg of beef	2 to 2½ lb
1 kg	chicken backs, necks and wing tips	2 to 2½ lb
About 5 litres	water	About 9 pints
1	bouquet garni, including leek and celery	1
1	garlic head	1
2	medium-sized onions, 1 stuck with 2 cloves	2
4	large carrots	4
	salt	

Place a round wire rack in the bottom of a large stock-pot to prevent the ingredients from sticking. Fit all the meat, bones and chicken pieces into the pot and add enough water to cover them by about 4 cm (1½ inches). Bring very slowly to the boil, using a spoon to skim off the scum that rises. Keep skimming, occasionally adding a glass of cold water to retard the boil, until no more scum rises—10 to 15 minutes. Add the bouquet garni, garlic, onions, carrots and a little salt, and skim once more as the liquid returns to the boil. Reduce the heat to very low, cover the pot with the lid ajar and simmer for at least 5 and preferably 7 hours. From time to time, skim off any fat that rises to the surface.

Strain the stock into a large bowl, then strain it again through a colander lined with dampened muslin. Leave the stock to cool, then refrigerate it. When the stock has set to a jelly, scrape off the solid layer of fat and discard it. Remove any remaining traces of fat by pressing kitchen paper gently on to the surface of the stock.

Glace de viande: Prepare a veal stock as above but do not add salt to it. When it has been cleansed of all fat, put it into a saucepan just large enough to hold it and bring it to the boil. Set the pan half off the heat and let the stock boil gently. From time to time, skim off the skin of impurities that collects on the cooler side of the pan. When the stock has reduced by about a third, after 1 hour or somewhat longer, strain it through a fine-meshed sieve into a smaller pan; continue to simmer the stock gently, skimming occasionally, for another hour or so, when it will again have reduced by about a third. Strain it again into a smaller pan and let it reduce for another hour. The liquid will now be thick and syrupy. Pour it into a bowl, leave it to cool, then refrigerate it. It will keep in the refrigerator almost indefinitely.

Coconut Milk

To make about ¼ litre (8 fl oz)

1	coconut	1
	hot water	

Remove the fibrous husk from the coconut and use a skewer to pierce the three indentations, or eyes, at the top of the coconut. Turn the coconut upside down over a bowl and allow the liquid to drain out through the holes. Reserve the liquid.

Place the coconut lengthwise on a hard surface, grasp it firmly at the pierced end and tap it sharply with a hammer about one-third of the way from the opposite end. The coconut will fracture along a natural seam. Continue tapping until the nut cracks open along this line. Break the coconut into several pieces with a hammer. Use a sharp knife to remove the coconut flesh from the shell and cut off the brown skin. Grate the coconut pieces coarsely, either with a grater or in a food processor. Add the grated coconut to the bowl of reserved coconut liquid. Pour hot water over the grated coconut to cover and leave the mixture for 1 hour.

Line a sieve with dampened muslin and set it over a clean bowl. Pour the grated coconut and liquid into the sieve, a little at a time, making sure that all the liquid has drained through the sieve before adding more. Once all the liquid has passed through the sieve, pick up the four edges of the muslin and twist the muslin tightly to release as much coconut milk as possible. Discard the coconut flesh.

Recipe Index

English recipe titles are listed by categories such as "Beef", "Chili Peppers", "Kebabs, Fish", "Kebabs, Meat", "Marinade", "Spit-Roast" and "Stuffing", and within those categories, alphabetically. Foreign recipe titles are listed alphabetically without regard to category.

General Index/Glossary

Included in this index are definitions of many of the culinary terms used in this book: definitions are in italics. The recipes in the Anthology are listed in the Recipe Index on page 168.

Recipe Credits

The sources for the recipes in this volume are shown below. Page references in brackets indicate where the recipes appear in the Anthology.

Allen, Jana and Gin, Margaret, *"Offal" Gourmet Cookery from Head to Tail.* © Jana Allen and Margaret Gin, 1974. © Pitman Publishing 1976. Published in Great Britain 1976, by Pitman Publishing, London. First published in the United States 1974 by 101 Productions as "Innards and Other Variety Meats". By permission of 101 Productions (*page 124*).

Alperi, Magdalena, *Tratado Completo de Comidas y Bebidas.* © Magdalena Alperi. First edition June 1977. Second edition December 1978. Translated by permission of the author, Gijon, Asturias (*pages 125, 137 and 148*).

Ashbrook, Frank G. and Sater, Edna N., *Cooking Wild Game.* Copyright, 1945, by Orange Judd Publishing Co., Inc. Published by Orange Judd Publishing Co. Inc., New York (*page 136*).

Aragones Subero, Antonio, *Gastronomia de Guadalajara.* Published by Institucion de Cultura "Marques de Santillana". Excma. Diputacion Provincial de Guadalajara, 1973. Translated by permission of the author, Madrid (*pages 107, 135 and 150*).

Barbecue, Le (Les Cahiers de la Cuillère d'Argent). © Editoriale Domus S.p.A., Milan-Italie. Published by Editoriale Domus S.p.A. Translated by permission of Editoriale Domus S.p.A. (*page 160*).

Beard, James, *James Beard's New Fish Cookery.* Copyright 1954, © 1976 by James A. Beard. Published by Little, Brown and Company, Boston, Massachusetts. By permission of Little, Brown and Company (*page 158*).

Beard, James A. and Brown, Helen Evans, *The Complete Book of Outdoor Cookery.* Copyright © 1955, by Helen Evans Brown and James A. Beard. Published by Pyramid Publications Inc. By permission of John Schaffner Associates, Inc., Literary Agents, New York (*page 102*).

Bertholle, Louisette (Editor), *Secrets of the Great French Restaurants.* English translation copyright © George Weidenfeld and Nicolson Ltd, 1973. Published by George Weidenfeld and Nicolson Ltd. First published in France under the title "Les Recettes Secretes des Meilleurs Restaurants de France" by Albin Michel, Paris, 1972. Copyright © Opera Mundi Paris 1972. By permission of George Weidenfeld and Nicolson Ltd. (*pages 104, 108 and 125*).

Bettonica, Luis (Editor), *Cocina Regional Española.* © 1981 Ediciones Hymsa (Barcelona) y Arnoldo Mondadori Editore S.p.A (Milano). Published by Ediciones Hymsa. Translated by permission of Arnoldo Mondadori Editore S.p.A., Verona (*page 140*).

Bickel, Walter and Kramer, René, *Wild en Gevogelte in de Internationale Keuken.* © 1974/1980 Zomer & Keuning Boeken B.V., Ede. Published by Zomer & Keuning Boeken B.V., Ede., Holland. Translated by permission of Zomer & Keuning Boeken B.V. (*page 130*).

Blackman, Grant, *Australian Fish Cooking.* © Copyright Grant Blackman 1978. Published by Hill of Content Publishing Company, Melbourne. By permission of Hill of Content Publishing Company (*pages 137, 143, 146 and 147*).

Bondanini, Mario V. (Editor), *Gastronomie de Plein Air.* © Copyright 1970 by Editions Melior, CH-1020 Renens/Suisse. Published by Editions Melior. Translated by permission of Editions Melior, Bussigny-Lausanne (*pages 144, 160*).

Boni, Ada, *Italian Regional Cooking.* Copyright © 1969 s.c. Arnoldo Mondadori. English translation copyright © 1969 s.c. by Thomas Nelson & Sons Ltd., and E. P. Dutton and Co., Inc. Published by Bonanza Books, a division of Crown Publishers, Inc., New York. By permission of Arnoldo Mondadori Editore, S.p.A., Milan (*page 159*).

Bonomo, Giuliana, *La Buona Cucina.* © 1976, Curcio Periodici S.p.A. Published by Curcio Periodici S.p.A., Rome. By permission of Curcio Periodici S.p.A. (*pages 90, 95 and 105*).

Bottiger, Theodor, *Das Grill-Buch.* Copyright © 1968 by Wilhelm Heyne Verlag München. Published by Wilhelm Heyne Verlag. Translated by permission of Wilhelm Heyne Verlag (*pages 93, 95 and 105*).

Bottiger, Theodor, *Schalen Und Krustentiere.* Copyright © 1972 Wilhelm Heyne Verlag München. Pubished by Wilhelm Heyne Verlag. Translated by permission of Wilhelm Heyne Verlag (*page 156*).

Brown Derby Cookbook, The. Copyright, 1949, by The Brown Derby Service Corporation. Published by Doubleday & Company, Inc. (*pages 93, 155*).

Brown, Helen Evans, *Helen Brown's West Coast Cook Book.* Copyright 1952, by Helen Evans Brown. Published by Little, Brown and Company, Boston. By permission of Little, Brown and Company (*page 93*).

Bugialli, Giuliano, *The Fine Art of Italian Cooking.* Copyright © 1977 by Giuliano Bugialli. Published by Times Books, a division of Quadrangle/The New York Times Book Co., Inc., New York. By permission of Times Books, a division of Quadrangle/The New York Times Book Co., Inc. (*pages 104, 124*).

Buonassisi, Vincenzo, *Cucina All'Aria Aperta.* © Arnoldo Mondadori Editore 1972. Published by Arnoldo Mondadori Editore S.p.A., Milano. Translated by permission of Arnoldo Mondadori Editore S.p.A. (*pages 98, 129, 142 and 150*).

Burros, Marian, *Pure & Simple.* Copyright © 1978 by Marian Fox Burros. Published by William Morrow and Company Inc., New York. By permission of William Morrow and Company (*page 145*).

Burrows, Lois M. and Myers, Laura G., *Too Many Tomatoes, Squash, Beans and Other Good Things.* Copyright © 1976 by Lois M. Burrows and Laura G. Myers. Published by Harper & Row, Publishers, Inc., New York. By permission of Harper & Row, Publishers, Inc. (*pages 92, 109*).

Callahan, Ed, *Charcoal Cookbook.* © 1970 Pacific Productions. Published by Nitty Gritty Productions, California. By permission of Nitty Gritty Productions (*pages 93, 94*).

Cantrell, Rose, *Creative Outdoor Cooking.* Copyright © 1979 by Ottenheimer Publishers, Inc. Published by Weathervane Books. By permission of Ottenheimer Publishers, Inc., Baltimore, Maryland (*page 116*).

Catenius van der Meijden, J. M.J., *Groot Nieuw Volledig Indisch Kookboek.* © W. van Hoeve, Amsterdam, 15th printing 1980. Translated by permission of B.V. Uitgeversmaatschappij Elsevier, Amsterdam (*page 140*).

Chablani, Mohan and Dixit, Brahm N., *The Bengal Lancers Indian Cookbook.* Copyright © 1976 by Mohan Chablani and Brahm N. Dixit. Published by Henry Regnery Company, Chicago. By permission of Contemporary Books, Inc., Chicago (*page 111*).

Chandonnet, Ann, *The Complete Fruit Cookbook.* Copyright © 1972 Ann Chandonnet. Published by 101 Productions, San Francisco. By permission of 101 Productions (*page 126*).

Chekenian, Jane and Meyer, Monica, *Shellfish Cookery.* Copyright © 1971 by Jane Chekenian and Monica Meyer. Published by the MacMillan Company, New York. By permission of MacMillan Publishing Co., Inc. (*page 157*).

Clusells, Sylvain, *Cooking on Turning Spit and Grill.* Copyright by Bonne Table et Tourisme, Paris 1959. English translation © Arthur Barker Limited 1961. Published by Arthur Barker Limited, London. By permission of Arthur Barker Limited (*pages 134, 148 and 157*).

Cocina Regional Española. Published by Editorial Almena, Madrid 1976. Translated by permission of Editorial Doncel, Madrid (*pages 92, 103 and 149*).

Comelade, Eliana Thibaut, *Cuina Rossellonesa i de la Costa Brava.* Published by Editorial Barcino, Barcelona 1968. Translated by permission of the author, Montpellier, France (*pages 133, 153 and 155*).

Consumer Guide Publications, the editors of, *Smoke Cookery.* Copyright 1978 by Publications International Ltd. Published by Crown Publishers, Inc., New York. By permission of Publications International Ltd., Illinois (*page 103*).

Cronin, Isaac, *The International Squid Cookbook.* Copyright © 1981 by Isaac Cronin. Published by Aris Books, Berkeley, California. By permission of Aris Books (*page 158*).

Culinary Arts Institute, the Staff Home Economists (Editors), *The Outdoor Grill Cookbook.* Copyright © 1960, 1954, 1953 by Spencer Press. Published by Grosset & Dunlap, Publishers, New York. By permission of Grosset & Dunlap, Inc. (*pag 128*).

David, Elizabeth, *Italian Food.* Copyright © Elizabeth Davi 1954, 1963, 1969, 1977. Published by Penguin Books Ltd London. By permission of Penguin Books Ltd. (*pages 10 146*).

David, Elizabeth, *French Provincial Cooking.* Copyright Elizabeth David, 1960, 1962, 1967, 1970. Published by Per guin Books Ltd., London in association with Michael Josep Ltd., London. By permission of the author, London (*pages 14 147*).

Davidson, Alan, *Mediterranean Seafood.* Copyright © Ala Davidson, 1972. Published by Penguin Books Ltd., London. B permission of Penguin Books Ltd. (*pages 142, 145, 148 an 151*).

Day, Irene F., *Kitchen in the Kasbah.* Copyright © 1975 b Irene F. Day. First published by André Deutsch Limited, Lor don 1976. By permission of André Deutsch Limited (*page 109, 113*).

Department of Commerce, Bureau of Fisheries. Econom Circular No. 18, Revised, Issued 14th March 1918. Publishe by U.S. Department of Commerce, Washington D.C. B permission of Department of Commerce, National Marin Fisheries Service (*page 158*).

Domenech, Ignasi, *Apats.* Copyright Archivo Gastronomic Ignasi Domenech. Published by Editorial Laia S.A., Barcelon 1979. Translated by permission of Jose C. Balague Domer ech, Barcelona (*pages 120, 147*).

Domenech, Ignacio, *Pescados y Mariscos.* Texto © Archiv Gastronomico Domenech 1979. Published by Editorial Br guera, S.A., Barcelona. Translated by permission of Jose C Balague Domenech, Barcelona (*pages 138, 155*).

Donovan, Maria Kozslik, *The Far Eastern Epicure.* Copyrig © 1958 by Maria Kozslik Donovan. Published by Willia Heinemann Ltd., London. By permission of the author, Gen va (*page 98*).

Donovan, Maria Kozslik, *The Blue Danube Cookboo* Copyright © 1967 by Maria Kozslik Donovan. Pubished b Doubleday & Company, Inc., New York. By permission of th author, Geneva (*page 123*).

Elkon, Juliette, *A Belgian Cookbook.* Copyright © 1958 b Farrar, Straus and Cudahy, Inc. Published by Farrar, Stra and Cudahy Inc., New York. By permission of Farrar, Stra and Giroux, Inc., New York (*page 149*).

Ermo, Dominique D', *Dominique's Famous Fish, Game Meat Recipes.* © Copyright 1981 by Acropolis Books Lt Published by Acropolis Books Ltd., Washington D.C. By pe mission of Acropolis Books Ltd. (*page 132*).

Famularo, Joe and Imperiale, Louise, *The Festive Famula Kitchen.* Copyright © 1977 by Joe Famularo and Louis Imperiale. Published by Atheneum Publishers Inc., New Yor By permission of Atheneum Publishers Inc. (*page 109*).

Feast of Italy. Copyright © 1973 by Arnoldo Mondad Editore. Published by Galahad Books, New York. Origina published in Italy under the title "Cucina all'Italiana" © 19 by Arnoldo Mondadori Editore. By permission of Arnol Mondadori Editore, Milano (*page 120*).

Finn, Molly, *Summer Feasts.* Copyright © 1979 by Molly Fin Published by Simon & Schuster, a division of Gulf & Weste Corporation, New York. By permission of Simon & Schuster, division of Gulf & Western Corporation (*page 129*).

Frisch vom Grill. © Walter Hadecke Verlag, 7252 Weil d Stadt. Published by Walter Hadecke Verlag, West German Translated by permission of Walter Hadecke Verlag (*pag 91, 140 and 158*).

Froidl, Ilse, *Das Geflügel-Kochbuch.* Copyright © 1966 Wilhelm Heyne Verlag, München. Published by Wilhe Heyne Verlag. Translated by permission of Wilhelm Hey Verlag (*page 130*).

Gin, Margaret and Castle, Alfred E., *Regional Cooking China.* Copyright © 1975 Margaret Gin and Alfred Cast Published by 101 Productions, San Francisco. By permissi of 101 Productions (*page 118*).

Great Cook's Guide to Fish Cookery, The. Copyright © 19 by David Russell. Published by Random House, New York. permission of Cook's Catalogue, New York (*page 143*).

Green, Henrietta, *The Marinade Cookbook.* © Text: Henri ta Green. Published by Pierrot Publishing Limited, Lond 1978. By permission of the author, London (*pages 108, 135*

Green, Karen and Black, Betty, *How to Cook His Goose* (*a*

Other Wild Games*). Copyright © 1973 by Karen Green and Betty Black. Published by Winchester Press Inc., Oklahoma. By permission of Winchester Press Inc. (*page 150*).
Greene, Bert, *Honest American Fare.* Copyright © 1981 by Bert Greene. Published by Contemporary Books, Inc., Chicago, Illinois. By permission of Contemporary Books, Inc. (*page 125*).
Grigson, Jane, *Fish Cookery.* Copyright © Jane Grigson, 1973. Published by Penguin Books Limited, London. By permission of Pitman Books Limited (*pages 144, 152*).
Grigson, Jane, *Jane Grigson's Vegetable Book.* © 1978 by Jane Grigson. Published by Michael Joseph Limited, London. By permission of David Higham Associates Ltd., London (*page 127*).
Guasch, Juan Castello, *¡Bon Profit! (El Libro de la Cocina Ibicenca*). Copyright by the author. Published by Imprenta ALFA, Palma de Mallorca 1971. Translated by permission of the author, Palma de Mallorca (*page 149*).
Guardiola y Ortiz, José, *Conduchos de Navidad y Gastronomia Alicantina.* Published by Agatangelo Soler Llorca, Editorial, Alicante, Spain 1972. Translated by permission of Agatangelo Soler Llorca, Editorial (*page 142*).
Hachten, Harva, *Kitchen Safari.* Copyright © 1970 by Harva Hachten. Published by Atheneum Publishers Inc., New York. By permission of Ann Elmo Agency Inc., New York (*page 99*).
Hawkes, Alex D., *The Flavors of the Caribbean & Latin America.* Copyright © The Estate of Alex D. Hawkes, 1978. Published by The Viking Press, New York. By permission of John Schaffner Associates Inc., Literary Agents, New York (*pages 97 and 100*).
Hawkes, Alex D. (Editor), *The Shrimp Cookbook.* Copyright © 1966 by Delair Publishing Company Inc. Published by Culinary Arts Institute, Chicago. By permission of Delair Publishing Company Inc., New York (*page 154*).
Hawliczkowa, Helena, *Kuchnia Polska.* Copyright by Helena Kulzowa-Hawliczkowa. Published by Panstwowe Wydawnictwo Ekonomiczne, Warszawa 1979. Translated by permission of Agencja Autorska, Warsaw, for the author (*pages 106, 130, 139 and 149*).
Hazelton, Nika, *The Picnic Book.* Copyright © 1969 by Nika Hazelton. Published by Atheneum Publishers Inc., New York. By permission of the author, New York (*page 99*).
Hornberg, Ulrike, *Schlemmereien vom Grill.* © Droemer Knaur Verlag Schoeller & Co., Locarno 1976. Published by Droemer Knaur Verlag. Translated by permission of Droemersche Verlagsanstalt Th. Knaur Nachf. GmbH & Co., Munich (*pages 98, 101 and 106*).
Horvath, Maria, *Balkan-Küche.* Copyright © 1963 by Wilhelm Heyne Verlag, München. Published by Wilhelm Heyne Verlag. Translated by permission of Wilhelm Heyne Verlag (*pages 121, 122 and 141*).
Hyun, Judy, *The Korean Cookbook.* Copyright © 1970 by Judy Hyun. Published by Follett Publishing Company, Chicago. By permission of the author, New York (*pages 119, 122 and 127*).
Jans, Hugh, *Vrij Nederland.* June 1972; October 1975; June 1976; October 1978 (magazine). Translated by permission of Hugh Jans (*pages 96, 106, 118 and 151*).
Jekyll Island Garden Club, The (Editors), *Golden Isles Cuisine.* Copyright © 1978 by Dot Gibson Publications, Waycross, Ga. By permission of Dot Gibson Publications (*page 153*).
Johnson, Ronald, *The Aficionado's Southwestern Cooking.* © The University of New Mexico Press, 1968. Published by the University of New Mexico Press, New Mexico. By permission of the University of New Mexico Press (*pages 103, 118*).
Kamman, Madeleine, *Dinner Against the Clock.* Copyright © 1973 by Madeleine Kamman. Published by Atheneum Publishers, Inc., New York. By permission of Atheneum Publishers, Inc. (*page 119*).
Keasberry, Oma, *Oma's Indische Keukengeheimen.* © Copyright 1978 Vermande Zonen bv, IJmuiden. Published by Vermande Zonen bv. Translated by permission of H. J. W. Becht's Uitgevers-Mij. B.V., Amsterdam (*page 111*).
Khawam, René R. *La Cuisine Arabe.* © Editions Albin Michel, 1970. Published by Editions Albin Michel, Paris. Translated by permission of Editions Albin Michel (*page 113*).
Laasri, Ahmed, *240 Recettes de Cuisine Marocaine.* © 1978, Jacques Grancher, Editeur. Published by Jacques Grancher, Editeur, Paris. Translated by permission of Jacques Grancher, Editeur (*page 134*).
Ladies' Home Journal, The Editors of, *Ladies' Home Journal Adventures in Cooking.* © 1968 by The Curtis Publishing Company & MacLean-Hunter Limited. Published by Prentice-Hall, Inc., New Jersey. By permission of The Ladies' Home Journal, New York (*page 154*).
Lane, Lilian, *Malayan Cookery Recipes.* © Lilian Lane 1964. Published by Eastern Universities Press Ltd. in association with University of London Press Ltd., London. By permission of Hodder & Stoughton Ltd., Kent (*page 101*).
Lemnis, Maria and Vitry, Henryk, *Ksiazka Kucharska.* Published in 1972. Translated by permission of Agencja Autorska, Warsaw for the authors (*page 91*).
Lemnis, Maria and Vitry, Henryk, *Old Polish Traditions in the Kitchen and at the Table.* © Interpress Publishers, Warsaw 1979. Published by Interpress Publishers. By permission of Agencja Autorska, Warsaw for the authors (*page 134*).
Logan, Barbara, *Barbecue and Outdoor Cookery.* © Ward Lock Limited, 1978. Published by Ward Lock Limited, London. By permission of Ward Lock Limited (*pages 139, 156*).
Lujan, Nestor and Perucho, Juan. *El Libro de la Cocina Española.* © Ediciones Danae, S.A. 1977. Published by Ediciones Danae, S.A., Barcelona. Translated by permission of Editorial Baber S.A., Barcelona (*page 137*).
Mallos, Tess, *Greek Cookbook.* © Copyright Tess Mallos 1976. Published by The Hamlyn Publishing Group Limited, London. By permission of Landsdowne Press, Dee Why and the author, Australia (*page 116*).
Mark, Theonie, *Greek Islands Cooking.* Copyright © 1972, 1973, 1974 by Theonie Mark. Published by Little, Brown and Company, Boston, Massachusetts; also published in the United Kingdom by B. T. Batsford Ltd., London. By permission of the author, Carlisle, Massachusetts (*pages 133, 145*).
Marković, Spasenija-Pata (Editor), *Veliki Narodni Kuvar.* Copyright by the author. First Edition "Politika", Belgrade, 1938. Published by Narodna Knjiga, Belgrade 1979. Translated by permission of Jugoslovenska Autorska Agencija, Belgrade, for the heir to the author (*page 116*).
Marks, James F., *Barbecues.* Copyright © James F. Marks, 1977. Published by Penguin Books Ltd., London. By permission of Penguin Books Ltd. (*page 92*).
Marshall, Mel, *Cooking over Coals.* Copyright © 1971 by Mel Marshall. Published by Winchester Press, New York. By permission of Winchester Press, Tulsa, Oklahoma (*page 142*).
Martin, Peter and Joan, *Japanese Cooking.* Copyright © 1970, by Peter and Joan Martin. Published by Bobbs-Merrill Company, Inc. Indianapolis. By permission of The Bobbs-Merrill Publishing Company, Inc. (*pages 126, 129 and 151*).
McIntyre, Nancy Fair, *It's a Picnic!* Text Copyright © 1969 by Nancy McIntyre. Published by Viking Press, New York. By permission of Viking Penguin Inc., New York (*pages 90, 154*).
Mégnin, Paul, *250 Manières de Cuire et Accommoder le Gibier.* © Albin Michel 1922. Published by Editions Albin Michel, Paris. Translated by permission of Editions Albin Michel (*page 136*).
Mitcham, Howard, *The Provincetown Seafood Cookbook.* Copyright © 1975 by Howard Mitcham. Published by Addison-Wesley Publishing Company Inc., Reading, Massachusetts. By permission of the author, New Orleans, Louisiana (*page 137*).
Mitchell, Kenneth (Editor), *The Flavour of Malaysia.* Copyright © 1974, Four Corners. Published by Four Corners Publishing Co. (Far East) Ltd., Hong Kong. By permission of Four Corners Publishing Co. (Far East) Ltd. (*page 111*).
Mostar, Katinka, *Feine Wildbret-Rezepte.* Copyright © by Kochbuchverlag Heimeran KG, München. Published by Wilhelm Heyne Verlag, München 1977. Translated by permission of Poldner Literary Agency, München (*page 130*).
Nicolau, M. del Carme, *Cuina Catalana.* © Editorial Miquel Arimany, S.A., Barcelona. Published by Editorial Miquel Arimany, S.A., 1971. Translated by permission of Editorial Miquel Arimany, S.A. (*pages 94, 122 and 138*).
Norman, Barbara, *The Russian Cookbook.* Copyright © 1967 by Bantam Books, Inc. Published by Atheneum Publishers Inc., New York. By permission of the author and her agent, Robert P. Mills, New York (*page 122*).
Novak, Jane, *Treasury of Chicken Cookery.* Copyright © 1974 by Jane Novak. Published by Harper & Row Publishers, New York. By permission of the author, Sherman Oaks, California (*page 128*).
Oaks II Collection, The. 1981. By permission of Carol Fanconi, Laytonsville, Maryland (*page 117*).
Ochorowicz-Monatowa, Marja, *Polish Cookery* (translated by Jean Karsavina). © 1958 by Crown Publishers, Inc. Published by Crown Publishers, Inc., New York. By permission of Crown Publishers, Inc. (*pages 102, 136*).
Olney, Richard, *House & Garden Magazine.* Copyright © Richard Olney. Published by House & Garden Magazine, New York 1971. By permission of the author, Sollies-Toucas, France (*page 128*).
Olney, Richard, *Simple French Food.* Copyright © Richard Olney 1974. Published by Jill Norman & Hobhouse Ltd., London 1981. By permission of Jill Norman & Hobhouse Ltd., (*pages 112, 156*).
Ortiz, Elisabeth Lambert, *Caribbean Cooking.* Copyright © Elisabeth Lambert Ortiz, 1973, 1975. Published by Penguin Books Ltd., London. By permission of Penguin Books Ltd. (*page 100*).
Paradissis, Chrissa, *The Best Book of Greek Cookery.* Copyright © 1976 by P. Efstathiadis & Sons. Published by Efstathiadis Group, Athens, 1977. By permission of P. Efstathiadis Group (*page 108*).
Pezzini, Wilma, *The Tuscan Cookbook.* Copyright © 1978 by Wilma Pezzini. Published by Atheneum Publishers, New York. Also published in the United Kingdom by J. M. Dent & Sons Ltd., London. By permission of Hughes Massie Limited (*pages 121, 123 and 126*).
Piepenbrock, Mechthild, *Grill Vergnugen.* © Grafe und Unzer Verlag, München. Published by Grafe und Unzer GmbH. Translated by permission of Grafe und Unzer GmbH. (*pages 94, 131 and 152*).
Pourounas, Andreas, *Aphrodite's Cookbook.* Copyright © by Andreas Pourounas and Helene Grosvenor. Published by Neville Spearman (Jersey) Limited, Jersey, Channel Islands 1977. By permission of Neville Spearman Limited, Sudbury, Suffolk (*page 122*).
Puga y Parga, Manuel M. (Picadillo), *La Cocina Practica.* Copyright by Libreria-Editorial "Gali". Published by Libreria-Editorial "Gali", Santiago 1966. Translated by permission of Libreria Editorial "Gali" (*page 138*).
Ramazani, Nesta, *Persian Cooking.* Copyright © 1982 by Nesta Ramazani. Published by The University Press of Virginia, Charlottesville, Virginia. By permission of The University Press of Virginia (*page 115*).
Ripoll, Luis, *Nuestra Cocina.* 600 Recetas de Mallorca, Menorca, Ibiza y Formentera. © by Luis Ripoll. Published by Editorial H. M. B., S.A. Barcelona 1978. Translated by permission of the author, Palma de Mallorca, Spain (*pages 107, 148*).
Roberson, John and Marie, *The Complete Barbecue Book.* Copyright 1951 by Prentice-Hall, Inc., New York. Published by Prentice-Hall, Inc. By permission of Mrs. Marie Roberson Hamm, New York (*pages 135, 160*).
Roden, Claudia, *Picnic.* Copyright © Claudia Roden, 1981. Published by Jill Norman & Hobhouse Ltd., London. By permission of Jill Norman & Hobhouse Ltd. (*pages 97, 114, 139 and 159*).
Rosselli, Anna Baslini, *100 Ricette per la Colazione sull'Erba.* Copyright © by G. C. Sansoni S.p.A., Firenze. Published by G. C. Sansoni Editore Nuova S.p.A., 1973. Translated by permission of G. C. Sansoni Editore Nuova S.p.A. (*pages 95, 100, 106 and 120*).
Sahni, Julie, *Classic Indian Cooking.* Copyright © 1980 by Julie Sahni. Published by William Morrow and Company, Inc., New York, By permission of Jill Norman & Hobhouse Ltd., London (*page 127*).
Schoon, Louise Sherman and Hardesty, Corrinne, *The Complete Pork Cook Book.* Copyright © 1977 by Louise Sherman Schoon and Corrinne Hardesty. Published by Stein and Day Publishers, New York. By permission of Stein and Day Publishers (*page 117*).
Semeyno Sukrovishte. © by the authors. Published in Sofia, c.1916. Translated by permission of Jusautor Copyright Agency, Sofia (*pages 132, 133*).
Serra, Victoria, *Tia Victoria's Spanish Kitchen.* English text copyright © Elizabeth Gili, 1963. Published by Kaye & Ward Ltd., London 1963. Translated by permission of Elizabeth Gili from the original Spanish entitled "Sabores: Cocina del Hogar" by Victoria Serra Sunol. By permission of Kaye & Ward

Ltd. (*page 90*).

Sewell, Elizabeth, *Barbecue Cookbook.* © Copyright Paul Hamlyn Pty., Ltd. 1971. Published by Paul Hamlyn Pty., Ltd., Dee Why West, N.S.W., Australia. By permission of Lansdowne Press, Australia (*pages 96, 107 and 154*).

Shelton, Ferne (Editor), *Pioneer Cookbook.* Copyright © 1973 by Ferne Shelton. Published by Hutcraft, High Point, North Carolina. By permission of Hutcraft (*page 96*).

Shishkov, Dr. Georgi and Vouchkov, Stoil, *Bulgarski Natzionalni Yastiya.* © by the authors 1978 c/o Jusautor, Sofia. Published by Projuzdat, Sofia 1959. Translated by permission of Jusautor Copyright Agency (*page 141*).

Singh, Dharamjit, *Indian Cookery.* Copyright © Dharamjit Singh, 1970. Published by Penguin Books Ltd., London. By permission of Penguin Books Ltd. (*pages 110, 114 and 138*).

Skipwith, Sofka, *Eat Russian.* © Sofka Skipwith 1973. Published by David & Charles, Newton Abbot, Devon. By permission of David & Charles (*page 110*).

Sotirov, Natsko, *Suvremenna Kouhnya.* © by the author. Published by 'Technika', Sofia 1959. Translated by permission of Jusautor Copyright Agency, Sofia (*page 112*).

St. Mary's Cathedral Ladies Guild, Caracas (Editors), *Beun Provecho.* Copyright St. Mary's Cathedral Ladies Guild. By permission of Jill A. Treneman, on behalf of St. Mary's Cathedral Ladies Guild (*page 96*).

Tante Marie, *La Véritable Cuisine de Famille.*© Editions A. Taride, Paris, 1980. Published by Editions A. Taride. Translated by permission of SARL Cartes Taride, Paris (*pages 132, 134 and 157*).

Tiano, Myrette, *Les Meilleures Recettes: Piques-Niques, Barbecues.* © Solar, 1981. Published by Solar, Paris. Translated by permission of Solar (*pages 96, 97*).

Trent, May Wong, *Oriental Barbecues.* Copyright © 1974 by May Wong Trent. Published by MacMillan Publishing Co., Inc., New York. By permission of MacMillan Publishing Co., Inc. (*page 131*).

Tsolova, M., Stoilova, V. and Ekimova, Sn., *Izpolzouvane na Zelenchoutsite i Prodovete v Domakinstovo.* Copyright © by the authors. Published by Zemizdat, Sofia 1978. Translated by permission of Jusautor Copyright Agency, Sofia (*page 94*).

Valldejuli, Carmen Aboy, *Puerto Rican Cookery.* Copyright © 1957, 1963 by Carmen Aboy Valldejuli. By permission of the author, Santurce, Puerto Rico (*page 121*).

Vazquez Montalban, Manuel, *La Cocina Catalana.* © Man-uel Vazquez Montalban, 1979. Published by Ediciones Peninsula, Barcelona. Translated by permission of Carme Balcell Agencja Literaria, Barcelona (*pages 107, 141 and 142*).

Vence, Céline, *Le Barbecue en 10 Leçons.* © Librairie Hachette, 1975. Published by Librairie Hachette, Paris. Translated by permission of Librairie Hachette (*pages 152, 159*).

Vergé, Roger, *Cuisine of the Sun.* © MacMillan London 1979. First published in 1981 by Papermac, a division of MacMillan Publishers Limited, London and Basingstoke. Originally published by Editions Robert Laffont S.A., Paris, as "Ma Cuisine du Soleil". © Editions Robert Laffont S.A., 1978. By permission of MacMillan Publishers Limited (*page 155*).

Waldron, Maggie, *Fire & Smoke.* Copyright © 1978 Maggi Waldron. Published by 101 Productions, San Francisco. By permission of 101 Productions (*pages 99, 102 and 132*).

Wolter, Annette, *Das Praktische Grillbuch.* © by Grafe und Unzer Verlag, München. Published by Grafe und Unzer GmbH Verlag, München. Translated by permission of Grafe und Unzer GmbH Verlag (*pages 91, 92, 94 and 115*).

Zane, Eva, *Greek Cooking for the Gods.* Copyright © 1970 by Eva Zane. Published by 101 Productions, San Francisco. By permission of 101 Productions (*pages 117, 150*).

Acknowledgements and Picture Credits

The Editors of this book are particularly indebted to Janet Bartucci, Myers CommuniCouncil, New York; Gail Duff, Maidstone, Kent; Ann O'Sullivan, Deya, Mallorca; Anna Maria Perez, Barcelona; David Schwartz, London; and Arthur W. Seeds, Naperville, Illinois.

They also wish to thank the following: Alison Attenborough, London; Ursula Beary, London; Markie Benet, London; Nicola Blount, London; Brinkman Corporation, Dallas, Texas; Mike Brown, London; Tom Calhoun, Culpeper, Virginia; Nora Carey, Paris; Joan Chasin, London; Emma Codrington, Richmond-upon-Thames, Surrey; Sara Jane Evans, London; Scott J. Feierabend, National Wildlife Federation, Washington D.C.; Dr. George J. Flick, Blacksburg, Virginia; Neyla Freeman, London; Susan Gaible, Richmond, Virginia; Jane Havell, London; Maggi Heinz, London; Hudson Brothers Greengrocers, Washington D.C.; Maria Johnson, Sevenoaks, Kent; Wanda Kemp-Welch, Nottingham; Larimer's Markets, Washington D.C.; Margot Levy, London; Mr. and Mrs. Norton W. Mailman, New York; Peter Mazzeo, Washington D.C.; MECO Metals Engineering Corporation, Greeneville, Tennessee; Ginny McCarthy, Tappan, New York; Philippa Millard, London; Wendy Morris, London; Neam's Market, Washington D.C.; North Carolina Yam Council, Raleigh, North Carolina; Rosemary Oates, London; Nancy Pollard, Alexandria, Virginia; Jorge W. Ramirez, Acme Barbecue College, Alhambra, California; Harold Reeves, Alexandria, Virginia; Sylvia Robertson, Surbiton, Surrey; Vicki Robinson, London; Royal Horticultural Society Gardens, Wisley, Surrey; John Sanders, Washington D.C.; Santullo's Market, Alexandria, Virginia; Holly Shimizu, Washington D.C.; Straight from the Crate, Alexandria, Virginia; Derek Walker, Port City Seafood, Alexandria, Virginia; Tina Walker, London; Rita Walters, Ilford, Essex; Dr. R. L. Wesley, Blacksburg, Virginia.

Photographs by Aldo Tutino: 4, 8—bottom, 9 to 11, 12—bottom, 14—top, 18 to 20, 21—bottom, 22—top, 23—top, 26, 28 to 33, 34—top, 35—top, 36, 37, 42 to 55, 56—bottom, 57—bottom, 58—top, 59—top, 66—top, 67—top, 74—top, 75—top, 78—top left, 80 to 85, 88.
Photographs by Bob Komar: Cover (barbecue), 8—top and centre, 12—top, 13, 14—bottom, 15, 16, 21—top, 22—bottom, 23—bottom, 24, 25, 34—bottom, 35—bottom, 38 to 41, 56—top, 57—top, 58—bottom, 59—bottom, 60, 62 to 65, 66—bottom, 67—bottom, 68 to 73, 74—bottom, 75—bottom, 76, 78—bottom, 79, 86, 87. Other photographers (alphabetically): Martin Brigdale: Cover (background); Louis Klein: 2.

Illustrations on pages 6 and 7 by Frederic F. Bigio of B-C Graphics. Line cuts from Mary Evans Picture Library and private sources.

Colour separations by Scan Studios Ltd.—Dublin, Ireland.
Typesetting by Camden Typesetters—London, England.
Printed and bound by Brepols S.A.—Turnhout, Belgium.